Film Fab

Talking Images Series

edited by Yann Perreau

Series ISSN 1744-9901

Previously published in this series

Cinema: The Archaeology of Film & the Memory of a Century
Jean-Luc Godard & Youssef Ishaghpour

Film Fables

JACQUES RANCIÈRE

Translated by Emiliano Battista

Oxford • New York

This work is published with the support of the French Ministry of Culture – Centre National du Livre.

Ĩi institut français

This book is supported by the French Ministry for Foreign Affairs as part of the Burgess Programme headed for the French Embassy in London by the Institut Français du Royaume-Uni

First published in France, 2001, by Editions Seuil
© Seuil 2001, *La Fable cinématographique*
Preface and English translation © Berg Publishers 2006

Paperback reprinted 2006

Berg
Editorial offices:
First Floor, Angel Court, 81 St Clements Street, Oxford OX4 1AW , UK
175 Fifth Avenue, New York, NY 10010, USA

Berg is the imprint of Oxford International Publishers Ltd.

Library of Congress Cataloging-in-Publication Data
Rancière, Jacques.
[Fable cinématographique. English]
Film fables / Jacques Rancière ; translated by Emiliano Battista.
p. cm. — (talking images series)
Includes bibliographical references and index.
ISBN-13: 978-1-84520-168-5 (pbk. : alk. paper)
ISBN-10: 1-84520-168-X (pbk. : alk. paper)
ISBN-13: 978-1-84520-167-8 (cloth : alk. paper)
ISBN-10: 1-84520-167-1 (cloth : alk. paper)
1. Motion pictures. I. Title. II. Series.

PN1995.R336 2006
791.43—dc22

2005032509

British Library Cataloguing-in-Publication Data
A catalogue record for this book is available from the British Library.

ISBN-13   978 1 84520 167 8 (Cloth)
           978 1 84520 168 5 (Paper)

ISBN-10   1 84520 167 1 (Cloth)
           1 84520 168 X (Paper)

Typeset by JS Typesetting Ltd, Porthcawl, Mid Glamorgan
Printed in the United Kingdom by Biddles Ltd, King's Lynn.

www.bergpublishers.com

Contents

Translator's Preface

Cinema is the combination of the unconscious eye of the camera and the conscious eye of the director, of the intimate face of things recorded on celluloid and their intentional arrangement during the editing process, of the will of the artist and the silent impression of things with neither will nor meaning.

This identity of opposites had been formulated and circulated as an idea and ideal of art for a good hundred years before the first public screenings, in philosophy, painting, theater, and literature. Flaubert had dreamed of writing a book that effaced the line between its prose and the ordinary prose of the world, and cinema's pioneers were quick to hail film as the art that would realize that dream and bid a final farewell to Aristotle's insistence on the primacy of plot by confronting it with the intimate presence of things and the naked truth of life: "Cinema is true. A story is a lie," wrote Jean Epstein in 1921. And yet, it became clear early on that cinema was never going to make a clean break with Aristotle and that the identity of opposites secured at the outset by the new art was by the same token lost from the outset. Little by little, plots, genres, types, identification with the characters—everything literature and painting had struggled so hard to subvert—were rehabilitated by the cinema, which turned out to be their strongest champion.

Film Fables is about the two poetics constitutive of the art of cinema. It has been standard to side with one of these two poetics over the other, to indict cinema's involution and its betrayal of its vocation, or, alternatively, to extract a work of pure plastic forms from the body of its fictions. Rancière doesn't take sides, but shows us on page after page that the power of cinema emerges from the conflict between the two poetics that animate its images. There are not two images—one aesthetic, the other representative, one commercial, the other a work of pure plastic forms—just as there is no simple option for one poetics over the other, but only one beauty against another in one and the same image. The film fable is a thwarted fable.

I take this opportunity to express my gratitude to everyone who contributed to the realization of this project: Tristan Palmer at Berg Publishers, who believed I was the right person for the job; Jacques Rancière for taking the time to answer my queries; Gabe Rockhill, who first suggested this project to me; Daniel Franco, who went over passage after passage of the text with me; Rochelle Maxwell and Fabien Gerard, for tracking down so many of the films mentioned in the book; Scott Newstok and Daniel Marcelle, for finding so many of the references; Jason Howard, Scott Samuelson, and Fintan Power, for their valuable suggestions; Peggy Donnelly, with whom I spent some of the best moments of this project going over the manuscript; all the staff at Berg. Lastly, I would like to dedicate this to Michelle and Gato, a token for all those films we saw together time and time again.

Prologue
A Thwarted Fable

Cinema, by and large, doesn't do justice to the story. And "dramatic action" here is a mistake. The drama we're watching is already half-resolved and unfolding on the curative slope to the crisis. The real tragedy is in suspense. It looms over all the faces; it is in the curtain and in the door-latch. Each drop of ink can make it blossom at the tip of the pen. It dissolves itself in the glass of water. At every moment, the entire room is saturated with the drama. The cigar burns on the lip of the ashtray like a threat. The dust of betrayal. Poisonous arabesques stretch across the rug and the arm of the seat trembles. For now, suffering is in surfusion. Expectation. We can't see a thing yet, but the tragic crystal that will turn out to be at the center of the plot has fallen down somewhere. Its wave advances. Concentric circles. It keeps on expanding, from relay to relay. Seconds.

The telephone rings. All is lost.

Is whether they get married in the end really all you want to know? Look, really, THERE IS NO film that ends badly, and the audience enters into happiness at the hour appointed on the program.

Cinema is true. A story is a lie.[1]

In these lines, Jean Epstein lays bare the problem posed by the very notion of a film fable. Written in 1921 by a young man of twenty-four, they welcome, under the title *Bonjour cinéma*, the artistic revolution he believes cinema is bringing about. Jean Epstein sums up this revolution with remarkable brevity, in terms that seem to invalidate the very argument of this book: cinema is to the art of telling stories [*l'art des histoires*] what truth is to lying. Cinema discards the infantile expectation for the end of the tale, with its marriage and numerous children. But, more importantly, it discards the "fable" in the Aristotelian sense: the arrangement of necessary and verisimilar actions that lead the characters from fortune to misfortune, or vice versa, through the careful construction of the intrigue [*noeud*] and denouement. The tragic poem, indeed the very idea of artistic expression, had always been defined by just such a logic of ordered actions. And along comes this young man to tell us that this logic is illogical. Life is not about stories, about actions oriented towards an end, but about situations open in every direction. Life has nothing to do with dramatic progression, but is instead a long and continuous movement made up of an infinity of micro-movements. This truth about life has finally found an art capable of doing it justice, an art in which the intelligence that creates the reversals of fortune and the dramatic conflicts is subject to another intelligence, the intelligence of the machine that wants nothing, that does not construct any stories, but simply records the infinity of movements that gives rise to a drama a hundred times more intense than all dramatic reversals of fortune. At the origin of the cinema, there is a "scrupulously honest" artist that does not cheat, that cannot cheat, because all it does is record. We mustn't confuse this recording with the identical reproduction of things in which Baudelaire had discerned the negation of artistic invention. Cinematographic automatism settles the quarrel between art and technique by changing the very status of the "real." It does not reproduce things as they offer themselves to the gaze. It records them as the human eye cannot see them, as they come into being, in a state of waves and vibrations, before they can be qualified as intelligible objects, people, or events due to their descriptive and narrative properties.

This is why the art of moving images can overthrow the old Aristotelian hierarchy that privileged *muthos*—the coherence of the plot—and devalued *opsis*—the spectacle's sensible effect. It isn't that the art of moving images is an art of the visible that managed to annex, thanks to movement, the capacity for narrative, or that it is a technique of visibility that replaces the art of imitating visible forms. It is just that the art of moving images provides access to an inner truth of the sensible that settles the quarrels for priority among the arts and among the senses because it settles, first and foremost, the great quarrel between thought and sensibility. Cinema revokes the old mimetic order because it resolves the question of *mimesis* at its root—the Platonic denunciation of images, the opposition between sensible copy and intelligible model. The matter seen and transcribed by the mechanic eye, says Epstein, is equivalent to mind: a sensible immaterial matter composed of waves and corpuscles that abolishes all opposition between deceitful appearance and substantial reality. The eye and hand that struggled to reproduce the spectacle of the world, as well as the play that explored the most secret reaches of the soul, belong to the old art because they belong to the old science. In the writing of movement with light, fictional matter and sensible matter coincide: the darkness of betrayal, the poison of crimes, and the anguish of melodrama come into contact with the suspension of specks of dust, the smoke of a cigar and the arabesques of a rug. And this same writing reduces all of this to the intimate movements of an immaterial matter. That is the new drama to have found its artist in the cinema. Thoughts and things, exterior and interior, are captured in the same texture, in which the sensible and the intelligible remain undistinguished. Thought impresses itself on the brow of the spectator in "bursts of amperes," while love on the screen "contains what no love had contained till now: its fair share of ultra-violet."[2]

Admittedly, this is a way of looking at things that belongs to another time than our own, but there are many ways to measure the distance. One such way is nostalgia. It notes that, outside the faithful fortress of experimental cinema, the reality of cinema long ago relinquished the beautiful hope of becoming a writing with light that confronted the fables and characters of other ages with the intimate presence of things. The young art of cinema did more than just restore ties with the old art of telling stories: it became that art's most faithful champion. Cinema wasn't content just to use its visual power and experimental means to illustrate old stories of conflicting interests and romantic ordeals, it went further and put those at the service of restoring the entire representative order that literature, painting, and the theater had so deeply damaged. It reinstated plots and typical characters, expressive codes and the old motivations of pathos, and even the strict division of genres. Nostalgia indicts cinema's involution, which it attributes to two phenomena: the breakthrough of the talkies [la coupure du parlant], which dealt a severe blow to the attempts to create a language of images; the Hollywood industry, which reduced directors to the role of illustrators of scripts based, for commercial reasons, on the standardization of plots and on the audience's identification with the characters.

At the other end of nostalgia is condescension. It tells us that if that dream is remote today, as it no doubt is, it is simply because it had never amounted to more than an inconsistent utopia. It just happened to synchronize with the great utopia of the times—with the aesthetic, scientific, and political dream of a new world where all material and historical burdens would find themselves dissolved in a reign of luminous energy. From the 1890s to the 1920s, this para-scientific utopia of matter dissolving itself in energy inspired both the symbolist reveries of the immaterial poem and the Soviet project of building a new social world. Under the guise of defining an art through its technical apparatus, Jean Epstein would have given us nothing more than his own particular version of the great ode to energy that his epoch sung and illustrated in myriad ways: in symbolist manifestoes à la Canudo and in futurist manifestoes à la Marinetti; in the simultaneist poems of Appolinaire and Cendrars to the glory of neon lighting and wireless communication, and in Khlebnikov's poems of transmental language; in the dynamism of dances à la Severini and in the dynamism of chromatic circles à la Delaunay; in Vertov's kino-eye, in Appia's stage lighting and designs, and in Loïe Fuller's luminous dances... Epstein wrote his poem about thought captured in bursts of amperes and love endowed with its fair share of ultra-violet under the spell of this utopia of a new electric world. He welcomed an art that no longer exists, for the simple reason that it never did. It is not our art, but it was not Epstein's either. It was not what filled the movie-theaters of his day, nor was it the art he himself made, in which he, too, told stories of ill-starred lovers and other old-fashioned heartbreaks. He hailed an art that existed only in his head, an art that was just an idea in people's heads.

It is by no means certain that condescension instructs us better than nostalgia. After all, what is this simple reality of the cinematographic art that condescension refers us to? How is this link between a technical apparatus for the production of visible images and a manner of telling stories forged? There is no shortage of theoreticians who have attempted to ground the art of moving images on the solid base of the means specific to it. But the means specific to yesterday's analogical machine and to today's digital machine have shown themselves equally suitable for filming both love stories and abstract dances and forms. It is only in the name of an idea of art that we can establish the relationship between a technical apparatus and this or that type of fable. *Cinema*, like *painting* and *literature*, is not just the name of an art whose processes can be deduced from the specificity of its material and technical apparatuses. Like painting and literature, cinema is the name of an art whose meaning cuts across the borders between the arts. Perhaps, in order to understand it, we should take another look at the lines from *Bonjour cinéma* and at the idea of art implied in them. Epstein pits the "real tragedy," that is, the "tragedy in suspense," against the old "dramatic action." Now, this notion of the tragedy in suspense is not reducible to the idea of the automatic machine inscribing the intimate face of things onto celluloid. It is something else altogether that Epstein identifies with the peculiar power of mechanical automatism: an active dialectic in which one tragedy takes form at the expense of another—the threat of the cigar, the dust of betrayal, or the poisonous power of the rug at the expense of the traditional narrative and expressive arrangements of expectation, violence, and fear. Epstein's text, in other words, undertakes a work of de-figuration. He composes one film with the elements of another. He is not describing an experimental film—real or imaginary—made expressly to attest to the power of cinema. We learn later that he has extracted this film from another film, from a melodrama by Thomas Harper Ince entitled *The Honour of His House*, with Sessue Hayakawa, a fetish-actor of the period, in the lead role. Epstein extracts the theoretical and poetical fable that describes the original power of the cinema from the body of another fable, from which he erased the traditional narrative aspect in order to create another dramaturgy, another system of expectations, actions, and states of being.

The cinema-unity thus undergoes an exemplary split. Jean Epstein welcomes an art that restores the duality of life and fictions, of art and science, of the sensible and the intelligible, to their original unity. And yet, Epstein only arrives at this pure essence of the cinema by extracting a work of "pure" cinema from the filmed melodrama. This particular penchant for making a fable with another is not a fad of the period, but a constitutive fact of the cinema as experience, art, and idea of art. It is also a fact that puts cinema in a contradictory continuity with a whole regime of art. From Jean Epstein to today, making a film on the body of another is exactly what the three main figures spawned by the cinema have been doing all along—directors, who "film" scripts they themselves have nothing to do with, the audience, for whom cinema is a potpourri of mixed memories, and critics and cinephiles, who extract a work of pure plastic forms from the body of a commercial fiction. The same is true of those two encyclopedic works that attempt to sum up the power of cinema: Deleuze's *Cinema 1* and *2*, and Godard's *Histoire(s) du cinéma*, in eight episodes. These two works constitute an ontology of the cinema argued for with bits and pieces gleaned from the entire *corpus* of the cinematographic art. Godard offers as evidence for his theory of the image-icon the pure plastic shots he extracts from the functional images Hitchcock had used to convey the enigmas and affects of his fables. Deleuze builds his ontology on the claim that cinematographic images are two things in one: they are the things themselves, the intimate events of universal becoming, and they are the operations of an art that restores to the events of the world the power they had been deprived of by the opaque screen of the human brain. Deleuze's dramaturgy of ontological restitution, like Epstein's or Godard's dramaturgy of origin, depends on the same process of extracting from the details in the fiction. For Deleuze, Jeff's broken leg in *Rear Window* and Scottie's vertigo in *Vertigo* are embodiments of the "rupture of the sensory-motor schema" through which the time-image splits itself off from the movement-image. Deleuze and Godard both repeat Jean Epstein's dramaturgy, they both extract, after the fact, the original essence of the cinematographic art from the plots the art of cinema shares with the old art of telling stories [*l'art des histoires*]. Cinema's enthusiastic pioneer, its disenchanted historiographer, its sophisticated philosopher, and its amateur theoreticians all share this dramaturgy because it is consubstantial with cinema as an art and an object of thought. The fable that tells the truth of cinema is extracted from the stories narrated on its screens.

The substitution operated by Jean Epstein's analysis is not the work of youthful illusion. He presents a fable of the cinema that is consubstantial with the art of the cinematograph, though it was not a fable born with the cinema. The dramaturgy Jean Epstein grafted onto the cinematographic machine has come down to us because it is as much a dramaturgy of art in general as of the cinema in particular, because it belongs more to the aesthetic *moment* of cinema than to the distinctiveness of its technical means. Cinema as an artistic idea predated the cinema as a technical means and distinctive art. The opposition between the "tragedy in suspense" that reveals the intimate texture of things and the conventions of "dramatic action" was instrumental in pitting the young art of cinema against the outdated art of the theater. And yet, cinema inherited this opposition from the theater, where it was first played out in the time of Maeterlinck and Gordon Craig, Appia and Meyerhold. These playwrights and stage directors had already countered Aristotle's arrangement of incidents with the intimate suspense of the world. They were also the ones who taught the cinema to extract the tragedy in suspense from the body of old plots. It is quite tempting, in fact, to see Jean Epstein's "tragedy in suspense" as deriving from the "motionless tragedy" that, thirty years earlier, Maeterlinck had thought of extracting from Shakespeare's stories of love and violence: "The mysterious chant of the Infinite, the ominous silence of the souls and of God, the murmur of Eternity on the horizon, the destiny or fatality we are conscious of within us, though by what tokens none can tell—do not all these underlie King Lear, Macbeth, Hamlet? And would it not be possible, by some interchanging of the roles, to bring them nearer to us, and send the actors further off? ... I have grown to believe that an old man, seated in his armchair, waiting patiently, with his lamp beside him; giving unconscious ear to all the eternal laws that reign about his house, interpreting, without comprehending, the silence of doors and windows and the quivering voice of the light, submitting with bent head to the presence of his soul and his destiny—an old man, who conceives not that all the powers of this world, like so many heedful servants, are mingling and keeping vigil in his room … or that every star in heaven and every fiber of the soul are directly concerned in the movement of an eyelid that closes, or a thought that springs to birth—I have grown to believe that he, motionless as he is, does yet live in reality a deeper, more human and more universal life than the lover who strangles his mistress, the captain who conquers in battle, or 'the husband who avenges his honor.'"[3]

The automatic eye of the camera so celebrated in *Bonjour cinéma* does no more than the poet of the "motionless life" dreamed up by Maeterlinck. Even the crystal metaphor Gilles Deleuze borrows from Jean Epstein is already there in the theoretician of symbolist drama: "Let but the chemist pour a few mysterious drops into a vessel that seems to contain the purest water, and at once masses of crystals will rise to the surface, thus revealing to us all that lay in abeyance there where nothing was visible before to our incomplete eyes."[4] Maeterlinck adds that this new poem about the sudden appearance of fabulous crystals in a liquid in suspension needs a new actor, a being that is not human, but closer in kind to the wax figures of a museum, and not the traditional actor with his old-fashioned feelings and means of expression. This android has enjoyed a not undistinguished life in the theater, from Edward Gordon Craig's Übermarionettes to Tadeusz Kantor's Theater of Death. The being of celluloid, whose "dead" chemical materiality jars with the actor's living gestures, is certainly one of its possible incarnations. Maeterlinck's description of the character who sits motionless beside his lamp conjures up for us a cinematographic shot; film directors, whether narrative or contemplative in temperament, have given this motionless character a great number of diverse incarnations.

But we are not so concerned here with the specific nature of the debt the film fable owes to symbolist poetics. It is not influence, or the fact of belonging to a particular lexical or conceptual universe, that leads Jean Epstein to work by extracting one fable from the body of another in Maeterlinck's wake and before Deleuze and Godard. The logic of a whole regime of art is implicated in the process. The work of de-figuration undertaken by Epstein was already being practiced by those nineteenth century art critics—Goncourt and others—who extracted from Rubens' religious scenes, Rembrandt's bourgeois ones, and Chardin's still-lives the same dramaturgy of the painterly gesture and the adventures of pictorial matter being brought to the foreground while relegating to the background the painting's figurative content. The Schlegel brothers were already proposing this Romantic fragmentation, this process of picking apart old poems only to turn those parts into the seeds for new poems, in the texts they published in the *Athenäum* at the beginning of that century. The whole logic of the aesthetic regime of art finds its footing at this time.[5] This logic rejects the representative model of constructed incidents and expressive codes appropriate to the subjects and situations in favor of an originary power of art initially distributed between two extremes: a pure creative activity thenceforward thought to be without rules or models, and the pure passivity of the expressive power inscribed on the very surface of things, independently of every desire to signify or create. It confronts the old principle of form fashioning matter with the identity, at the core of this new regime, between the pure power of the idea and the radical impotence of sensible presence and of the mute writing of things. But this union of contraries, where the work required by the artistic idea and the originary power coincide, is the result of the long work of de-figuration that in the new work contradicts the expectations borne by the subject matter or the story, or that reviews, rereads, and rearranges the elements of old works. This process undoes the arrangements of fiction and of representational painting, and draws our attention instead to the painterly gesture and the adventures of matter lurking beneath the subject of figuration, to the glimmer of the epiphany and the splendor of pure reasonless being glowing just beneath the conflict of wills of the play or novel. It hollows out or exacerbates the gestures of expressive bodies, slows down or speeds up narrative progression, suspends or saturates meanings. The art of the aesthetic age wants to identify its unconditioned power with its contrary: the passivity of reasonless being, the specks of elementary particles, and the originary upsurge of things. Flaubert dreamed of writing a book without subject or matter, a book that would be held together by nothing more than its "style," though he himself realized that the only way to achieve this sovereign style, the pure expression of his artistic will, was to create its opposite: a book stripped of every trace of the writer's intervention and composed instead of the indifferent swirl of specks of dust and of the passivity of things with neither will nor meaning. This splendor of the insignificant had to be realized in the infinitesimal gap opened up at the heart of representative logic: in stories about individuals who help or thwart one another in the pursuit of their goals, these goals being, incidentally, of the most commonplace sort: seducing a woman, attaining a social position, earning money... The work of style was to affect the passivity of the empty gaze of reasonless things in its exposition of everyday actions, and it would only succeed in its task if it itself became passive, invisible, if it painstakingly effaced the difference between itself and the ordinary prose of the world.

Such is the art of the aesthetic age. It is an art that comes afterwards and undoes the links of representative art, either by thwarting the logic of arranged incidents through the becoming-passive of writing, or by re-figuring old poems and paintings. [This work presupposes all past art to be available and open to being reread, reviewed, repainted or rewritten at will. It presupposes also that anything and everything in the world is available to art.] Banal objects, a flake peeling from a wall, an illustration from an ad campaign, are all available to art in their double resource: as hieroglyphs ciphering an age of the world, a society, a history, and, inversely, as pure presences, as naked realities brought to light by the new-found splendor of the insignificant. The properties of this regime of art—identity of active and passive, elevation of everything to the dignity of art, work of de-figuration that extracts the tragedy in suspense from the dramatic action—are the properties Jean Epstein attributes to cinema. Cinema, in the double power of the conscious eye of the director and the unconscious eye of the camera, is the perfect embodiment of Schelling's and Hegel's argument that the identity of conscious and unconscious is the very principle of art. It is easy, then, to see how one may be tempted to conclude, with Epstein and others, that cinema is the dream come true of this regime of art. After all, it really does seem that Flaubert framed his micro-narrations like "film shots": Emma at the window absorbed in her contemplation of the bean props knocked down by the wind; Charles leaning out of another window and gazing distractedly at the laziness of the summer evening, at the skeins of cotton drying in the air and at the dirty water of an industrial river. Cinema seems to accomplish naturally the writing of *opsis* that reverses Aristotle's privileging of *muthos*. The conclusion, however, is false, for the very simple reason that cinema, being by nature what the arts of the aesthetic age had to strive to be, invariably reverts their movement. Flaubert's frames are the work of a way of writing that contradicts narrative plausibility and expectation by reaching for the dreamlike stasis of paintings. Painters and novelists had to work to make themselves the instruments of their becoming-passive; the mechanical apparatus, conversely, suppresses the active work involved in this becoming-passive. The camera cannot be made passive because it is passive already, because it is of necessity at the service of the intelligence that manipulates it. The camera-eye Dziga Vertov uses at the beginning of *Man with a Movie Camera* to explore the unknown face of things seems at first to illustrate Jean Epstein's claim. Just then, a cameraman enters the frame and installs the tripod of a second camera on top of the first, the instrument of a will that has prior access to the discoveries of the first and is free to

arrange them into bits of celluloid appropriate for every use. The fact is that
the mechanic eye lends itself to everything: to the tragedy in suspense, to the
work of Soviet Kinoks, and not least to the illustration of old-fashioned
stories of interest, heartbreak, and death. Those who can do everything are
usually doomed to servitude. And indeed it turns out that the "passivity"
of the machine that supposedly crowns the program of the aesthetic regime
of art lends itself just as well to the work of restoring the old representative
power of active form arranging passive matter that a century of painting and
literature had struggled to subvert. At the end of the day, the whole logic of
representative art finds itself restored, piece by piece, by this machine. And
the artist who rules over the passive machine with a sovereign hand is, more
than any other artist, doomed to transform his mastery into servitude, to
put his art at the service of companies whose business is to control and cash
in on the collective imaginary. In the age of Joyce and Virginia Woolf, of
Malevich and Schönberg, cinema arrives as if expressly designed to thwart a
simple teleology of artistic modernity, to counter art's aesthetic autonomy
with its old submission to the representative regime.

We must not map this process of thwarting onto the opposition between
the principles of art and those of a popular entertainment subject to the
industrialization of leisure and the pleasures of the masses. The art of the
aesthetic age abolishes all of these borders because it makes art of everything.
The novel of the aesthetic age grew to maturity with the serial; its poetry
beat to the rhythm of the masses; its painting adorned guinguettes and
music halls. In Epstein's day, the new art of directing films drew inspiration
from acrobatic feats and athletic performances. It was also in his day that
one started seeing scraps of consumer goods hanging from picture rails
or illustrating poems. There is no doubt that very early on pressure from
the industry turned film directors into "craftsmen" who had to struggle
to impress their logo on scenarios they were more often than not obliged
to illustrate with actors not of their choosing. And yet, a basic law of the
aesthetic regime of art is to come afterwards, to graft one's art onto a
preexisting art and render its operations almost indiscernible from the prose
of everyday stories and images. The film industry, in a sense, is only the most
radical form of this law. It is true that today we seem more than willing to
rehabilitate a cinema of craftsmen in the face of the impasses of an "auteur
politics" whose culmination seems to be the aestheticism of publicity
campaigns. Nobody needs to be prompted to reiterate Hegel's diagnosis
that the work of the artist who does only what he wants succeeds in showing
no more than the image of the artist in general. All we add today is that this

image is bound in the end to be confused with the image of a name brand on a product.[6] If the art of cinema accepts to come after producers and scriptwriters and to illustrate the program they provide—which it invariably thwarts with its own logic—it isn't just because of the pressure the harsh laws of the market exert on it. It is also, and more importantly, because of an indecisiveness at the heart of its artistic nature. Cinema literalizes a secular idea of art in the same stroke that it actualizes the refutation of that idea: it is both the art of the afterwards that emerges from the Romantic de-figuration of stories, and the art that returns the work of de-figuration to classical imitation. Hence the paradoxical nature of the continuity between cinema and the aesthetic revolution that made it possible. Even though the basic technical equipment of the cinema secures the identity of active and passive that is the principle of that revolution, the fact remains that cinema can only be faithful to it if it gives another turn of the screw to its secular dialectics. The art of cinema has been constrained, empirically, to affirm its art against the tasks assigned to it by the industry. But the visible process by which it thwarts these tasks only hides a more intimate process: to thwart its servitude, cinema must first thwart its mastery. It must use its artistic procedures to construct dramaturgies that thwart its natural powers. There is no straight line running from cinema's technical nature to its artistic vocation. The film fable is a thwarted fable.

We must then call into question the idea of a continuity between the technical nature of the machine of vision and the forms of the cinematographic art. Filmmakers and theoreticians have been quick to suggest that the art of cinema attained its perfection there where its fables and forms succeeded in expressing the essence of the cinematographic medium. A few exemplary figures and propositions punctuate the history of this identification of form and fable: the burlesque automaton—whether Chaplinesque or Keatonian—that fascinated the generation of Delluc, Epstein, and Eisenstein before resurfacing at the core of André Bazin's film theory and inspiring systematizations being worked out today;[7] the gaze cast by Rossellini's camera at "non-manipulated things"; Bresson's theory and practice of the "model," which pits the truth of cinematographic automatism against the artifice of theatrical expression. It would be easy to show, however, that none of these dramaturgies properly belong to the cinema. Better yet, it would be easy to show that if they belong to cinema at all, it is because they put a thwarting logic in motion. There are some brilliant pages in Bazin where he tries to demonstrate that Charlie's mime is the incarnation of cinematographic being, of the form silver nitrate prints

on strips of celluloid.[8] But the burlesque automaton was an aesthetically
constituted figure, a hero of the pure spectacle that flew in the face of
traditional psychology, long before the advent of cinema. We might also
add that its role in the cinema wasn't to be the embodiment of the technical
automaton, but to make itself the instrument that derailed every fable, the
equivalent, in the art of moving images, to the becoming-passive characteristic
of the prose of the modern novel. The burlesque body is constantly shuttling
between total impotence and absolute power, its actions and reactions are
always overshooting or falling short of the mark. The best example here is
the Keatonian hero, divided as he is between a look that spells defeat from
the outset and a movement that nothing can stop. The Keatonian hero is
always looking on as things slip right through his fingers, and he is also a
moving body [le mobile] whose forward thrust knows no resistance, as in that
scene in Sherlock Junior where he clears, in a straight line, all the obstacles
in his way while sitting on the handlebars of a motorcycle whose driver
had fallen off at the beginning of the course. The burlesque body cuts the
links between cause and effect, action and reaction, because it throws the
elements of the moving image into contradiction. This is why, throughout
cinema's history, the burlesque body has been the preferred dramaturgic
machine for transforming one fable into another. Today, we have Kitano
using the mechanics of burlesque to turn the logic of the action film on its
head. With acceleration, he turns the violent confrontation of wills into a
pure mechanics of action and reaction divested of all expressivity; he then
dissolves these automatic movements in pure contemplation by subjecting
them to the inverse principle of distension, of a growing gap between
action and reaction. The policemen at the end of Hana-bi have become
pure spectators observing the suicide of their old colleague, perceptible
only as a sound resonating in the indifference of sand and waves. Burlesque
automatism drives the logic of the fable to what we might call, with Deleuze,
pure optical and sound situations. But these "pure" situations are not the
rediscovered essence of the image: they are the result of those operations
whereby the cinematographic art thwarts its own powers.

At the risk of parting ways with Bazin and Deleuze, I would say that
Rossellini's dramaturgy proves the same point: all of these "pure" situations
result from a set of specific operations. Bazin argues that Rossellini, in the
great fables of wandering he brings to the screen, realizes the fundamental
vocation of the automatic machine to follow, ever so patiently, the minute
signs that allow a glimpse into the spiritual secret of beings. Deleuze
sees Rossellini as the director par excellence of the pure optical and sound

situations that reflect the realities besetting Europe in the aftermath of the war, a time when individuals who had lost all their bearings were forced to confront situations they had no answers for. But the situations of narrative rarefaction Rossellini dramatizes on the screen are not situations indicative of the "impossibility to react," or of the inability to bear intolerable spectacles or coordinate gaze and action. They are experimental situations that Rossellini uses to superimpose onto the normal movement of narrative continuity another movement directed by a fable of *vocation*. In *Rome, Open City*, Pina tears herself free from a line of soldiers who clearly should have been able to restrain her and dashes after the truck driving away her fiancé. Originating in the mode of the burlesque movement only to end in a mortal fall, Pina's dash after the truck at once exceeds the visible of the narrative situation and of the expression of love. Similarly, the jump into the void that brings Edmund's wanderings to a close in *Germany Year Zero* exceeds every (non)reaction to Germany's material and moral ruin in 1945. These movements are not oriented towards a fictional end, nor have they been disoriented by an intolerable situation: they've been deflected by the imposition of another movement. Rossellini has transferred a dramaturgy of the call from the religious to the artistic level. That is what drives his characters from one mode of movement and gravitation to another mode, where they cannot but free-fall. Even if Rossellini achieves in that movement the coincidence of a fictional and a plastic dramaturgy, this unity of form and content is not the realized essence of the cinematographic medium, producing a "non-manipulated" vision of things; it is instead the product of a dramaturgy where the character's extreme liberty coincides with his or her absolute subjection to a command. The logic of the "rupture of the sensory-motor schema" is a dialectic of impotence and excessive power.

We reencounter this same dialectic in Bresson's "cinematography." Bresson had thought to sum it up with his well-known couple: the "passive" model who mechanically reproduces the gestures and intonations dictated by the director, and the director—painter—editor who uses the screen as if it were the blank canvas whereon to assemble the "pieces of nature" offered up by the model. Still, we need a more complex dramaturgy than this one to separate the art of the cinematographer from the stories he tells. A Bresson film is always the *mise-en-scène* of a trap and a hunt. The poacher (*Mouchette*), the rogue (*Au hasard, Balthazar*), the rejected lover (*Ladies of the Bois de Boulogne*), the jealous husband (*A Gentle Woman*), the thief and the chief of police (*Pickpocket*), all set their traps and wait for their victims to get caught. The film fable realizes its artistic essence by thwarting the scenarios concocted by these volitional agents. It's a mistake, however, to think that visual fragmentation and the passivity of the model do in fact thwart those scenarios, since what they actually do is erase the line between the hunter awaiting his prey and the director trying to surprise the truth of the "model." There must be, in other words, a counter-logic that opposes the visible complicity between these two hunters. What protects the prey from the hunter and the film fable from the story illustrated in Bresson is, first of all, a fleeing movement, a fall into the void. The door that slams shut as somebody opens a window and the flowing silk scarf in *A Gentle Woman*, or the girl who rolls down the slope time and again to the edge of the pond where she'll drown herself in *Mouchette*, mark the counter-movement, initial or final, by which the preys elude their hunters. The beauty of these scenes comes from how the visible contradicts narrative meaning: the veil gently suspended by the wind hides the fall of a suiciding body, the child playing at rolling down the slope both fulfills and denies the suicide of a teenager. That the authors thwarted by these scenes that Bresson himself added to the storyline are not obscure scriptwriters but Dostoevsky and Bernanos highlights all the more the counter-movement that keeps cinema from every simple effectuation of its visual essence. The role Bresson assigns to the voice in his films is the other part of this counter-effect logic. Far from being just the expression of the truth wrenched from the model, the so-called "white" voices of Bresson's films are, more radically, how cinema accomplishes the project of literature by inverting it. Literature, to thwart the arrangement of incidents and the conflict of wills, let itself be infiltrated by the great passivity of the visible. The addition of image to literature amounted to a subtraction of sense. Cinema, for its part, can only appropriate this power by reversing the game and hollowing out the visible with the word. That is the function of these "white voices" that melt together all the different intonations required by the classical expression of the characters. Paradoxically, it is this sound invention, and not the framing of the painter and the montage of the editor, that defines the art of the model representative of a "pure cinema." The counterpart of the image that cuts the literary narrative is this voice that simultaneously lends body to the image and subtracts from it. It is like a thwarted narrative voice in literature [*une parole littéraire contredite*]: neutrality of the narrative voice attributed to bodies it has disowned and that distort it in turn. Ironically, the voice that defines Bresson's cinematographic art was first imagined in the theater as the voice of the "third character," the Unknown or the Inhuman, Maeterlinck thought inhabited Ibsen's dialogues.

All these great figures of a pure cinema whose fables and forms would easily be deducible from its essence do no more than offer up the best examples of the film fable, split and thwarted: *mise-en-scène* of a *mise-en-scène*, counter-movement that affects the arrangement of incidents and shots, automatism separating image from movement, voice hollowing out the visible. Cinema can only make the games it plays with its own means intelligible to itself through the games of exchange and inversion it plays with the literary fable, the plastic form, and the theatrical voice. The texts gathered here attest to the multiplicity of these games, with no pretensions, of course, to exhausting the field of possibilities of the art of cinema. Some of the chapters show the paradoxes of the film fable at their most radical. This is the case, for instance, with Eisenstein's efforts to create a cinema that opposes the fables of old with its capacity to translate an idea—in his case, that of communism—directly into signs-images that convey new affects. It is also the case with Murnau's transposition of Molière's *Tartuffe* to the silent screen. Eisenstein's project governs *The General Line*, where he identifies the demonstration of the new art with the political opposition of the new and mechanized world of the kolkhozes to the old world of the peasants. But to bring it off, Eisenstein has to line the opposition with a more secret aesthetic complicity between the Dionysian figures of the new art and the trances and superstitions of old. Murnau manages his transposition of *Tartuffe* into silent film by transforming Molière's schemer into a shadow, and his conquest operation into the conflict of visibilities conducted by Elmire to dissipate the shadow haunting her husband. But then, it is the very power of the cinematographic shadow that Murnau must lay to rest in order to unmask the impostor. A more discrete thwarting of the text it brings to the screen can be found in Nicholas Ray's *They Live by Night*, where Ray imbues the visual fragmentation with the poetic powers of metonymy in order to undo the perceptive continuum created by the "stream of consciousness" that the novelist in the 1930s had used, inversely, to capture the sensory character of the moving image. Even the most classical of cinematographic forms, the ones most faithful to the representative tradition of carefully arranged incidents, clearly defined characters, and neatly composed images, are affected by this gap, evidence enough that the film fable belongs to the aesthetic regime of art. Anthony Mann's Westerns are a good example. There can be no doubt that Mann's Westerns are model representatives of that most coded of cinematographic genres, or that they obey all the fictional needs dictated by a narrative and popular cinema. And yet they too are inhabited by an essential gap. The meticulous precision that connects the hero's perceptions and gestures cuts his actions off from all those things—the stability of ethical values, and the frenzy of desires and dreams that transgress them—that normally give meaning to the action. Ironically, it is the perfection of the "sensory-motor schema" of action and reaction that causes problems for these tales of quarrels with desire and the law by substituting them with the confrontation between two perceptive spaces. A constant principle of what is known as *mise-en-scène* in the cinema is to supplement—and thwart—narrative continuity and the rationality of the goals by not aligning two visibilities, or two relationships of the visible to movement, either by means of visual reframings, or by means of the aberrant movements imposed by a character who simultaneously aligns himself with the scenario of the pursuit of goals and perverts it.

We should not be surprised to find here two other classical incarnations of this figure, namely the child (*Moonfleet*) and the psychopath (*M, While the City Sleeps*). The child in the cinema oscillates between two roles, traditionally playing either the victim of a violent world or the mischievous observer of a world that takes itself too seriously. In *Moonfleet*, Fritz Lang confronts these banal and representative figures with the aesthetic figure of the child director, who is determined to impose his own script and to mount the visual refutation of the narrative game of intrigues and the visual game of appearances that normally conspire to pigeonhole the child into the role of naïve victim. The obstinacy that exceeds every rational pursuit of goals is likewise the trait by which the psychopath, in the cinema, upsets the scenarios of the trap where the criminal is at once hunter and prey. In its aberration, this obstinacy mirrors the equality of action and passion where cinema metaphorizes itself. The murderer in *M* escapes visually because the automatism of his movements dovetails into the double trap set by the police and the mob that will in the end get the better of him. Unlike his pursuers, who trace circles on maps and post detectives on street corners, the murderer doesn't pursue a rational goal, he could not do something other than what he does. When he meets a child's gaze reflected in a shop window, he must pass from the insouciance of the anonymous *flâneur* to the automatism of the hunter, just as he must regain the image of a contented observer an instant later, as he stands side by side with another little girl. The shot of the murderer and his next victim looking happily at the window display of a toy shop belongs to the same counter-effect logic as the flowing scarf in *A Gentle Woman*, the rolls down the slope of *Mouchette*, the rectilinear trajectory of *Sherlock Junior*, the meticulous and indifferent gestures of James Stewart in Mann's Westerns, and the mythological elation of the bull's wedding in *The General Line.*

This same logic abolishes the borders between document and fiction, between the politically committed work and the pure work. The plastic extravagance of Eisenstein's communist film is part and parcel of the same dream that produced the indifferent "shot" of Emma Bovary gazing out of her window, and this indifference sometimes rubs off on the images of the politically committed documentary. This is the case in that moment of *Listen to Britain* when Humphrey Jennings' camera, positioned into the light, shows two characters in silhouette peacefully watching the sun set over the waves before a change of angle reveals their function and identity: they are two coastguards scanning the horizon for signs of the enemy. *Listen to Britain* is a limit example of the counter-effect characteristic of the film fable. Although meant to rally support for England's war efforts in 1941, the film never shows a country at war and mobilized militarily for its defense. Jennings only shows the soldiers during their moments of leisure: in a train compartment singing a song about distant lands, in a dance or concert hall, at a village procession. His camera slides seamlessly from one furtive image to another: a man at his window at night, holding a light with one hand and drawing the curtains with the other, a school courtyard where children dance in a circle, the two men watching the setting sun. The paradoxical political choice of showing a country at peace in order to win support for its war efforts succeeds because Jennings makes exemplary use of the paradox inherent to the film fable. The peaceful moments that make up the film—a face and light glimpsed behind a window, two men chatting as they watch the sunset, a song in a train, a dance contest—are nothing other than the moments of suspension that punctuate fiction films and that invest the constructed verisimilitude of the action and the story with the naked truth, the meaningless truth of life. The fable tends to intersperse these moments of suspension/moments of the real with action sequences. Jennings, by thus isolating them in this strange "documentary," highlights just how ambivalent this play of exchanges, between the verisimilar action characteristic of representative art and the life without reason emblematic of aesthetic art, really is.[9] The ordinary, the zero-degree of cinematographic fiction is for these two to complement one another, in order to provide a sort of double testimony to the logic of the action and the effect of the real. The artistic work of the fable, conversely, is to vary the values, to increase or diminish the gap, to invert the roles. The privilege of the so-called documentary film is that it is not obliged to create the *feeling* of the real, and this allows it to treat the real as a problem and to experiment more freely with the variable games of action and life, significance and insignificance. If this play is at its zero-degree in Jennings' documentary, it takes on an altogether different complexity when Chris Marker composes *The Last Bolshevik* by interlacing images from the post-Soviet present with various types of "documents": images of the imperial family in 1913 and those of a Stalin lookalike "helping" tractor drivers in their difficulties; the buried film-reports Alexander Medvekin shot from his film-train, the comedies he directed and which got brushed under the carpet, and the films he was obliged to make of the huge pageants put on by Stalinist athletes; the accounts gathered from interviews, the massacre on the Odessa steps of *Battleship Potemkin*, and Simpleton's lamentation on the stage of the Bolshoi Theater. Marker, by putting all of these in dialogue in the six "letters" to Alexander Medvekin that make up the film, can deploy better than all illustrators of made up stories the polyvalence of images and signs, the potential difference between values of expression—between the image that speaks and the one that silences, between the speech that conjures up an image and the one that is simply enigmatic—that make up, in contrast to the episodes of before, the new forms of fiction of the aesthetic age.

Documentary fiction invents new intrigues with historical documents, and thus it touches hands with the film fable that joins and disjoins—in the relationship between story and character, shot and sequence—the powers of the visible, of speech, and of movement. When Marker replays, under the shadow cast by the color images of restored Orthodox pomp, the "doctored" images of the massacre on the Odessa steps and images from Stalinist propaganda films, his work resonates with Godard's, who filmed, in the Pop age, the Maoist theatricalization of Marxism and, in the "Post-Modern" age, the fragments of the intermingled history of the cinema and the century. Marker also touches hands with Fritz Lang, who replays the same story of the chase for a psychopathic killer at two different ages of the visible: the first in *M*, where maps and magnifying glasses, inventories and drag-nets trap the murderer and prosecute him in a theatrical court; the second in *While the City Sleeps*, where all these accessories have disappeared and been replaced by a machine of vision, the television that places Mobley "face to face" with the murderer and transforms an imaginary capture into a weapon for a real capture. The TV monitor isn't the instrument of "mass consumption" that spells out the death of the great art. It is, more profoundly and also more ironically, the machine of vision that suppresses the mimetic gap and that thus realizes, in its own way, the new art's panaesthetic project of immediate sensible presence. This new machine doesn't annul the power of cinema, but its "impotence." It annuls the process of thwarting that has always animated its fables. The task of the director is then to invert, once again, the game where television "realizes" cinema. A longstanding lamentation in contemporary thought wants us to bear witness to the programmed death of images at the hands of the machine for information and advertisement. I have opted for the opposite perspective and have tried to show that the art and thought of images have always been nourished by all that thwarts them.

NOTES

1. Jean Epstein, *Bonjour cinéma*, in *Écrits sur le cinéma* (Paris: Seghers, 1974) 86. A previous translation of this text, by Tom Milne, originally published in *Afterimage* 10 (Autumn 1981) 9–16, can be found in Richard Abel, ed. *French Film Theory and Criticism: A History/Anthropology, 1907–1939*, volume 1: 1907–1929 (Princeton, NJ: Princeton University Press, 1988), 242.

2. Epstein, *Bonjour cinéma* (Paris: Seghers, 1974) 91. Abel, *French Film Theory*, vol. 1, 244.

3. Maurice Maeterlinck, "The Tragical in Daily Life," in *The Treasure of the Humble*, trans. Alfred Sutro (London: George Allen, 1897) 98–9; 105–6.

4. Maeterlinck, "The Tragical in Daily Life," 110.

5. For a more elaborate discussion, please see my *The Politics of Aesthetics*, trans. Gabe Rockhill (London: Continuum Books, 2004), and *L'Inconscient esthéthique* (Paris: Galilée, 2001).

6. Serge Daney has worked out the most rigorous form of this dialectic of art and commerce. See especially his: *L'Exercice a été profitable, monsieur* (Paris: P.O.L., 1993) and *La Maison cinéma et le monde* (Paris: P.O.L., 2001). I discuss these in my: "Celui qui vient après. Les antinomies de la pensée critique," *Trafic* 37 (2001) 142–50.

7. Cf. Thérèse Giraud, *Cinéma et technologie* (Paris: PUF, 2001), which argues for the opposite thesis to the one I argue for here.

8. André Bazin, "The Myth of Monsieur Verdoux," in *What is Cinema?*, vol. 2, trans. Hugh Gray (Berkeley: University of California Press, 1971) 104. "Before any 'character' ... there exists a person called Charlie. He

is a black-and-white form printed on the silver nitrate of film." Bazin's analysis does not limit itself to the onto-technological identification of the Chaplinesque character with cinematographic being, though that is one of its major concerns, hence his opposition to the "ideology" of *Modern Times* and *The Great Dictator*. Both these films, Bazin argues, destroy Charlie's "ontological" nature because they make Charlie Chaplin's hand and thought too visible.

9.   For a more detailed analysis of this film, please see: Jacques Rancière, "L'Inoubliable," in *Arrêt sur histoire*, eds. Jean-Louis Comolli and Jacques Rancière (Paris: Éditions du Centre Georges Pompidou, 1997) 47– 70.

Part I

Fables of the Visible

Between the Age of the Theater and the Television Age

CHAPTER I

Eisenstein's Madness

Eisenstein pretends to tell us everything about his transition from theater to cinema, from the time of the theater to the time of the cinema, with two anecdotes. In the first, about his last experience as a director at the Proletcult Theater, Eisenstein tells us that while at work on his production of Tretiakov's *Gas Masks*, he was seized by the idea of staging the play in its actual setting and for the public it supposedly addresses. And so it was that *Gas Masks* was staged in the Moscow Gas Factory. There, Sergei Mikhailovitch tells us, the reality of the factory overwhelmed the production of the play and, more generally, overwhelmed the very project of a revolutionary theater whose stage performances would be the direct assimilation of the technical gestures and operations of labor. The new factory and labor needed a new art, one of their dimensions.[1]

Although it all seems very simple at first, a matter of pitting the realities of Soviet labor against the old mirages of representation, the second anecdote complicates matters right away. During the preparation of an Ostrovsky play, at the Proletcult still, the face of a young boy attending rehearsals caught the director's eye. The boy's face mimetically reflected every sentiment and action represented on the stage, as though it were a mirror. This chance glimpse of the boy's face was supposedly the source of a completely different project. Instead of annulling the omnipotence of *mimesis* so clearly visible on the boy's face by destroying the illusions of art in the interests of the new life, Eisenstein decided to do the reverse. He now wanted to capture its principle and break down its mechanism, not for the sake of a critical demonstration of its powers of illusion, but for the sake of rationalizing and optimizing its use.[2] *Mimesis*, it must be remembered, is two things. It is the psychic and social power through which a word, a behavior, or an image prompts its analogue; and it is the particular regime of art that embeds this very power in the laws of genres, the construction of stories, and the representation of characters acting and expressing their sentiments. The point, then, was not to pit, wholesale, the realities of the construction of a new life against the fables and images of yore, as was fashionable at the time, but to wrench the psychic and social powers of *mimesis* from the grip of the mimetic regime of art. It was to transform the powers of *mimesis* into a power of thought capable of producing, directly and within a specific mode of sensorialization, the effects that mimetic art had until then entrusted to the episodes of the stories and the audience's identification with the characters. This meant replacing the traditional effects achieved by identification with the story and the characters by the direct identification with the affects programmed by the artist. Eisenstein opened a new path to those who had nothing else to do besides range in opposition the construction of new forms of life and the prestige of *mimesis*: an *aesthetic* art, an art where the idea is no longer translated into the construction of a plot dependent on identification, fear, and pity, but is directly impressed onto an adequate sensible form.

Cinema was the exemplary form of this art. We must be sure that we don't mix up our terms: cinema designates more than just a mode of producing images. An art is more than the expressive use of a material medium and a determinate means of expression—an art is an idea of art. Eisenstein stresses this same point in his essay about "the *cinema* of a country that has no *cinematography*."[3] He is thinking of Japan. The essence of cinema, Eisenstein says, is to be found everywhere in Japanese art, save for in Japanese cinema. One finds it in the haiku, in Japanese prints, in the Kabuki Theater, in every art, in short, that mobilizes the ideogrammatic principle of the Japanese language. The principle of the cinematographic art and the principle of ideogrammatic language are one and the same. But this language, in itself, is double. Meaning, in an ideogram, results from the meeting of two images. And so, just as the combination of the image for water and the image of an eye signifies "to weep," the combination of two shots, or of two visual elements of a shot, produces a meaning that contradicts the mimetic value of the elements represented. It produces, in other words, an element in a discourse where the idea is put directly into images in accordance with the dialectical principle of the union of contraries. The "ideogrammatic" art of the Kabuki is the art of montage, of the contradiction that opposes the integrity of the character with the parceling of bodily attitudes and the "nuances" of the mimetic translation of sentiments with the shock of antagonistic expressions. Cinematographic montage inherits the power of this language. But the ideogram is also an element in a fusional language that does not recognize the difference between substratum and sensible components. Cinema, like the ideogram, is a fusional art that reduces the audiovisual elements to a "single unit of *theater*": not an element in a determinate art or sense, but a stimulant for "the cortex of the brain as a whole, irrespective of the paths by which the accumulated stimuli have been brought together."[4] Put differently, Japanese "theater" gives the new "cinema" its program: the constitution of a "language" of the elements that properly belong to the art, such that the art's direct effects on the brain to be stimulated can be doubly calculated: as the exact communication of ideas in the language of images, and as the direct modification of a sensory state through the combination of sensory stimuli. This is how the theater of a country with no cinematography pointed the way to a country in the process of going from the age of the theater to the age of the cinematograph.

The passage from "theater to cinema" is not the replacing of an art by another, but a manifestation of a new regime of art. That does not mean, however, that the procedures of this new art are new in and of themselves. Unable to find the means to shoot and constrained to devote his energies to writing, the celebrated director of *Battleship Potemkin* put all his efforts into showing that the principles of montage were already at work not only in the haiku and the Kabuki, but also in El Greco's paintings and Piranese's drawings, in Diderot's theoretical texts and in Pushkin's poems, in the novels of Dickens and Zola, and in innumerable other manifestations of the art of montage. Cinema presents itself as the synthesis of the arts, as the material fulfillment of the utopian goal that Père Castel and Diderot had sought in the ocular clavichord, Wagner in his musical drama, Scriabin in his colored concertos, and Paul Fort in his theater of perfumes. But the synthesis of the arts does not mean bringing together words, music, images, movements, and perfumes on one stage; it means reducing the heterogeneous procedures and the different sensory forms of the arts to a common denominator, to a common fundamental [*principielle*] unity of ideal and sensory elements. This is what is summed up in the term montage. In cinematographic language, the image of the world captured by the machine is stripped of its mimetic function and becomes instead a morpheme for a combination of ideas. This abstract morpheme is also a sensory stimulus that does precisely what Artaud will want to do later: it reaches the nervous system directly, without having to rely on the mediation of a plot acted out by characters expressing their sentiments. Cinema is not the language of light sung by Canudo. It is, more soberly, the art that guarantees the non-mimetic decomposition and re-composition of the elements of the mimetic effect by reducing the communication of ideas and the ecstatic explosion of sensory affects to a common unit of measurement.

Apollonian language of images that gives discourse its plastic form and
Dionysian language of sensations: Nietzsche's model of tragedy had been,
especially in Russia, at the basis of symbolist theories about poetry and
theater, and it is easily recognizable in the "dialectical" couple of the organic
and the pathetic. An outcome of the Revolution had been the coupling
of Dionysus' drunken unconscious with the rational calculations of the
builders of the Soviet world and of the bio-mechanic athletes of the new
theater. In a provocative vein, Eisenstein radicalized this union by identifying
it with Pavlov's calculations of the conditioned reflexes that would "plough
the psyche of the viewer like a tractor" and make it the field for the growth
of a new conscience. The entirely mathematical rigor of "organic" montage
is supposed to bring about the qualitative leap to the "pathetic" and secure
the exact adequation between the propagation of the communist idea and
the manifestation of a new idea of art.

It is exactly this program that, in an exemplary manner, governs *The General
Line*, a film without a "story," without another subject than communism itself.
In all his other films, Eisenstein had put the means of montage at the service
of an already constituted subject or theme. It is true that *Strike* brings to the
screen a concept of strike that doesn't correspond to any strike in particular;
and it is also true that the historical films enjoy their fair share of invention,
beginning with the massacre on the Odessa steps in *Battleship Potemkin*, a
scene, says Eisenstein, born of the sensation of flight materially evoked by
those steps. But the subject matter of these films, like that of *October*, brings
with it a ready-made plot, scenes that can be recognized, shared affects and
emblems. The same cannot be said about *The General Line*, where Eisenstein
uses the pure means of montage to pathetize an idea that cannot count
on the helping hand offered by identification: the superiority of collective
over individual farming. The construction of sequences that alternate
between the old (the procession praying for relief from the drought) and
the new (the cream-separator mechanically transforming milk into cream)
has to reveal that the power of the communist idea and the power of the
cinematographic art are equivalent. The rapid multiplication of shots in
the scenes with the cream-separator, cross-cutting from the separator to the
faces—now suspicious, now joyous, now darkened—is there to exalt the
rather unattractive event of milk condensation. A constructive mathematics
has to supplant all Dionysian orgies, and yet, who cannot see that it can
only do so on the condition that it has itself been made Dionysian? The
demonstration of the cream-separator—together with the water jets,
waterfalls, and flashes of lightning that are used as its metaphors—is

followed by abstract numbers that, in the absence of all represented crowds, flash upon the screen the growing number of members of the kolkhoz. These abstract numbers are plastic and meaningful elements whose size swells with the numerical progression and whose flashings harmonize with the lightning and the flowing milk and water. Eisenstein wants us to see these sequences as the cinematographic equivalent of Malevich's suprematist painting. But, more than an abstract painting, what these scenes conjure up for us is a common language that is also a common sensorium of words, rhythms, numbers, and images: the common language of the "I feel" that Eisenstein opposes to Cartesian dualism in his reflections on the Kabuki. He sets this new language of the immediate union of the intelligible and the sensible in opposition to the old forms of mimetic mediation, just as he sets the mechanical miracles of the cream-separator, of the tractor, and of collectivization in opposition to the old prayers asking heaven and its priests for the means to remedy the uncertainties of nature and the evils of property. But it could be that the opposition is a *trompe l'oeil* and that the strange logic, a sort of Dionysian Pavlovism, Eisenstein opposes to the gesticulations of ancient superstitions is very quickly turned on its head. The "abstract" frenzy of the lightning and numbers dancing on the screen that impose the Dionysus-like mathematics of the new world must already have been anticipated in the scenes of the "old," it must have already forged a more profound alliance with the irrationality of superstition.

What really counts in the procession scenes, much more than the "dialectical" play of oppositions Eisenstein enumerates rather offhandedly years after the making of the film, is the frenzied pantomime of genuflecting and signs of the cross. This pantomime is more than the ancient submission to superstition that has to be replaced by the sober attention to the verifiable performance of the machine. It is the power of the idea to become incarnate that cinematographic procedures have to be able to capture if they hope to convert the idea into another body. Montage cannot ensure this conversion through the simple calculation of "attractions," so it must liken itself to this body possessed by an idea in order to bring it about. In his memoirs, Eisenstein says that the principle of montage is captured in its entirety in the superstitious person's belief that a cat is not just a furry mammal, but a combination of lines that has been on intimate terms with all that is dark and ominous since the beginning of time.[5] There is no doubt an element of provocation in all of this: the filmmaker, forced to spend years writing, multiplies the paradoxes and the foggy clues. Still, Eisenstein isn't just being witty and whimsical. Nor is he just shuffling for a reply in the paradox he hurls at the participants at a congress who denounce his formalism and suggest that he should rediscover the warm values of humanity. His supposed formalism, he tells them, relying on Wundt, Spencer, and Lévy-Bruhl, is nothing less than the recovered language of pre-conceptual thought. His use of metaphor and synecdoche in *The General Line* and in *Battleship Potemkin*, Eisenstein tells them, is governed by the same logic that governs the paratactic structures characteristic of Bushman language and Polynesian rituals of childbirth. The formal operations of the cinema assimilate the pure and conscious calculations of the communist project to the unconscious logic governing the deepest layers of the sensory thought and habits of primitive peoples.[6]

If cinema's formal operations secure this assimilation, it must be because the montage that rearranges the sensory affects of superstition is superstition's accomplice. The young komsomol in *The General Line* can turn his head away when the members of the kolkhoz post cow skulls on fence poles to exorcise the bull's malady, and the director can show his allegiance to this attitude by underscoring the return of superstition with an intertitle. But the *mise-en-scène* cannot separate its powers from these exorcisms. It cannot do without these animal masks, skulls, metaphors, and masquerades. Undoubtedly, the taste for masks and hybridization was quite common in Eisenstein's era, though they were most commonly used for the purposes of "critique." In Dix's paintings, in Heartfield's photo-montages, or in the shot of the croaking frogs in *You Only Live Once*, the metaphor or masquerade denounces a certain inhumanity in the human being. Eisenstein's bestiaries do something else entirely. Beyond caricature and metaphor, his bestiaries are a positive affirmation of the original unity of the human and the inhuman, the site where the rational powers of the new rediscover the ecstatic powers of the old. The frenzied speed of the fake competition between the young komsomol and the old Hercules-like peasant and the fairy-like wedding of the bull both exceed everything that may have been required for the depiction of the "new life." Between them, they form what we could properly call a mythology, maybe the last version of the mythology of reason becoming sensible where "the oldest program of German idealism" saw, at the dawn of the nineteenth century, the tasks of art converging with those of the new community.

The heart of the problem is not that we have come to regard this program with suspicion. Our unease as we watch the cascading milk or the wedding of the bull in *The General Line* is not ideological, but aesthetic. It is about what we see. We would love to shake off our discomfort by indicting the film as pure propaganda, but that argument fizzles out quickly. For one because the shots in question are the freest and most beautiful ones Eisenstein ever composed, and for another because propaganda films function differently. A propaganda film must give us a sense of certainty about what we see, it must choose between the documentary that presents what we see as a palpable reality or the fiction that forwards it as a desirable end, all the while keeping narration and symbolization in their respective places. Eisenstein systematically denies us this sense of certainty. Consider the scene of the two brothers who divide up their meager inheritance in accordance with the "old" law. They remove the thatched ceiling and saw the logs of the isba in half, literalizing the metaphor of "dismantling" property. What we expect to see at the end of the scene is the isba surrealistically cut in two, whereas what we actually see is different and distributed over two incompatible registers. On the symbolic level, the sawed off logs instantaneously become a new enclosure fencing in the whole field; on the narrative level, the brother's family leaves, their wagon loaded with the logs the metaphor had already "used" to build the fence. The director has borrowed a figure of speech from classical rhetoric, the syllepsis, where an expression is taken both in its literal and figurative senses. The syllepsis does not distinguish between the specific scene and the world it symbolizes. Here, though, it does so at the price of leaving the elements disjointed and the eye uncertain of what it sees. The end of the famous scene of the cream-separator presents the same counter-effect. On the narrative level, the milk should thicken into cream. Metaphorically, the thick stream has been anticipated by an equivalent symbol that nevertheless contradicts it visually: an ascending jet of water, synonym of prosperity. Visually, both meanings have to be borne by Marfa's kneeling body: the liquid flowing down her outstretched arms, the opposite of the water from the sky of the procession, and the thick cream that dots her cheeks as if it were make-up, the opposite of the dirt-smeared brow of the peasant woman who rises from the old genuflexions.

This is at once too much and too little for a single body to bear. Everything that today's viewers find unbearable about the film is there in Marfa's body. The film wants to present collectivization as desirable, and the most common strategy for making an idea desirable is to project it onto desiring, and desirable, bodies, onto bodies that traffic in the signs of desire. Marfa should do a little more to seduce us than just loosen her headscarf from time to time. She should also convey, however slightly, a *human* desire, a desire for something other than her cream-separator, her bull, or her tractor. A little weakness in the body, a breach in the law, is necessary to make the law

lovable. The carefree and likeable fellow in Boris Barnet's *By the Bluest of Seas*
who abandons communist work for the beautiful eyes of one of the women
in the kolkhoz does more to make communism lovable than Marfa's figure in
all its devotion. A woman without a man, whether husband or lover, with no
parents or children, Marfa only desires communism. Things might even have
worked had she been a virgin of the pure idea, but there is nothing ideal in
Marfa's communism. Quite the contrary: the film is constantly mobilizing
romantic affects that culminate in the true–false love scene where Marfa
is coupled not with the tractor driver, but with the tractor. Some fabric
is needed to mend the belt of the broken-down tractor, and the tractor
driver, who has already sacrificed his shirt-front to the same cause, is about
to use the red flag when Marfa's hand stops him. A silent dialogue ensues.
Marfa half-opens her coat, shows her skirt, and the driver tears off part of
it. Crouching next to the tractor, the driver tears the fabric rip by rip while
Marfa, in her underskirt, hides her face in her hands and laughs, like a
prudish virgin who laughs and cries as she offers herself. The tension in the
scene is as superb as it is intolerable, as had already been the case in the scene
of the dispute over the use of the profits, where the furious determination
of the greedy farmers to distribute the common money subjects Marfa to
what she experiences as gang rape.

That is what leaves us cold: this enormous rerouting of energies that
invests the communist tractor with the affects "normally" found in the
relationship between one human body and another. But, once again, ideology
is not the heart of the matter. This excess—or ecstasy—of the idea that
today's viewers object to in *The General Line*, calling it a "propaganda film,"
is essentially what Soviet propagandists also objected to when they indicted
the film as an exercise in "formalist cinema," as completely antithetical to
the representation of "living men." We want to convince ourselves and
others that Eisenstein's cinema suffers only from its identification with the
Soviet regime. But the problem goes much deeper. Other artists who are
also emblems of the commitment to communism have fared better. Brecht
succeeded in identifying the figure of the cynical observer with that of the
engaged critic, and the lessons of dialectical pedagogy with the athleticism
of the boxing ring or the mockery of the cabaret, the first under the
aesthetic canon of Dadaism, the second under that of the New Objectivity.
He identified the work of the Marxist playwright with a certain artistic
modernity, with an art that stages the denunciation of the age-old ideals
of art. This ironic modernity not only survived communism's political fall,
it has actually become the most banal form of the alliance between artistic

novelty and the critique of dominant imaginaries. This banal version is a threat to Brecht, but also a protection, the very protection Eisenstein lacks. The discomfort Eisenstein creates today has less to do with communism than with the aesthetic project he identified with the propagation of the communist idea. Unlike Brecht, Eisenstein never wanted to instruct or to teach his audience how to see and create a distance. Brecht set out to purge theatrical representation of identification, fascination, absorption. Eisenstein, instead, wanted to capture all of them and multiply their power. Rather than saying that he put the young art of cinema at the service of communism, it would be more accurate to say that he put communism through the test of cinema, through the test of the idea of art and modernity that Eisenstein saw incarnated in cinema: that of a language of ideas becoming a language of sensations. A communist art was not for him a critical art aimed at bringing about a new consciousness; it was an ecstatic art that directly transformed the links between ideas into chains of images in order to bring about a new regime of sensibility.

That is the heart of the problem. Our grudge with Eisenstein has less to do with the ideals he wanted us to share with him than with the fact that he turns our supposed modernity on its head. He reminds us of that idea of artistic modernity to which the cinema once thought it could identify its technique: the anti-representative art that was going to replace the stories and characters of yore with a language of ideas/sensations and with the direct communication of affects. Marfa's lovingly torn skirt doesn't just refer us to a century of revolutionary illusions that have faded into the background. It also asks us what century we ourselves live in to derive so much pleasure—our Deleuzes in our pockets—from the love affair upon a sinking ship between a young woman in first class and a young man in third.

NOTES

1. Sergei Eisenstein, "Through Theater to Cinema," in *Film Form*, ed. and trans. Jay Leyda (New York: Harcourt, Brace and Company, 1949) 8.
2. Sergei Eisenstein, "How I Became a Director," in *Selected Works Volume 3: Writings, 1934–1947*, ed. Richard Taylor, trans. William Powell (London: British Film Institute, 1996) 285–6.

3. Sergei Eisenstein, "The Cinematographic Principle and the Ideogram," in *Film Form*, 28.
4. Sergei Eisenstein, "The Filmic Fourth Dimension," in *Film Form*, 67.
5. Sergei Eisenstein, *Mémoires*, vol. I, trans. Jacques Aumont (Paris: UGE, 1978) 59.
6. Sergei Eisenstein, "Film Form: New Problems," in *Film Form*, 122–49.

CHAPTER 2

A Silent *Tartuffe*

Friedrich Murnau's film versions of *Tartuffe* (1925) and *Faust* (1926) offer
the perfect opportunity to point out that the relationship between cinema
and theater is a little more complex than the champions of the purity of
the cinematographic art, from Jean Epstein to Robert Bresson, would have
us believe. Some filmmakers, including some of the greatest, were never
really convinced by the notion that the two "languages" were radically
heterogeneous, and they tried, even during the silent period, to bring the
masterpieces of the stage to the silver screen. The question then is: how did
they hope—indeed how were they able—to pull this off when the silent
image was all they had at their disposal? How were they going to make
cinematographic language say: "Cover up that bosom, which I can't / Endure
to look on" or "Heaven forbids, 'tis true, some satisfactions"? In some
respects, this is Lessing's classic question in the *Laocoön* about the relation
of the arts to one another. We might even say that the cinematographic
transposition of Molière's play poses still more formidable problems than
those attendant on the attempt to determine whether sculpture, like poetry,
can represent pain. *Tartuffe* is a play that represents hypocrisy, which is to
say a difference between being and appearance that, by definition, lacks a
specific expressive code, else no one would fall for it. Moreover, everyone
knows that "hypocrite" comes from the Greek word *hupokrites*, meaning actor,
someone who speaks through a mask. The comedy of the hypocrite is such a
standard of the theater because of how well it showcases the theater's ability
to play with appearances. In the play, the confrontation between the lie and
the truth that unmasks it is secondary to the sequence of appearances that
succeeds in transforming an appearance into its opposite. Showing that the
devout man is really a lecherous lout doesn't interest Molière half as much
as the process whereby he transforms Tartuffe's edifying discourse into a
discourse of seduction. Playing on the ambiguity of the words (heaven/
heavenly/divine, devotion/altar), he turns a speech of religious devotion

into one of romantic devotion right under Elmire's nose. The success of the comedy of the hypocrite depends on its use of the oldest dramatic trick in the book: the double meaning of words. If it works, it is because Tartuffe, like Oedipus, says something other than what he is saying, because, in general, words say something other than what their speakers intend them to say. Which explains, by the by, why we can always be taken in by Tartuffe, even though, as Madame Bordin says in *Bouvard and Pécuchet*, "everyone knows what a Tartuffe is." Knowing what a Tartuffe is doesn't prevent seduction, but enables it: our knowledge frees us to savor for its own sake the seduction of words that say something other than what they are saying.

We are now in a position to formulate the problem posed by the cinematographic representation of the hypocrite: can a shot show something other than what it shows? The problem is laid bare by the modern prologue, the "properly cinematographic" prologue that scenarist Carl Meyer invented for this version of *Tartuffe*. In it, we're introduced to a contemporary hypocrite, an elderly housekeeper who cajoles her master with an eye to his inheritance. The opening of the film shows the housekeeper getting up, grumbling, to shake the shoes of the unfortunate old dotard she abandoned behind her in the corridor, before she goes back and flashes him a false little smile. We immediately see that she's a hypocrite because we see the deception going on behind the old dotard's back. Our position as spectators is already separated from his position as a character, and our superior knowledge results in a deficit in pleasure: we suffer from not being taken in ourselves, as we are taken in by the charms of the speeches that aim at seducing Elmire. The image does not have the power to show two things at once, unless it is in the didactic mode of the symbol: the image of the housekeeper carefully sharpening the barber's razor on a leather strap also reveals her intentions. In matters of appearance, cinema's real strength isn't that it can show us who this being that we take for someone else really is, but that it can show, in the subsequent shot, that what we saw happen in the preceding shot is in fact something else. This other barber, furiously sharpening his razor in the grip of anger, is simply getting ready to give his client a close, neat shave (*The Great Dictator*). The cuckolded husband who stands in front of his wife and shoots himself in the mouth is actually just taking a bite out of a chocolate revolver and enjoying scaring the pants off of his wife (*Adam's Rib*). That is what we are shown in the subsequent shots: one more shot is always needed to thwart appearances.

Cinema's appropriation of the comedy of the hypocrite is plagued from the outset by two principles of cinematographic representation. The first is a principle of non-duplicity: an image always shows what it shows and no more. The image tendentiously annuls the duplicity of speech. We could call this the *Moonfleet* effect: the image, all by itself, contradicts the one who says: "Don't believe me, I'm lying to you."[1] The second is a principle of supplementarity: making a shot say something other than what it says requires another shot that completes, and reverses, what the previous shot had started. This principle of course presupposes the continuity of the dramatic chain of events. It is almost impossible to correct a shot from a distance, the problem John Ford faced in *The Man Who Shot Liberty Valance*. We see the clumsy Ransom Stoddard (James Stewart) miraculously shoot and kill Liberty Valance (Lee Marvin). A scene much later in the film shows us *who* actually shot and killed Liberty Valance: Tom Doniphon (John Wayne), who was standing across the street on the night of the showdown. But we cannot harmonize the truth proposed by this later scene with our visual experience. It is impossible to modify the point of view after the fact, to reinsert into the field of vision what had not been there before, to change the direction of the fatal bullet. This later truth doesn't depend on visual agreement; its only substance is in the *words* Doniphon uses to reveal it to Stoddard. It may just be that this is the most intimate meaning of the famous "Print the legend" on which the film closes: not the banal idea that people prefer pretty lies to the naked truth, but the much more troubling observation that the image, unlike language, is incapable of transforming another image.

What, then, can cinema do with the theatrical comedy of the hypocrite? What can the silent cinema do with Tartuffe? How will Murnau use cinema to show that "the clothes don't make the man" when he had just used all the resources of film to show the opposite in *The Last Laugh*? The clothes do make the man. Is the demoted doorman, bereft of his striped uniform, anything more than a human wreck? Two possible ways of dealing with these difficulties are available. The first is to let the difficulties, the citations, and the theater play themselves out in the theater. Scenarist Carl Meyer opts for this solution and embeds the cinematographic transposition of Molière's *Tartuffe* in a contemporary story of hypocrisy. The old man's nephew, suspecting the housekeeper's scheme to swindle him out of his inheritance, arrives disguised as a traveling filmmaker and tries to unmask the hypocrite with his projection of *Tartuffe*. The plot structure is the same as we find in *Hamlet*: the spectacle within the spectacle will force the hypocrite into the open. This dramatic structure, as it turns out, is ineffective, since *Tartuffe* doesn't fit into either of the cases where it can be effective. In one case, the spectacle within

the spectacle works, as it does, for instance, in Minnelli's *The Pirate*, where
the spectacle allows the false Macoco, a traveling actor mistakenly taken for
the notorious pirate, to reveal the real pirate, who passes himself off for a
respectable bourgeois. But it works in *The Pirate* due to the introduction of
a very particular motivation: the real pirate, now a rotund bourgeois, would
rather reveal his true identity than let the actor steal his role. The pleasure
in theatrical impersonation and swagger brings about a "truth" prejudicial
to the reality of the character, and celebrates much less the defeat of the
criminal than the victory of the actor, who appears to the young Bovaryst
bride as the real incarnation of her romantic image of the pirate. In the
other, it fails, as for instance in *Hamlet*, where the representation does not
force the hypocrite into the open. But the failure in the fiction is still one
of fiction's successes. It confirms the impossibility of knowing constitutive
of the character and the futility of the desire to know that, perhaps, hides a
more secret desire to remain ignorant. It also confirms the superiority of the
actor, who neither lies nor tells the truth, over the liar who hides the truth
and the truth seeker determined to smoke him out.

Tartuffe doesn't fit into either of these fictional "successes." The spectacle
within the spectacle unmasks no one and reveals nothing. The representation
doesn't unmask the hypocrite; for that, the film will need a poison flask taken
directly from melodrama, the word "poison" written all over it. The fact is
that the purpose of this whole machinery isn't to unmask the hypocrite,
but to serve as an abstract signifier of modernity that invests this modern
cinematographic adaptation with a self-imposed alienation effect. But what
exactly is this, then, this doubly alienated *Tartuffe*?

The cinematographic transposition has to rely on something other than
the scenario's recourse to the theatrical machinery of showing a spectacle
within a spectacle. It must, in other words, have its own built-in principle of
conversion, its own way of making the variations in the bodily movements
of the characters act like slips and slides of speech. The playwright displaces
a speech. The filmmaker must entice a silhouette, this black silhouette
that stands in such sharp relief against the white walls, into movement.
In Molière, Tartuffe is a being composed of words twice over: of his own
words and of the words spoken about him before he ever appears on the
stage. Murnau's film, conversely, is characterized by a refusal to use words
that goes beyond the constraints of silent film and the economic use of
intertitles. There are symbols for this refusal in the film itself, in Tartuffe
yawning in reply to Orgon's request that he convert Elmire to his faith, and,
possibly, in Dorine's advice to the same Orgon—"Ask nothing, just come

and see." Murnau's Tartuffe is not a man of words, but a tall and somber silhouette, a long overcoat, a black pole crowned by a white ball, a round head perpetually hidden behind a book. The film opts for a radical solution to our opening question about how to make cinematographic language say: "Cover up that bosom, which I can't / Endure to look on." It makes Tartuffe and Dorine's meeting a non-meeting. The black silhouette walking down the stairs, its head buried in a book, takes no notice of the soubrette mounting the stairs. The problem for the cinematographic fiction will be how to make this silhouette move, how to transform it into its opposite, into the lewd man in shirtsleeves with large, gaping mouth sprawled out on Elmire's bed at the end of the film.

How will Murnau bring about this transformation? Molière's Tartuffe is done in by words, by the predilection for seducing with words common to the priest and the lecher. What equivalent power does silent film have at its disposal to animate, and betray, the silhouette, to lead it to lower its guard? A first answer might be: Tartuffe can give himself away, to others and to the camera, by his gaze. All the variations in Tartuffe's expressions are variations of the gaze. The face the devout man buries behind his book is animated by his eyes, or by one of them to be exact. The film visualizes hypocrisy with this eye that steals a sidelong, appreciative glance at a morsel of food, a ring, or a breast, while the other continues to look straight ahead. Tartuffe, in other words, betrays his real character by leering. It remains to find out what leering means. Are the sidelong glances of Emil Jannings/Tartuffe different from those of Emil Jannings/Haroun-al-Rachid, the lustful sultan of *Waxworks*? Lotte Eisner writes: "He [Murnau] gets Karl Freund's camera to explore all the crevices, every wrinkle, every twitch, every blink, in order to reveal, along with the freckles and bad teeth, the dissimulated vices."[2] But what the camera shows us in *Tartuffe* is a being on the lookout, a being fearful of being found out. It just so happens that an eye looking askance can be an illustration of two opposing things. It can be a covetous eye susceptible to the provocation trying to surprise the lustful being who lurks behind the black silhouette. And it can also be the opposite, an eye surveying the traps set to reveal his desire. Tartuffe's eye leers because it is constantly tracking the lateral and oblique movements that should escape its notice. The attraction drawing his eye towards the desired object is always preceded by the eye's observation of who is, or could be, looking. Elmire's machinations to show the hidden Orgon the truth about Tartuffe fail because the bosom she puts right under his nose is less visible to Tartuffe than the hazy reflection of Orgon's face in the tea kettle. Elmire's powerlessness, however, is also

Tartuffe's. This silent hypocrite, bereft of the seductive power of words, is in a situation akin to that of the "saboteurs" of the Stalinist regime, who never sabotaged anything lest their identity as saboteurs be revealed. Tartuffe, above all, must not let anyone notice he is a hypocrite. This explains why the seduction scene, in which Elmire is the one doing all the work, seems so forced. Elmire's whole show [*mimique*], unless it is meant for someone other than Tartuffe, is forced, just as is, indeed even more so, the relationship between the shots of Tartuffe's leering eye and the shots of the objects offered up to his desire—her lower legs and heaving chest. These objects are not so much what Tartuffe the lustful being sees but what should arouse his desire. They are objects of desire in general—the exposed flesh between the boot and skirt and the quivering, palpitating bosoms that went to young men's heads in nineteenth-century novels. The film shows us these objects of desire so that *we* can attribute them to Tartuffe's desire. It seems, though, that what should arouse his lust actually arouses in him the more prosaic desire of making sure no one is watching.

At first sight, it seems that the fiction adopted strives in vain for an operation that never takes place: the conversion of Tartuffe's body into another *gestus*. And yet, the set designs, composed entirely of two types of places, seem to have been created precisely for the purpose of bringing about this conversion. We have, in the hallway, the landing, and the staircase, the classic "passageways" of theatrical fiction, passageways that are, as a matter of principle, always open (even when they happen to be a bedroom, like Marschallin's in *The Rose-Bearer*). This theatrical space where it need not speak but only parade about is the black silhouette's place of choice. And then we have the closed spaces of cinematographic intimacy. These spaces are not secretive but, on the contrary, closed volumes where bodies are locked in, trapped, and threatened by the eye looking in through the keyhole. The task is to entice Tartuffe to move from the theatrical space where he parades his cinematographic silhouette at ease to these trap rooms. But this fictional as well as decorative strategy doesn't work, least of all if we think of it as a mechanism designed to induce the hypocrite to confess and reveal his true character. A character who's unable to control appearances and who has been reduced to the role of a suspicious beast cannot be caught at his own game. Someone else has to be caught in his place. In the last scene, the passive and transfixed Elmire, wearing a flirtatious décolleté dress that makes her seem more mummy-like than attractive, is joined in her room by a different character, who has, without any transition, taken the place of the black silhouette: a drunken and lewd tramp reminiscent of those characters we find in Labiche and Offenbach, the sort one recruits from the bottom of the barrel to play the roles of distinguished guests at a dinner party meant to impress a sucker, but who resume their natural state at the most inopportune moment. The cinematographic transformation of the body never takes place because the hypocrite has not been allowed to command the play of appearances. The character Orgon chases violently from his home at the end of the film is a different theatrical character than the one who had duped him.

If the cinematographic transposition of *Tartuffe* relies on making the character's gaze do the work that words with their double meanings do in the theater, then it does not succeed. There remains another possibility. Murnau's *Tartuffe* tells a radically different story from Molière's, a story, incidentally, perfectly suited to the resources of cinema. The real difference between the film and theater versions is not to be found in the "modern" prelude and epilogue, but rather manifests itself once the "story itself" gets under way. In the film, as in Molière's play, Tartuffe is absent, but the status of this absence is different. The two first acts of the play manage to sketch the image of the (falsely) devout man by means of what the characters have to say about him, Tartuffe being the object of everyone's obsession. The film doesn't use words to fill out the character, but instead identifies him with a shadow. More than the falsely devout man who shows up to swindle the family, Tartuffe is the shadow that comes to separate Orgon and Elmire, the shadow that darkens Orgon's eyes as he lowers Elmire's arms when she is about to embrace him. I spoke above about sentences with double meanings. Now at least one made its way into the film, in Orgon's reply to Elmire's declaration of love ("I'm so happy!"): "If you only knew how happy I am!" Orgon is obviously thinking of a different happiness than hers, of the other love object he is contemplating through Elmire's now transparent body. While she rejoices in her husband's return, he is dreaming of the new friend he made during his trip. This new friend is the shadow that comes between them, the one Elmire confronts again only a little later, when she goes to Orgon's room to try to win him back and the camera leaves us behind his door. This meeting with the shadow accounts for the intensity of Elmire's incredible exit, her crinoline dress gaining formidable weight as she descends the stairs. The crinoline dress, like the powdered valets, is of course an anachronism in this late eighteenth century set, but not a random one. The Marie-Antoinette dress crushing Elmire's body as she hastens down the stairs captures the whole transformation: rather than a historical discrepancy, her dress is a fictional displacement. Elmire has been transformed into the Countess Almaviva from *The Marriage of Figaro*, who painfully realizes that her husband doesn't love her anymore. Her incredible descent and the tears that fall on Orgon's medallion are the equivalent of two arias from Mozart, a *Dove sono* and a *Porgi amor*. Similarly, the scene of Elmire writing, with Dorine's help, the letter she hopes will entice Tartuffe into her room transposes the celebrated duet between the Countess and Susanna.

Everything we had found confusing about this *Tartuffe sans* seduction falls into place as a result of this fictional displacement. Murnau's story is not the story of a hypocrite's machinations and designs, but of Orgon's malady and the treatment Elmire concocts to cure it. Everything revolves around Elmire and Orgon, around Elmire and Orgon's love for this shadow. Hence the importance of those scenes of Orgon anxiously preparing Tartuffe's lunch or lovingly watching over his rest. These scenes visualize, in a sense, Dorine's ironic quips about her master's folly in Molière's play. Here is the principle of transforming lines from the play into film images. Instead of showing what the characters say in the play, the images show what is said about them. The bustle and commotion of valets we see at the beginning of the film visualize Madame Pernelle's harsh words about her daughter-in-law's servants; the shot of Orgon standing in front of the arbor and looking at Tartuffe napping on a hammock visualizes Dorine's words. In this over exposed setting, we see Orgon's dream, this dream that traverses the sordid reality we see with Elmire's eyes: an enormous tomcat, hideous and sated, curled up on a hammock.

This principle of visualization, more than the determined cinemato-graphic transposition of the elements of the theatrical fable, inscribes the image and fable of Tartuffe into a series that belongs to cinema in general, to expressionist cinema in particular, and to Murnau's cinema even more so: a series of stories of appearances that are no longer stories of confession. Cinema, we've already seen, doesn't lead hypocrites to confess, but tells the stories of substantial and beguiling shadows that have to be destroyed. A shadow doesn't confess, it vanishes, disappears. The story of Orgon falling prey to a shadow resembles other stories Murnau has told us in his films. Think of the young poet and civil servant in *Phantom*, who is literally knocked down by the staggering force of a white apparition; of the young Hutter rushing to the land of ghosts in *Nosferatu*; of the farmer, in *Sunrise*, standing before the apparition of the foreigner.

All of these shadows have to be dissipated. But dissipating shadows is a tall order for the cinema, since it excels at doing exactly the opposite, at giving shadows substance, at making them objects of love and fascination from which only a miracle or violent blow can deliver us. That's what this *Tartuffe* is all about. Murnau's film is about Elmire's machinations to win back her husband, about the operation she must perform to excise from Orgon's heart the intruder who has made her invisible to him. It's an act of exorcism, the chasing of a specter. This change of fable explains why Tartuffe's character is so impoverished in the film. He who, in Molière, is in control of everything, including his own perdition, has become, from the very start, the intruder to be expelled, the one who must be tempted into error so he can be expelled. The film deprives Tartuffe of all initiative, so much so that even his assault on Elmire's virtue is singularly ambiguous. The missal he places upon the bosom exposed by the décolleté dress is certainly blasphemous, but not devouringly sensual; at most, it replaces the handkerchief from the play. And the intertitles pare down whatever erotic charge the gesture may have even further. The initiative belongs to Elmire, the one who wants to chase out the shadow, unmask it. I suggested above that the big seduction scene is quite strange, that Elmire's whole show is a bit too mechanical, and that the relationship between Tartuffe's gaze and the objects of desire is problematic inasmuch as it has to work through us. This would all be very strange unless Elmire's show is actually meant for someone else, which indeed it is. Elmire has put on this décolleté dress for the third party hidden behind the curtain, Orgon. Recall Madame Pernelle's words to Elmire: "A woman who would please her husband's eye / Alone, wants no such wealth of fineries."

But one must tell Madame Pernelle that Elmire is not out to please only her husband, but also this person infatuated with Tartuffe. We should add that Elmire, by thus offering her bosom, does two things at once: she offers to Tartuffe's hard-to-elicit desire what should be the object of Orgon's desire, and she offers herself in sacrifice to dissipate the shadow. She offers her neck to the dark man, just as Hutter's fiancée offers hers to Nosferatu's fangs to free Hutter and the others from the vampire when the cock crows. Elmire offers herself to Tartuffe to restore Orgon, like the corrupted peasant of *Sunrise*, to the world of the living, to enable him, like the selfish and ambitious son of *Burning Soil*, to be reunited with his family. Her erotic show is a sacrificial rite. In *Nosferatu*, the sacrifice causes the shadow to vanish, whereas in *Tartuffe* the shadow does not vanish, but is annihilated by substitution.

We should pause a moment and examine closely the difference between these two solutions, as it encapsulates the problem of the cinematographic fable, that is, of the relationship between cinema and the appearances it creates. Cinema showcases its powers of illusion with these shadows that hold the characters captive. To say that the visual narrative must dissipate these shadows is tantamount to saying that it must dissipate the immediate powers of the cinema. There are two ways to dissipate shadows. One uses the phantasmatic power itself to this end: the *phantasmata*-producing machine takes it upon itself to dissipate the shadows it has itself created—the magic of the machine dissolves Nosferatu's black shadow right before our eyes. This first way is, as it were, a family affair: cinematographic technique dissipates the shadows of cinematographic fiction. The second way is completely different. It assumes that cinema has renounced the power to dissipate *its* shadows, that it was stepped out of its domain and confiscated its figures. That is what happens in *Tartuffe*. The dark shadow, set so clearly in relief against the white walls, is as much a figure of the cinema as that hazy and overexposed universe, Orgon's kingdom. To dissipate its own shadows, cinema must back up Elmire's strategy, it must help her lure Tartuffe out of the relationship that ties his black shadow to Orgon's hazy kingdom. Elmire has to lure him out of the land of cinematographic immediacy. Her whole fictional strategy boils down to separating Tartuffe from the mode of being of cinematographic *phantasmata* that protects him. This shadow that cannot be tricked into confession, as it might be in the theater, can likewise not be dissipated cinematographically. The only remaining alternative is to move the shadow into another, intermediary, set. The cinematographic silhouette walks into the bedroom where Elmire tries to trap it only to find itself confined by the frames of a genre painting. Elmire's romantic bedroom, at first reminiscent of a Fragonard, becomes a Dutch interior, a pictorial space where bodily proximity and the distribution of light and shadow lead the black silhouette to be lost from sight.

Murnau eliminates Tartuffe by substituting one body for another. The body that enters Elmire's bedroom is a different body, the rustic and satisfied body of a farmer, a bit drunk and loud-mouthed, just like the bodies we find in the paintings of van Ostade or Adriaen Brouwer. Unable to dissipate the shadow, Murnau eliminates it by the exactly inverse procedure: he turns the shadow into a body that cannot hide the identifying traits of its origin, the evidence of its difference. The plebeian body sprawled out on Elmire's bed is a body out of its element, a body that clearly does not belong in Orgon's aristocratic abode, a total stranger to the ways of being exemplified by Elmire's transfixed body. Its more natural habitat is a tavern scene. The difference in social class is also a difference in the distribution of arts and genres. While the cinematographic shadow belongs to the Romantic poetics that breaks with the generic principle of adapting artistic forms to the subjects represented, Elmire's, and Murnau's, strategy is to lead the cinematographic shadow back to a classical universe where a genre corresponds to a subject and where characters have the physiognomy and language befitting their status. The unsettling and elusive cinematographic body reverts to being an easily identifiable pictorial body that can be put in its place, which is clearly not the home of Elmire and Orgon. Tartuffe is visually expelled from their universe well before he is physically thrown out by Orgon.

We would be wrong to regard Murnau's cinematographic transposition of the theatrical fiction of the hypocrite as a straightforward translation. Tartuffe's story must be changed in the land of cinematographic shadows. Cinema deprives the seducer of the theatrical means of seduction and creates a shadow to be dissipated. But what can no longer be entrusted to the double meaning of words in the theater can likewise not be guaranteed by the means proper to cinematographic magic. The shadow has to be re-embodied and restored to a mode of representation where bodies, and the differences between them, are clearly identifiable. To resolve the fictional problem, Murnau identifies Tartuffe with a pictorial figure, a character from genre painting. But this solution, to place the camera in front of a figure from genre painting, means that cinema has in some ways renounced what had until then seemed its own way of imitating painting and substituting the theater, its own way of creating and dissipating shadows, its own immediate magic. Murnau's film fictionally eliminates Tartuffe at the very high price of having aesthetically to eliminate with him all of cinematographic expressionism. Hence the film's grayness of tone. The problem isn't really that the platitude of the intertitles awakens at every turn our nostalgia for the lost enchantment of Molière's words, but that, to appropriate Tartuffe, cinema must work against its own enchantments. With *Tartuffe*, Murnau puts the last nail in the coffin of expressionism by annihilating with his hero a certain idea of what makes cinema unique.

NOTES

1. For an extended discussion of this effect in Fritz Lang's *Moonfleet*, see "The Child Director," Chapter 4 below.

2. Lotte Eisner, *The Haunted Screen: Expressionism in the German Cinema and the Influence of Max Reinhardt*, trans. Roger Greaves (Berkeley: University of California Press, 1973) 269. Translation slightly modified.

CHAPTER 3

From One Manhunt to Another

Fritz Lang between Two Ages

Since its release in 1955, Fritz Lang's *While the City Sleeps* has been seen as an expression of radical pessimism by an artist who had grown disenchanted with democracy and with the art of cinema through the combined forces of the American people and Hollywood. If that is the case, then what is really the object of Lang's pessimism, and how does he turn it into fable? It is standard to assume that the heart of the plot is the all-out competition between the big shots of Amos Kyne's news empire: the editor, the head of wire services, and the manager of picture services fight it out to see who gets the position of managing director of the empire when its founder dies and the business is turned over to his spoiled and incompetent son. The son gets the competition going by promising the position to the one who succeeds in unmasking the maniacal woman-killer whose crimes are at that moment terrorizing the city. A whole web of feminine intrigues is deployed for the service of the competitors. As for the visual space of the film, it seems to be entirely composed of the bodily movements and exchange of glances that cast these schemers into always unstable relationships of inferiority or superiority; in the huge glass office, they spend their days spying on what is happening on the other side of the corridor in the hopes of catching a meaningful smile or motion by surprise, all the while hiding what they themselves are doing, fashioning a mask meant to deceive the others about the power relationships at play. The assumption, in short, is that everything revolves around the competition and the secrets permanently lodged in the bowels of the immense machinery whose business is to bring to the people the light of information. Lang's pessimism consists in observing, and making us observe, that all these people hunting down the murderer are as unpleasant as he is, perhaps even more so.

But it could be that the show put on by these schemers is only a comforting illusion, and that the plot's black heart is really made up of the actions of the only two honest members of Kyne's empire, the reporter Ed Mobley and his fiancée Nancy, a secretary. Mobley is not angling for a promotion, nor is he interested in getting tangled up in any schemes. All he really wants to do is unmask the murderer, and he has his own idea about how he's going to do that: he'll lead the murderer to reveal himself by talking to him. Mobley's project is, a priori, contradictory. To speak to the murderer, he must first know who the murderer is, and if he knows who he is, it is because he has already been caught. Even the Machiavellian examiner Porphyry would be powerless if Raskolnikov hadn't bitten the bait and come out to meet him. Mobley is no examiner though, he's a television reporter, and speaking face to face with people he doesn't know is what he does every night at eight o'clock. On the night in question, he goes to the television studio ready to speak to his viewers, as he always does, and to speak to one viewer in particular, the murderer. Armed with the insubstantial pieces of evidence he got from a policeman friend, Mobley sketches the murderer's Identikit, tells him he has been identified and that soon it'll be all over for him. Without seeing the murderer, Mobley looks at him, he summons him with his voice to meet this gaze. And suddenly, mid-sentence, a spectacular camera movement anticipates the effect with a shot reverse-shot that places the camera in front of the murderer and the television monitor in the reverse angle. This literal rendition of the "face to face" that introduces the reporter into every home is at the same time a trope that inverses the very meaning of the word "television." The *televised* is no longer the one seen on television, but the one seen by it. In this scene, the televised is the murderer, who is told to recognize himself as the one of whom, and to whom, Mobley speaks.

Lang performs with this camera movement a standard theatrical operation, well known since Aristotle as recognition, the change from ignorance to knowledge. But, more than simply the process that leads from ignorance to knowledge, recognition is the operation that brings the identified and unidentified persons into alignment. The paradigmatic example is to be found in *Oedipus Rex*, where Oedipus learns that he himself is the murderer he's been looking for when the messenger, pointing at him, tells the herdsman: "here's the man that was that child." There is recognition in a nutshell, in the junction of the two demonstratives the herdsman had tried so hard to prevent. Indeed, all the other characters in the play who either know or suspect the secret spare no efforts to prevent the alignment of the two identities, to postpone the moment of recognition when Oedipus gets caught in his own trap—a trap set by the one who knew nothing and who above all had to remain ignorant, though he was, at the same time, the only one who insisted on knowing.

This is what our scene in the film is all about. Evidently, though, Lang has inverted everything in Aristotle's schema of recognition. For one, the audience has known the murderer's face ever since he was shown in action in the opening shots of the film, quite some time before this scene. For another, the moment of recognition is not the moment when the trap closes, but when it is set, when the character who does not know pretends to know and tells someone he doesn't know: "I know you're him." Feigning to know more than one does to get the suspect to fall into the trap and cough up the missing evidence is nothing new, but elementary police work. But that's not what's happening here, as is shown, *a contrario*, by an episode a little earlier on in the film, when the police arrest the unfortunate super of the building for seeming the ideal suspect and take him back to the station, where they put him through the usual treatment: the bright lights projected on the face, the harassing questions, the intimidation, etc. This whole show, Mobley tells his friend Lieutenant Kaufman, is useless and bound to get him nowhere. Mobley puts what he knows and doesn't know to a completely different use. There are no light projectors shining in the suspect's face, no questions, there's no harassment or intimidation. Mobley is not out to make the suspect on hand confess to having committed the crime, but to bring the unidentified criminal to the recognition that he has been recognized. That requires an apparatus that institutes a different kind of face to face: a face to face with someone who is closer to you than any policeman can ever be, precisely because he is farthest away, because he only sees you from far away; a face to face with someone who is instantly on intimate terms with you, who speaks to you while speaking to everyone else, and to you just as to everyone else.

What does Mobley do in this scene, then? Two things at once. While his words sketch the Identikit that tells the criminal what he is, his eyes lock the criminal in their gaze and direct him to where he must recognize himself: in the Identikit. The problem, of course, is that Mobley's Identikit is an insubstantial illusion, an amalgam of two heterogeneous elements: the set of individuating traits (age, physical strength, hair color) Mobley uses to describe *who* the murderer is, though these never suffice to individuate anyone; and a standard and well-known clinical portrait that says only *what* he is, to what category of criminal pathology he belongs. The police would have no use for such an Identikit, nor is it intended for them. The only person who can find it useful is the person who has to recognize himself in it: the one assumed to be there facing Mobley, the one instructed to identify his *who* to this hotchpotch of distinctive traits. The murderer, by the same token, is the

only one who can expose himself, who can go where he is expected through
the mediation of the pleasure of having been recognized for *what* he is, and
the terror of having been recognized for *who* he is. The visual counterpart to
this double mediation is the double grimace of Robert Manners, played by
John Barrymore Jr. Whether in front of the fictional screen of the television
or in front of the real screen of the camera, the double register of the actor's
expression is absolutely stereotypical. The initial feeling of satisfaction—a
broad smile, eyes shining—is superseded by a growing sense of panic—a
snarl, eyes widening in alarm, and hands that move into action and clutch
the crossbar of the chair, just as later on they'll clutch the mother's neck and,
towards the end, Dorothy Kyne's neck. The actor's performance exhausts
itself in the variations on this double register, particularly the snarl. It is all
he can do to convey the distress mechanically triggered in him by the sight of
a woman's legs, his feverishness before the projected action, his ambivalent
feelings towards his mother, or his attitude when confronted by Mobley's
imaginary gaze. The stereotypy of Barrymore's performance cannot but
remind us of a performance of much higher caliber from a quarter of a
century earlier, also by an actor playing the role of a psychopathic killer, a
sort of brother of Robert Manners. His stereotyped grimaces remind us of
all the expressive nuances—the transitions from carefree stroller to savage
beast to prostrate victim—that Peter Lorre brings to his role in *M*, another
manhunt story, for which *While the City Sleeps* is, in some ways, the American
remake.

It is of course possible to explain away the difference between the two
by appealing to the quality of the actors, and it is well known that Lang
had nothing but harsh words for the young Barrymore. But what is also well
known is that Lang left a very small margin of initiative to the personal talent
of his actors: when he discovered during the filming of *M* that Peter Lorre
couldn't whistle, he did the whistling for him instead of dropping it from
the film. In other words, even if John Barrymore Jr. couldn't act as well as
Lang might have wanted, it is reasonable to think that he acted as Lang told
him to. He may not have known how to give a *stereotyped performance*, but that
is what he was asked to do. The expressive simplification has nothing to do
with the incompetence of the actor, but is integral to the very apparatus of
the *mise-en-scène*: this apparatus is what has changed since *M*. If it has changed,
it isn't because Lang has lost his creative touch, but because an apparatus of
cinematographic *mise-en-scène* is a way of playing with a political and social
apparatus of visibility, a way of using one of its tacit resources, of rendering
its implicit activity explicit. The stereotypy of Robert Manners' grimace is

the polar opposite of M's savage and conquering whistling because Lang is working with different apparatuses of visibility in M and in *While the City Sleeps*.

It would be worthwhile then to backtrack and consider for a moment the episode in M that corresponds to the remote face to face between Mobley and the murderer that launches the manhunt. Midway through M, the police, following a microscopic search of psychiatric hospitals, identify the murderer and his whereabouts. Armed with a magnifying glass, a policeman examines the windowsill of his lodgings, where he finds, as he runs his fingers on the woodgrain, shavings from the red pencil the murderer had used to write his taunting messages. While they are searching his lodgings, the murderer is out and about. He is standing in front of a shop window with a little girl he has just met. Both are visibly quite happy: happy with what they are looking at, happy with being together. His eyes follow the child's hand as she points to the toy of her dreams. He loves being a *flâneur*, he loves looking at shop windows, he loves little girls, he loves pleasing them. He seems to have momentarily forgotten the goal of the operation: he is just delighting in the present. She, too, is happy, since she loves toys and adults who are kind to little girls. A little later, when she sees the chalk mark on his shoulder, all she thinks about is cleaning up the stain on the "poor old man." The manhunt is about to begin, and once it does there'll be no respite, so that this scene is the hero's last moment of grace, and we must understand "grace" in the strong sense of the term. It is not a last moment of respite, but something more like a grace granted to the character, the grace he has been allotted as a character. It was but a moment earlier that a masterfully arranged composition had shown us his transition from normal person to furious and pitiless beast hunting its prey; and it is but a moment later that the hunt against him will be in full swing. But for now, there is a moment of grace when the murderer is allowed to delight in a spectacle, a touch, a sensation, and to delight in it aesthetically, disinterestedly. Before the scenario condemns the character, before he is left with no chance of survival, the *mise-en-scène* grants him his chance at being human. Not at being a sick man in need of protection, but his chance at being a carefree *flâneur* in a crowd, nothing more than a peaceful image seen through a shop window. It grants him his photogenic chance, in Jean Epstein's sense of the term.

The issue here is not one of narrative suspension, but of poetics. Aristotle's requirement that the narrative must lead the criminal to the point where he'll be caught and unmasked runs into a new, and conflicting, requirement: the *aesthetic* requirement for suspended shots, for a counter-logic that at every turn interrupts the progression of the plot and the revelation of the secret. In these moments, we experience the power of empty time, the time of goals held in abeyance when young Cosettes contemplate the dolls of their dreams, and when those condemned to "misery" delight in a simple moment of reconciliation with a world wholly indifferent to them and from which all one really wants is the chance to share in a novel quality of the sensible. "Action too has its dreamy moments," says the author of *Les Misérables*, and rightly so. The important point is not that the progression of the episodes has to be punctuated with moments of rest, but that the very meaning of episode has changed. The new action, the aesthetic plot, breaks with the old narrative plot by its treatment of time. In the aesthetic plot, it is empty time, the lost time of a stroll or the suspended time of an epiphany—and not the time of projects, of goals realized or frustrated—that lends power to the narrative. Literature came upon this pure power of the sensible between Flaubert and Virginia Woolf, and Jean Epstein, along with a handful of others, dreamed of making this power the very fabric of the language of images. True, the allures of this language never fully seduced Fritz Lang, nor did he ever embrace the notion that cinema was the new art of *aisthesis* that would supplant the old arts of *mimesis*. Lang understood very early on that cinema was an art insofar as it was the combination of two logics: the logic of the narrative structuring the episodes and the logic of the image that interrupts and regenerates the narrative. Lang also noticed early on that the combined logic of cinematographic *mimesis* bore close ties to a *social* logic of *mimesis*, that it developed as much in reaction to that social logic as under its shelter.

Let's take a closer look at the moment of aesthetic happiness, which is also a moment when places are exchanged. While the police are searching his room, the murderer is casually wandering the streets. There is something strangely complementary between M's brief moment of peace as a man of the crowds and the punctilious organization of the police, its unflagging efforts to find in the visible what it hides by tracing circles on a map with a compass, by meticulously searching every bush, and by descending into the dingiest dives to subject their every nook and cranny to the magnifying glass. M's chance to exist as a character, both for himself and for us, paradoxically depends upon all these circles that spread the news of the murder while concentrically closing in on the murderer, who manages nonetheless to inch his way and trace his own path across the circles traced by the police, the mob, public opinion, and the anarchic spread of suspicion. He is sheltered, somehow, at the heart of the trap, much as the happiness of the scene in front of the shop window is embedded in an alternating montage that stresses that the hunt for the criminal is only gaining momentum. All the circles that close in on him in the scenario of the trap, all the social circles that imitate each other, preserve him as a character and give him his chance.

To grasp the principle of this chance, we must take a look at a singular moment in the murderer's already singular trial in the makeshift courtroom set up by the mob. What is so strange about this trial isn't that the members of the mob act out every single one of the roles that make up a real trial, down to the defense attorney who, his Penal Code in hand, so stubbornly defends the murderer that no one is quite sure how to ascertain "what he really thinks." It is, more profoundly, that the murderer's fate seems caught between two laws: the law pure and simple, the order that protects honest, as well as dishonest, people; and a second law: the *mimesis* of the social comedy, the way social roles have of living off of imitation, of being fueled by the social's penchant for the theatrical—for diffusing, performing, and reversing roles. The crime boss appoints himself the representative of the bereaved parents and honest citizens and confronts the murderer with photos of the young girls he has killed; the con man of the group plays the attorney for the defense. A prostitute interrupts the proceedings to voice the anguish and pain of the mothers. Is she herself a mother? Or is she playing the role of mother as the others play at being attorneys? It doesn't much matter. What does matter is the sudden change of tone in her voice: midway into her angry tirade against the murderer, her voice falters, and when she resumes, after a brief silence, she speaks more slowly, more tenderly, as if she were trying to express the ineffable pain of these mothers and to make us believe that she too has felt it. A woman caresses her shoulder while she speaks, a silent display of the solidarity of these bereaved mothers. "How could you know what it feels like? You should ask the mothers": that's the gist of what their "representative" has to tell him. The initial anger, the faltering voice, the continuation in a lower tone of lamentation, the simple words, we had heard all of it but a minute before—in the murderer's testimony. He, too, starts out by launching an angry tirade against his accusers, comes to a halt midway through, and then resumes his speech in the same lower register, the expression of his pure pain. And he, too, concludes by asking his prosecutors: "What do you know? How could you possibly know what I feel?" In both instances, the same "voice of pain" breaks the silence to invoke what the other does not know. There is something that remains unknown and that can only be imitated, vocalized, performed, something that can only be felt through an equivalent.

The murderer's chance and the happiness of the *mise-en-scène* both rest on the possibility of weaving the cry of distress and the appeased countenance into a *mimetic* fabric that is, simultaneously, a paradigm of how society functions. The *social* law of *mimesis* is that one must imitate, perform, what, whether true or false, is not there or not known. Sincerity and hypocrisy are equal before this imperative. The counterpoint to the naked order, to the social order of the law, is what we might call the freedom or chance of *mimesis*, which here grants an equal chance to the fictive mother and the fictional murderer. This is what protects M, and is precisely what has disappeared in *While the City Sleeps*. If there is a paradox in the relationship between the schemes going on inside Kyne's empire and the fate of the psychopathic killer, it isn't that these supposedly "honest people" seem more sordid and low than the criminal they are hunting down. It is rather that this empire of the democratic press and of public opinion has blotted from the field all public opinion, even the one that assumes the terrifying form of the lynching mob in *Fury*. No one is too concerned with Robert Manners in *While the City Sleeps*, no one makes the rounds of the psychiatric clinics to find out if any patients have been released, no one tries to find out the murderer's whereabouts. Even stranger, nobody reads the *New York Sentinel*, save for the journalists and the murderer. And it seems that nobody watches television either, except for Nancy, to admire her hero and, once again, the murderer. There is no list of the usual suspects and places, no need to pick up the scent of the murderer and track him down. The murderer himself, the televised, will of his own accord go where he is expected, and he'll do so because an image has come to him and directed him to sit down in front of it and to recognize himself in the imaginary Identikit of the murderer. He has to recognize himself in the Identikit and feel flattered that the identity of his case has been recognized, happy that his lipstick message worked and that his hateful glee has been recognized. But, at the same time, he must also recognize that he is trapped, that he has been recognized as the murderer. This double capture hurls the murderer into the trap and incites him to want to do what, till then, he had only done by automatic compulsion. He's now to do it as if he had been programmed to do it, either through the desire for vengeance or because he's been challenged. He has no choice but to respond in the same exact manner to every situation: he must equate his simple incapacity to bear the sight of a woman's legs with the deeper motivations of vengeance, hate, and challenge. Indeed, all of this yields only one symptom, it is all expressed in the same snarl, the same eyes widening in alarm, the same sequence of gestures.

The stereotypy of his performance, rather than reflecting the shortcomings of a deplorable actor, reflects the apparatus of visibility that sustains the character. The structure that would protect him from his pursuers is gone, and with it is gone also his chance for a moment of grace when he might be allowed to express something besides this simple facial automatism. The other's vocal address and binding gaze have locked him in this imaginary shot reverse-shot, and there is no escape. A murderer can elude the police; a man of the crowds can, like M, merge into the crowds. That is totally different from having to elude someone who looks you in the face from far away in order to make you coincide with what he knows about you, someone who, in and through you, brings what he knows and doesn't know into alignment. Face to face with the murderer, Mobley adds to the knowledge of the policeman the knowledge of the clinical doctor, the supposed knowledge of the psychoanalyst, the knowledge of the professor, and many other types of knowledge besides. He gathers all these types of knowledge under the aegis of one fundamental knowledge: he can pass himself off for the savant that he isn't. Put more generally, he knows how to act out what he is not. This is, essentially, the knowledge of the actor, and it is as an actor that the journalist combines in himself all these roles. Mobley confiscates the power of *mimesis* and its performances and identifies them with the position of the one who knows. He chains this power down to the place filled by his image, the place of the one who sees and knows.

A quick look at the classical formulation of the problem, Plato's in particular, will shed some light on the identification going on here between science and *mimesis*. The sovereign knowledge Mobley deploys in his broadcast is the ability to identify what he knows with what he doesn't know, what he is with what he isn't; in short, he deploys the knowledge of being what he is not. This defines, in Plato, the knowledge of the mimetician: a non-knowledge that passes itself off for knowledge. We're all familiar with how Plato calls this "knowledge" into question. There is Socrates, in the *Ion*, asking how the rhapsode Ion could possibly know everything he sings about in his epic poems. How could he know how to "do" everything he narrates, everything he identifies himself with? And, in the *Republic*, Socrates asking ironically if Homer knows everything his characters know. After all, his characters rule states, wage war, and so on. Does he, Homer, know how to do all that? If he doesn't, we must then conclude that his fabrications are just simulacra, appearances suitable only for nurturing the social comedy of appearances.

This social comedy of appearances, as we saw a minute ago, obliges the mob to parody both the pain of honest people and the impartiality of justice, and, in the same stroke, gives the character his chance at the very heart of the death hunt. Things have changed by the time we get to Edward Mobley, and what Homer could not do, he can. With his one iconic performance, Mobley actually manages to be everything at once: policeman, public prosecutor and judge, professor, doctor, interlocutor, and general commanding the battle. Mobley is all of these as an actor, which explains why he is no longer limited by the obligation to mimic justice or the police. The actor, having forged the imaginary synthesis of every type of knowledge, arrives in the place of the one who knows and imposes an imaginary face to face that banishes from the field every social space protecting the character, every social space granting the character the chance to be something other than what he is to knowledge, that is, a sick man, a well-documented clinical case, something akin to a Charcot photograph or an overhead projection in a pedagogical conference—a puppet of knowledge.

The apparatus of Ed Mobley in his TV studio, and the ruse used by his journalist colleague Casey Mayo in *The Blue Gardenia*, another film by Fritz Lang, are not at all alike. Mayo, angling for a spectacular story, also traps his victim by using the press to address himself directly to her. With his "Letter to an Unknown Murderess," he leads her to believe that she has already been identified and offers her his help as a ploy to get her to come out into the open. Mayo's trap, however, displays all the classical traits of seduction: set by a man for a woman, by a successful journalist for a petty switchboard operator, it trades on traditional hierarchies of sex and class. Nothing could be further from Ed Mobley's trap in *While the City Sleeps*. He offers no assistance to allure the weak one to come to him, but imposes his assistance upon the murderer in a different sense. He imposes his image, his presence, his identification of what he knows with what he doesn't know, of what he is with what he isn't. Mobley's trap trades only on the imaginary knowledge borne by the image that speaks to the televised and instructs him to act strictly in accordance with what it knows about him all the way up to where the trap engulfs him. This is no seduction, but an execution in some senses more radical than the one in the fictive trial: a scientific execution that robs the subject of the ability to be different than he is known to be. It is an execution in effigy at the same time that it is the setting of an effective trap.

This is something entirely different from Casey Mayo's *trick*, and also from the intrigues and schemes—the withholding of information, the adulteries, the hallway romances—that go on in Kyne's empire. That the honest and disinterested Mobley should despise all that is perfectly understandable. Here, at least, things are still as they were in Plato: to despise power one must know something better than power. And clearly Mobley knows something better than being the managing director of the empire: the thrill afforded by this play of knowledge that absorbs all relationships of domination and that ends up being an apparatus of execution. But, to get to the bottom of this face to face, we must look into the nature of the image Mobley places before the murderer, the nature of the power he exerts and that allows him to impose this face to face. We need a detour here, leaving behind Mobley king of the screen to follow Mobley as a man about town.

A truly peculiar love scene sheds light on our problem. Mobley downs a few shots of whiskey at a bar to muster up some courage and, a little tipsy, goes to call on Nancy. She won't let him in, but Mobley very stealthily manages to release the door's security lock so he can sneak back into the apartment unannounced and impose upon his beloved the embrace of reconciliation. This scene is, interestingly enough, modeled point for point on the murder scenes of the psychopathic killer. Everything is the same: the staircase, the fascination with women's legs, the quick side look at the released security lock, the intrusion into the apartment, the ensuing scuffle, and even the insistent inscription of the maternal signifier: "Didn't you ever ask your mother?" Nancy's reply to one of her suitor's saucy questions echoes the message the maniacal killer writes on the wall with his victim's lipstick: *Ask Mother*. Lang's camera develops a sustained analogy between the love scene and the murder scene. Where, then, is the difference? The answer visually suggested by these shots is simple: Mobley strikes the right flow, the proper motor coordination of speech, gaze, and hands. The point is to know the right way to use physical violence, to hold the neck with one hand while wrapping the waist with the other, to close one's eyes instead of rolling them or staring wide-eyed, to use vulgar language and saucy pitches instead of mute lipstick inscriptions. Mobley, in short, shows that with women there are things to do and say—they just have to be performed in the right order and with the proper timing. None of this, incidentally, requires a whole lot of subtlety: it works even when the motions and intonation are those of a man who's had a few too many whiskeys. It all comes down to starting off on the right foot, which means renouncing the position of papa's boy—à la Walter Kyne—and of mama's boy—à la Robert Manners; it means renouncing the superfluous question: are you what your parents wanted you to be? That's the price to pay for starting off on the right foot and for mastering the fluid coordination of one's motor skills, the price to pay if one hopes to turn out a good behaviorist and not a psychoanalytic Identikit.

The spectator no doubt feels that he too would fall for this mediocre pitch were he in Nancy's shoes, and that in spite of the fact that this is clearly less a love scene than a pedagogical one. Rather than making a show of his affections for Nancy, Mobley is giving the sexual psychopath a distant-learning lesson on the normal libido, on the libido that has gone through all the stages of infantile fixation and found the right objects to suck on—glasses of booze and the lips of secretaries. We're now in a position to explain Mobley's peculiar power, what he brings to this place, to the image the murderer has no chance of escaping. It is not the father, the law, order, or society that one cannot escape. Recall Mobley's attitude when Amos Kyne was going off about the duties of the press in a democracy, about the sovereignty of the people, the need to keep it abreast of all it is interested in, and so on. Mobley just turns his back to him. He is thinking about his imminent broadcast, and his silence seems to be saying: "Oh! come off it! The people, democracy, the free press, information. That's all a bunch of stuff and nonsense. What really matters is what I'm about to do. Yes, me, sitting in front of the camera and entering everybody's living room. The people don't exist. There are only tele-spectators and people like me unto infinity, people I can instruct, not as a father, but as an older brother."

This older brother is not a terrifying image of the "big brother" variety. The older brother is just someone who can project a normal image, an image of the norm, someone who has gone through all the stages of infantile fixation and "matured" his libido. Mobley faces the murderer as he would face his kid brother who never left the stage of intellectual and manual masturbation and of papa and mama stories, and is still wondering whether it was for wanting him that a man and a woman performed the series of movements known as making love. In short, he faces the murderer as an older brother, the image of the normal. The knowing actor occupies the place of the older brother, that image of the normal, the place of a fully absorbed, yet self-denied, *mimesis*. This is the new couple that replaces the duo of *mimesis* and the law. The actor has taken over the place of the expert, absorbed all of *mimesis*, and identified it from then on with the position of the one who knows and sees you. In Mobley's televised broadcast, the authority of the brother trumps the authority of the father. There are, as we know, two ways of understanding this substitution. Discussing Melville's *Bartleby, the Scrivener* and *Pierre*, Deleuze concocts a theoretical fable, an America of brothers and sisters founded on the destitution of the image of the father.[1]

Fritz Lang's fable confronts the fraternal utopia of American democracy with a counter-utopia: the world of older brothers is not the "high road" of the emancipated orphans but its opposite, a world with no escape. It is not the father and the law but their absence that closes all the doors. It is the destitution of social *mimesis* to this relationship between a knowing and seeing image and an image known and seen; its destitution to the benefit of the television image, of the played image of the one who is, and knows, normality itself, the "sexually mature" older brother.

More than a German *émigré's* expression of disillusionment with American democracy, *While the City Sleeps* is the *mise-en-scène* of democracy's identification with the tele-visual. But this identification is not just an object for Fritz Lang. It is a new apparatus of the visible that cinema as such has to confront. We've seen its effects on the fable and on the character of the murderer, so it should come as no surprise to find that the expressions of his vanquisher, the ubiquitous god of tele-visual presence, are also marked by the same stereotypy. We continue to follow Mobley about town, in his role of lover. Close to the denouement, just as the murderer bites the bait of the tele-viser and is about to fall into the trap, Mobley finds himself the victim of a lover's quarrel with his fiancée Nancy. She is angry with him because of his escapade with the provocative Mildred, a columnist working for one of the schemers. Put on the spot by Nancy's accusations, the actor-professor Mobley is singularly incapable of speaking, of finding the tone of conviction. He tells Nancy he would be devastated if she left him, but we don't believe him. It isn't that we think he isn't being sincere. He just comes across as someone who doesn't know how to imitate, how to strike the tone and assume the image of someone overcome by his feelings. Earlier on in the film we had seen the adulterous Dorothy Kyne dupe her husband and the wily Mildred put on a third-rate performance to seduce the reporter. But Mobley, it seems, either doesn't know or has forgotten how to act out even his sincere feelings for Nancy. A sincere feeling, after all, must be performed just as much as a feigned one. The prostitute in *M* knew how to express the pain felt by the mothers, making the question—is she a mother?—redundant. Mobley, conversely, is only capable of expressing two feelings: a vain and idiotic beatitude—self-satisfied smile, mouth wide open, eyes inspired—and exasperation—eyes rolling, hands fidgeting incessantly. "Don't bother me with all this," his hands seem to be saying at first; then they tighten up, recalling the hands of the murderer, and at any rate miming the thought: "I could strangle you"; finally clenched, his two fists bang on the table in the most commonplace of angry gestures. The stereotypy of these two expressions, inane beatitude and exasperation, of course mirrors the stereotypy of the murderer's two expressions. Perhaps Mobley, too, is a captured image, perhaps the mimetician's identification with the image-that-knows has rendered him inept at the old theatrical and social games of *mimesis*, inept at expressing a sentiment through performance. Mobley is reduced to stereotypy and made a prisoner of his own exclusive knowledge: to speak from far away, in the image of the one who knows, to those who are absent.

Faulting the actor in Mobley's case would be much harder than in the case of the murderer. For all the unkind words Lang had for Dana Andrews, he must have known at least two things about him long before he got the cameras rolling. Playing the passionate lover was never this actor's specialty. In *Laura*, his big romance film, he cut a strange figure for a lover. Conversely, the one thing he always played to perfection is impassiveness. In *Laura*, again, he let the humiliations the radio star and worldly socialite Waldo Lydecker hurls at the plebeian policeman Macpherson roll off of his supremely indifferent shoulders. He was certainly capable of investing Mobley's exasperation with all the nuances and half-tones Lang might have wanted. The problem isn't with Dana Andrews' performance, but with the strange sort of actor he plays, an actor who calls into question the very notion of mimetic performance. In *While the City Sleeps*, the policeman has become the journalist and the plebeian taken the place of the worldly socialite. He has taken over the position of the writer and replaced Lydecker's radio voice with his voice and tele-visual image. But this appropriation costs the promoted plebeian a double price: he loses the ability to speak and perform Lydecker's unending love, and he loses Macpherson's patience. He is now a prisoner of his new identity, that of the image-that-knows and that speaks to you from afar. It would seem that, outside of that relationship, there was nothing left to perform but insignificance or a grimace. The image-that-knows can no longer be a character that performs. The tele-visual image, by calling into question the social performance the actor is supposed to represent, calls into question the very *gestus* of acting.

As we watch the grimaces, the rolling eyes, and the exasperated hand gestures that characterize Mobley's performance with Nancy, we may be reminded of a statement by Dziga Vertov from the heroic days of the cinema: "The machine makes us ashamed of man's inability to control himself, but what are we to do if electricity's unerring ways are more exciting to us than the disorderly haste of active men and the corrupting inertia of passive ones?"[2] The disorder of active men, the inertia of passive ones, that is exactly what Dana Andrews gives us here, like a big kick in the face of this great cinematographic ideal. Lang never really shared the ideal of the exact mechanical man captured by the electric eye. Unlike Vertov, Lang was never very enthusiastic about a society where humans were as exact as machines, and equally devoid of psychology. Nor did Lang ever think, like Epstein, that a feeling could be x-rayed and that thought impressed itself in bursts of amperes upon the brows of spectators. Lang always believed that a feeling had to be performed, imitated, and if expressionism (a term Lang disliked) means anything at all, it is that. He always opposed the anti-mimetic utopia dear to the avant-garde of the 1920s; he always confronted it with that critical mode of *mimesis* that pits one of its modes against the other. Lang stuck to this personal credo from the days of the auteur cinema—the days of *M*, when he was master of the game—all the way through Hollywood, when he had a limited say in a process where actors, like scripts, were dictated by the producer and imposed by the industry. But he always managed to preserve a personal mimetic apparatus and to play his own art of mimesis against the art imposed upon him by the industry. The problem, though, is that in *While the City Sleeps* Lang confronts something other than the industry's financial constraints. He confronts one of the industry's other faces, this other version of the utopia of electricity, though one that is indeed quite real and called television. This new machine recasts the terms of the relationship between art and industry by redefining the very meaning of *mimesis*. It settles the quarrel between the utopists of the mechanical eye and the artists of a thwarted *mimesis* by replacing both of them, by fixing the status of the mechanical image of the masses as a self-suppressed *mimesis*.

What role does Dana Andrews play? He plays the tele-visual man, he performs the relationship between his ability and inability. He performs the tele-visual man's ability to perform only one thing: the position of the one who knows, the one who, speaking and seeing from far away, summons those who are far off to come and sit themselves down in front of him. This ability is of course a challenge to the mimetic arts in general, and to cinema in particular. We might then think of *While the City Sleeps* as the *mise-en-scène* of the tele-visual man. This explains why the trio—murderer, journalist chasing him down, and his aide—is more important than the schemes and intrigues that run rampant in the news empire. This trio is none other than the tele-visual trio: the tele-visual couple and its witness, Nancy. Mobley knows that at the heart of Kyne's news empire, at the heart of this enterprise of bringing information to the people and of this counter-enterprise of schemes and illusions, there is ultimately only one important thing: the TV studio. The all important thing is the apparatus that puts Mobley "face to face" with the murderer and that is of no interest at all to anyone in the place except for Nancy. I suggested earlier that this trio, and not the show put on by the schemers in the rat-race for the position, is what gives the film its formula. A more precise formulation is perhaps in order. The whole film turns on the threshold that separates the tele-visual trio from the world of schemes and schemers. The trio is set apart because it knows where the serious things are happening. That is the privilege it has over the others. The price the members of this trio pay for this privilege is a deficit in mimetic ability, a deficit in the ability to do what an actor is normally asked to do, since it is, after all, what is also done in real life: imitate feelings, regardless of whether they are felt and experienced.

It makes little sense, then, to spend a lot of time trying to determine what is more interesting, the hunt for the murderer or the schemes that surround it. The real point of interest is this threshold, this relationship between the tele-visual scenario and the old scenario of representation. No matter how sordid the ambitions and means that reign supreme in Kyne's empire, the ostentatious parade of interests, passions, ambitions, deceit, lies, seductions, that old scenario of representation is still what infuses appearances with a great mimetic glow. Besieged by the new power of the image-that-knows, *mimesis* deploys all its old charms, including the most hackneyed, as in Mildred's seduction scene, played by Ida Lupino. Through this huge glow, Lang shows us what is lacking in the image-that-knows, the loss of the mimetic power of seduction that goes hand in hand with its very authority. When he is not in front of the cameras, when he is not looking at a spectator from far away but rather seeing her up close, when he must act out a feeling, the tele-visual character is reduced to this grimace. The film dramatizes this relationship between ability and inability, each side criticizing and mocking the other. Lang's *mise-en-scène* seems to capture the filmmaker's foreboding that perhaps, in art as in this story, the tele-viser will carry the day and the weak image triumph over the strong one. Perhaps it was Lang's premonition of this fate, coupled with his desire to play with it, to drag it back into the very core of the art of appearances, that led him to insist on a short scene not originally in the script, a scene that, paradoxically, the producers wanted to suppress on the grounds that it was a touch coarse: the gag of the slide-viewer with whose secret the wily Mildred sparks Mobley's interest, though all it really hides is a crawling baby. All the powers of illusion are contained in this tiny and insignificant slide-viewer.

Let's not forget the silent commentary of the bartender who picks it up: a smile, a shake of the head. In his smile we see the smile, at once mocking and disenchanted, of the director, who senses that it may very well be the end of the line for the old box of illusions, but wants to play a bit anyway with what has supplanted it.

NOTES

1. Gilles Deleuze, "Bartleby; or, The Formula," in *Essays Critical and Clinical*, trans. Daniel W. Smith and Michael A. Greco (Minneapolis: University of Minnesota Press, 1997) 68–90.
2. Dziga Vertov, "We: Variant of a Manifesto," in *Kino-Eye: The Writings of Dziga Vertov*, ed. Annette Michelson, trans. Kevin O'Brian (Berkeley: University of California Press, 1984) 7.

CHAPTER 4

The Child Director

There is no denying that infancy is disarming. In either one of his twin figures, as pitiable or mischievous, the little animal was tailor made to reveal the world's brutality and falsehood with the guile of innocence. And so the mind, feeling vanquished from the outset, is immediately roused to its guard at the beginning of *Moonfleet*, when the image presents all the signs characteristic of the little animal, his essence, as it were. Age: ten; eyes: green; hair: red; distinctive traits: freckles; nationality: English; civil status: orphan; profession: chimney sweep; fictional type: child of dispossessed family. The identification with the young orphan becomes almost unstoppable once we add to our natural compassion for orphans our desire to always have been one, that most secret desire to have been our own parents that we express metaphorically in the open seas, the highway, and in worn-out shoe soles. Would any schoolboy today, upon seeing the little whistling animal push his finger through the bared soles of his shoes, feel glorified because he can recite *Ma Bohême*, just as his homologue, in Flaubert's time, could declaim *Rolla*? Fashioned from the most hackneyed longings for some sort of prelapsarian innocence, isn't the figuration of rediscovered infancy a zero-degree of art identical to a zero-degree of morals, both still stuck in the pathos of the origin: that green paradise where stories of infancy and innocence are interchangeable that Kant and Schiller, to say nothing of St. Augustine, have sufficiently warned us about?

It may be, though, that alleging such sluggishness of feeling only betrays a sluggishness of thought. After all, it is not always the same fable of infancy that we see being played out in beautiful or ugly images. Some have built figurations of a different force atop this commonplace seduction, figurations that identify the virtue of childhod with a dispute over the visible by transforming the commonplace fable of the child who casts a naked gaze on the appearances of the adult world into the site where an art confronts its own powers. Ozu made a film in the last days of the silent period about two children who go on a hunger strike after seeing a screening at the home of their father's employer of some home movies where the father plays the buffoon for the amusement of his boss (*I Was Born, but...*). In the mimes of these two children, the art of cinema was forced to confront the social uses of the camera and the service it paid to the hierarchy, and amusement, of the rich. But, Ozu's title says meaningfully, "I was born." Twenty-five years into the talkies, the boys' hunger strike had become a speech strike by a new generation of kids, striking this time around to get a television set (*Good Morning*). These two young rebels mount a visual confrontation between the conversational codes of adult civility and the anarchy—that other conformism—of infantile society. With their revival of the insolent disrespect for the social comedy that Chaplin and Keaton expressed in their silent choreography, these two boys push the cinema to confront its old powers, and, in the relationship between the fable and the figuration, the whole field of cinematographic representation gets re-disputed.

John Mohune's foolishness, his attachment to his mother's letter assuring him that he will find a friend in the villainous Jeremy Fox, might just be another instance of the combined suspension of a social and a representational code. "Sir, I object": it isn't just the cynicism of Lord Ashwood that John Mohune objects to; this young and naïve animal wreaks havoc in the very logic of the play of truth and falsehood, of the visible and its opposite, characteristic of cinema in general and of Langian figuration in particular. He may very well be insufferable to a director who can't stand naïve children, but the more important point is that he demands from Lang an exemplary stretching of his art, of the way he puts the play of appearances into images.

Let's see the little Tom Thumb at work. Attracted by a noise, the young John Mohune looks up and his eyes meet the terrifying stare of the bronze archangel who guards over the cemetery. A hand that seems to come from beyond the grave appears above the gravestone and invades the right side of the screen. John screams and faints. A low-angle shot now arranges the wax faces perched over the child in a nightmarish circle: a mocking reference to the means that the cinema in its infancy liked to use to evoke a subjective vision, portray the sense of the abyss, or incite fear in the audience. The child now opens his eyes, props himself up on his elbow, and redresses the vision. The whole story of the film is here in these few shots. This little chimney sweep, who's in the habit of going down chimneys and who spends his time falling into the subterranean coves where the villainous flipside of refined society can be seen, never stops redressing the perspective and making it horizontal. He goes through the film reframing the shots and imposing his own space, with never so much as a thought to what social custom and artistic mastery picture [*figure*] and express metaphorically in the vertical relationship of the glittering surface to the gloomy deeps, the outward appearance to the hidden secret: a certain economy of the visible, simultaneously social and narratological, that turns hidden knowledge into fictional capital. Lang extracts a cinematographic fable with different consequences from the *topos* of innocence braving corruption and triumphing: that of the redresser of appearances. Not a redresser of wrongs. He remains within the fable in the figure of the magistrate Maskew, who resembles those he fights against not so much because he is cruel but because he is absolutely incapable of uttering a sentence without a double meaning.

John, for his part, is as deaf to double meanings as he is to any sentence telling him that what he sees hides what is. He makes his way through the studios of the hidden truth imposing his own gaze and storyboarding the shots for his script, that of the letter that sent him off in search of someone who has no choice but to be his friend. Whether it is in the tavern, in the underground cove where the squire is revealed to be the leader of a band of smugglers, or through the windowpane of the dilapidated manor house where a gypsy woman dances on the table and toys with the squire's desire, John obstinately isolates the figure of the friend and shoots only this all important relationship, which must, by the way, be just as he has it in his script. And, indeed, it is true that the *mise-en-scène* of this script with only two characters has a childlike simplicity: all it does is invert the logic of the adult script where John is constantly being told not to believe what he is told. "Not words, deeds," declare the wise in their wisdom, and the child's *mise-en-scène* follows suit. He responds to the speeches telling him not to put any stock in words with the deaf tranquility of gestures that hear and yet don't hear, gestures that extract a different truth from the words. "What am I supposed to do with you, make you a pillar of society like myself?," asks the knavish gentleman, and the smugglers in the know all roar with laughter. The child, though, doesn't speak or laugh—he just looks, greets, smiles. Asked to promise "to laugh" now and then, John does so with his whole body, which is to say he makes a real promise out of their joke. His posture alone is enough to drain the sentence of its "second meaning," to force it to consummate all its meaning in the sole space of the manifest. John's naïveté is the polar opposite of Edmund's in *Germany Year Zero*. Edmund concentrates all his attention and tenderness on putting an end to a father who is suffering and socially useless. In so doing, Edmund does, and doesn't do, what his teacher tells him to do, that is, what his teacher, as yet another member of the huge Nazi army, has done and not owned up to doing: "You said it, I did it." John, at the end of *Moonfleet*, tells Jeremy Fox the opposite: "You said you would abandon me, but you didn't." But if Jeremy Fox hasn't abandoned him, it is because the child director has patiently constructed with his gaze and gestures a reality where the cynic's words lose their effectiveness.

This suspension strategy starts in the back-room of the tavern, where the cynic undertakes to educate the naïve boy and teach him that he is not the friend he might have thought. "A friend! You disabuse yourself of that whimsy," Jeremy Fox says, his back turned to the child that he assumes is listening all the more attentively now that his instructor isn't looking at him. If you know you needn't look, and Jeremy Fox knows full well that when he strikes the pose of a superior by turning his back to those he's talking to, he commands their full attention to his words all the better by their feeling of inferiority. The child makes no reply. He objects to Jeremy Fox's admonitions that he should disabuse himself of his whimsy by suspending his attention. He sleeps, just as he will sleep later on in the beach hut during the time that it takes Jeremy Fox to leave, and retrieve, the note telling John yet again that he was wrong to have trusted him; the same time that it takes for the duped trio of crooks to fall into the trap and kill each other off, thus awarding victory to the sleeping boy who's active even in his absence. What's the use in taking seriously words that instruct you not to believe them, save perhaps for those power games where you want the crook trying to sham you to know that you know what's up? These parlor games are good for the boudoir and for the coach of the Ashwoods, where the camera shows that hugging a Pekinese is as good as embracing a lover and that, when measured against the glitter of a diamond, the lie of a fake love scene and the truth of a real scene of adultery are entirely interchangeable. The film of the quiet child ("You don't speak much, do you?" comments the young Grace) cracks the mirrors where Jeremy Fox and Lady Ashwood confirm time and again that love and gold are as interchangeable as truth and lying. It hangs on a truth that the worldly wise have had to abandon to those still untutored in its ways: the statement "I lie" *in truth* makes no sense. The mother's letter telling John he'll find a friend in Jeremy Fox has more truth in it than Jeremy Fox's enjoinder: "Believe in the lying Jeremy Fox when he tells you not to believe him." The truth of the mother's letter, however, derives its strength and fragility from the same source: it hangs entirely on how well the child can arrange with his gaze and gestures the space of the visible so as to frame the figure of the friend, on how well he manages to extract this figure, and with it the space that secures the truth of the letter, from the space of pomp and falsehood.

The fictional work of the character and the action of the camera thus perform one and the same operation: both undo a posture and disband a group. They both undo the posture of this man in evening clothes who so theatrically enters the smugglers' lair with his conquering gaze and disdainful mouth, turns his back to the smugglers to indicate his superior position, and reaffirms his command with every new lesson in martial arts he gives to the infantry. The turning point here is not really that the jealous woman bares Jeremy Fox's shoulder to reveal the mass of scars left by the watchdogs the Mohunes had set on him in his youth. A prior and more subtle play was needed for the gaze and voice of the boy to frame the wound on Jeremy's face, for his *mise-en-scène* to arrange the barely perceptible signs of this assault: a gaze whose haughty pomp seems to recede, pursed lips that have changed expressive registers. We have to have seen this play at work earlier, in the interlacing of medium shots and close-ups, horizontal shots and vertical shots, shots and reverse-shots that the objector, the redresser of appearances, introduces at the party when he arrests the splendors of the flamenco and the ordinary games of easy seduction with his little song. Here's where the child's *mise-en-scène* extracts the visibility of a wound from the visible games of refined society, and where John draws his "friend" into his frame: in the close-up of Jeremy Fox, with John singing in the reverse angle, where we see the hand of the by now vanquished paid seductress resting on the shoulder of the man who has already been pulled away from her, her gesture of seduction now one of impotence; and in the long final shot of the staircase, where the ladies' favorite, standing on the threshold between two spaces just split asunder by the naïve boy, follows with his eyes the child who doesn't look back as he makes his way up the stairs. "Are you going to destroy him too?" his rejected lover asks him. "There is far more danger of him destroying me," he replies. And, in fact, in this extra step the destruction of the destroyer has already begun. The scene already announces the final exit from the beach hut—walking backwards to hide the fatal wound from the boy—of the man we first saw standing so arrogantly at the door of the tavern.

The film renders visible the trajectory of a wound. Much as the attentive gaze of the child director may search for traces of that wound in the set of the abandoned summerhouse, it is actually in the pursed lips of the adult that he manages to bring it to the light of day. But the film also traces the story of a higher seduction. The *mise-en-scène* of naïveté, with its total dependence on the scenario of the letter and what authorizes it—no more than the secret of a mutual love and reciprocal debt—is another distribution of the visible that offers the blasé libertine something like a Pascalian wager: the charm of a higher game, a principle of discernment that locks up the hidden/exposed games of deceit of the Ashwood household and turns the triumphant cynicism of dissolute gentlemen and alluring women into pure affectation. This reversal in the fable is of course matched by a corresponding reversal in the *mise-en-scène*. Jeremy Fox's exasperation with the spaniel-eyed child who keeps on pestering him was originally Fritz Lang's exasperation with this idiotic story and this child actor that, as always, he didn't think was "very good." Lang's whole experience as an exile, finding at the heart of the best political regime the penchant for lynching and organized lying, and his whole art as a filmmaker, as somebody who arranges images in their essential deceitfulness, were they not equally revolted by the obligation of having to put into beautiful images this unlikely story about a trusting child who disarms with his smile a world where deception is the rule? But perhaps the direction draws its strength from this very anger. After all, the "naïve" direction of the child is nothing other than the knowing direction of the director, who despises the sentimental script and can't stand the child's naïveté. The fact is that, since Schiller, sentimentality is one thing and "sentimental poetry" another. Naïve poetry is poetry that doesn't need to "induce a sentiment" because it is naturally attuned to the nature it presents; sentimental poetry, conversely, knows itself to be separated from the lost paradise of immanence by the distance of sentimentality, and so it must be shaped against that distance. The sentimental work, the modern work if you will, is a thwarted work. In the thwarted direction of the filmmaker Fritz Lang we encounter the same tension as in the style of the novelist Flaubert. The same, but reversed. For the "dry" subject of Emma Bovary's miserable love affairs, Flaubert abandoned the lyricism of *St. Anthony*. His project, and his torture, was "to write mediocrity well." Directing naïveté well amounts to the reverse: Lang has to accept the lyricism he abhors. Flaubert took his revenge writing *Salammbô*, Lang will take his shooting *While the City Sleeps*.

The lyrical film of victorious innocence and the film noir of triumphant villainy are intimately linked, each one seeming the other's mirror image as well as its exact opposite. Lang's direction of the child who sleeps every time he is told he's being lied to, and opens his heavy eyelids to ascertain each and every time that the facts belie the claim, foreshadows his direction of a sleeping populace ruled over equally by the crime coming from the bowels of the city and by the lies of the men in the glass office who pretend to bring to the darkness of night the light of democratic information. The portrayal of the obsessive criminal who writes 'Ask Mother' on the wall of one of his victims and of the reporter who "never asked" his mother will be Lang's revenge for everything he had to concede to this freckled orphan. And Mildred's (Ida Lupino) conquering seduction of the reporter, meant to help (though at his own expense) the same George Sanders, will compensate for all of Lady Ashwood's vain simpering. The real tension animating *Moonfleet*'s seemingly limpid surface and exemplary fluid narrative is that the direction has to efface its normal powers: it has to subject the play of day and night, of high and low, of appearance and its opposite, to the intrusions of the disarmed and disarming gaze of the child who comes looking for his "friend," his victim. All that's manifest in John Mohune's gaze, beyond the shared secret of an unhappy love and a hidden treasure, is the far from secretive secret of the equality of the visible, the very equality from which, when all is said and done, every demonstration of the game of appearances derives its power. Isn't the ultimate secret of the image that, to the frustration of the clever, it contains no more or less than what it contains? All the boy has to do to win is insist on the obstinacy of the cinematographic lens, which bares the image of all metaphor and sees in it nothing beyond what is horizontally available to the gaze. But the strength of the figuration, its implacable logic, is that it keeps collapsing everything to this one level, that it continuously subjects to this single equality the great and false-bottomed machinery of appearance.

The scene at the well is a microcosm for this narrative logic. Inside the well whence emerges, proverbially, the truth of the lying surface, and held aloft by the cord of adult machination, the child with heavy eyelids leans forward with all the strength a child usually reserves for the swing and stretches out his hand to get the diamond, horizontal with his gaze. This superb, if topographically implausible, shot condenses the redressing of appearances, the great game of converting verticals into horizontals. This is the higher game of the direction, of the director who can seduce because he has himself been seduced and thrown off kilter. How else can we explain Lang's irritation with a film he directed unwillingly, but is loved by cinephiles all the same? His notorious anger over the last shot, "added" at the insistence of the producers, expresses perhaps just the vexation of someone who, in order to make a film he could live with, had to fall for the pitch of the naïve boy. It cannot be denied that the final shot of the boy opening the grilled gates of the manor house to await the return of his friend is less beautiful than the shot of the boy watching the boat bear away his friend Jeremy Fox, whom he does not know is dead. But isn't it the case that what so vexes the director about the "added" shot is that it steals the unmistakable signature of the magician, who reasserts his mastery by parading before the child the cinematic truth that his friend is dead and that John, with his spaniel-eyes, doesn't see? The ending "imposed" upon him doesn't change anything at all in the meaning of the narration. The same cannot be said about the happy ending of *While the City Sleeps*, where Mobley, disgusted by Walter Kyne's decision to award the position to his wife's incompetent lover, learns over the radio while on his honeymoon that Kyne has gone back on his decision. This ending actually reverses the entire logic of the film by awarding the final victory to a moral that had not been given the least bit of substance in the narration. Lang, in other words, would have had every reason to be angry about it. If he wasn't, it must be because this reversal lends itself to the final pirouette of this master who renders equivalent the commercial constraints of the *happy end* and the casualness of the creator who returns his creation to the emptiness whence it came. The hat the reporter on his honeymoon throws over the telephone of intrigues becomes a mirror image of the cross of the Legion of Honor of the last line of *Madame Bovary. Moonfleet's* "bad ending" is not an instance of the artist being betrayed by the laws of commerce, but the incurably inane illustration of the law by which the idiot annuls the power of the cunning. The telephotographic signature is powerless against that: John Mohune, like Emma Bovary, misses the artist's self-affirmation as cunning. They both miss the game of mastery expressed in the disappearance of the artist as the work "closes in" on itself, and in the signature with which the artist reminds us he is himself the instrument of his own disappearance. The superior power of art is that it accepts another disappearance, that it traces the imperceptible line separating this other disappearance from the banalities of trade. In this, the child always trumps the man.

CHAPTER 5

Some Things to Do
The Poetics of Anthony Mann

Some things a man has to do, so he does 'em.

The formula is perfectly polished, like the film to which it gives its moral; *Winchester 73*, of all of Anthony Mann's Westerns, is undoubtedly the one whose formulas and images seem to have been most carefully polished. We know, though, that the hero in the film does, and very obstinately at that, only one thing, or rather two things in one: he chases after the man who stole his famous Winchester, which is to say that he chases after the bad brother who killed their father. The director, on his side, makes sure he diligently includes in the film everything a good director of Westerns should: strangers who ride into a little town in turmoil, a provocation in a saloon, sharpshooters showing off their stuff, a chase in the desert, a poker game that ends badly, the defense of a camp against the Indians, the storming of a house where some bandits have holed up, a bank holdup, and a final settling of scores amidst cacti and boulders. Mann includes all the episodes required for the exemplary construction of an exemplary fable. In the course of the chase that will, in good Aristotelian logic, reveal the identity of the parent and of the enemy and, in good Western moral, bring down the criminal under the blows of the man of justice, the Winchester of the title passes, in one close-up after another, from hand to hand until it comes to its final resting place under the words THE END. And the heroine, that eternal problem of Western narration, circles round with the rifle only to find the same owner in the end.

There seems to be a perfect harmony between the doing and the having-to-do of the director and his character, between a narrative logic that is sure to satisfy every semiotician and the moral of the story, where justice triumphs at the end of a number of trials. And yet, this neat harmony runs into trouble precisely in the identification that normally binds both logics: in the character's way of being. Lin Mac Adam (James Stewart) may assure Lola (Shelley Winters) all he wants that he is as scared as everyone else before the Indian attack, but his every gesture contradicts his words. He evidently has a knack for expressing himself in sententious formulas, but his gaze and demeanor seem incapable of embodying either justice or vengeance. The signs of reflection that constantly flash across his face and his unflagging attention to how the present circumstance may bring him closer to his goal, or distance him from it, only bring this incapacity into even sharper focus. He avenges a father much as he would do *anything else*. This perfectly accomplished justice, this rifle that eventually returns to its legitimate owner, just makes a certain absence all the more manifest. Pressed against the flank of a horse, the plaque on the butt still nameless, the Winchester itself seems frozen in its status as an exhibition piece, as alien even to its owner. It as if, like Stesichore's Helen, who never left Sparta, but whose phantom alone eloped to Troy to fuel wars and epics, it was only in a dream that the Winchester made its way from contest showcase to Western museum. As if all the others, all those blinded at the sight of this repeating rifle that shines only when we, the audience, are in the reverse angle, as if all of these—the merchant and the Indian, the weakling and the braggart—had died because they mistook this phantom for the good old rifle left in the care of Dodge City.

The whole story, in short, might have been no more than the dream of the children we see in the first images of the film pressing their foreheads against the glass of the showcase, the same children who were granted, because of their good behavior, the privilege of being the first to caress the object. This metafilmic hypothesis is not altogether incoherent. *Winchester 73* banishes from Mann's universe for a long time to come the childhood and family bliss that had been so present in the Indian fable *Devil's Doorway*, Mann's previous film. It is as if childhood and family bliss had been sent back to the reservation with the Indians who thought they were home and on their land, and as if this departure had closed all the doors on the dream of ever living harmoniously in one home and fatherland. Maybe this is what the "Indian turn" of the Western really means. Not the discovery that Indians are also human beings who think, love, and suffer, but rather the feeling that their expropriation spells out a common destiny and forecloses the romance that would engender, simultaneously, the virtuous American man and "his" land. Is it just chance that, seven years later, in *The Tin Star*, it is the son of an Indian who brings back the childhood and family bliss so radically absent from the cycle of Westerns shot with James Stewart?

The fiction of the expropriated Indian is the fiction of the closed door of the paternal home. There can be no doubt that this sober lawman draws all his strength from embodying nothing but this expropriation in the face of beings who've never quite recovered from their childhood. We don't need to read an Oedipal symptom into the family photo that, however implausibly, adorns the wall of the murderous son in *Winchester 73*. This much, though, is certain: even if the photo is an index of recognition for the heroine and for us, it does not give the least bit of substance to the family home, where nobody can imagine James Stewart savoring the tranquility of work done, the Winchester hanging on the wall, Shelley Winters in an apron, and a bunch of children with his same blue eyes. Lin's companion urges him to think about *after*, but in vain: that time will never come to distract the vigilance of this lawman and inscribe its imaginary in his present gestures.

That's the singular strength of this character who embodies nothing and that James Stewart plays with a meticulous attention that seems always to be the manifestation of a more profound distraction. The image of the father and of the paternal home, of law and morals, never really take hold in Stewart. It seems he's never heard of this sheriff called Wyatt Earp, who apparently doesn't care all that much about his star and who seems as attentive to the orderliness of his territory as he is indifferent to what goes on beyond its borders. Stewart is, at best, a cross-bred figure of the law—barely less fleeting than that of the sheriff of Crosscut in *Man of the West*, and barely more serious than the law embodied by the villainous Judge Gannon in *The Far Country*. No sense of law or of belonging to an ethical community introduces the slightest difference into the care Mann's hero takes in avenging a father or a brother and the care he takes in leading his herd or prisoners to the slaughterhouse. Is it even possible to imagine a father for this man who shows himself to be the son of his own actions with every collected step or gunshot? Mann's hero doesn't embody the power or the dream of justice, but is protected, instead, by his abstraction. It is this that renders him immune to the fascination that leads to their doom all those who see in the radiance of the rifle an object of desire within their reach. One need look no further than this for the secret behind the paradoxical invincibility of this hero who is so often wounded in the script and whom the camera, as if for the fun of it, loves to place so ostentatiously in the sharpshooter's line of fire.

The hero's invincibility, of course, is primarily a matter of the contract between the director and the audience, a contract Mann subscribes to without reservations. It is only fitting for the hero to triumph, for the man who said "I'll do this" to do it, for the hero to fulfill the desires of all the people out there in those darkened rooms who have gotten used to the fact that they'll never do what they would have hoped to do. Mann, though, still has to put the generosity of this contract into fables and images. And in truth, the one who has to do this, the actor, is not really made for the part. James Stewart, Mann said, is not the "broad-shouldered type," so that you must take a lot of "precautions" if you want to show him "taking on the whole world." This system of *precautions* is none other than the logic that puts the fable into images. Look at Dutch Henry at the top of the cliff, wasting all his ammunition on the pebbles methodically thrown by his brother. What exactly could make his arm so useless and his sight so troubled that a shadow is all he can shoot at with the Winchester of his dreams? What else, if not this absent lawman so removed from every fascination for every fleeting object that he assumes the illusory consistency of a specter? Look at the old rancher in *The Man from Laramie* charge full speed ahead and shoot *strictu sensu* into the scenery while his foe is leaning calmly against a tree. The simple materialist explanation—the old rancher is losing his sight—cannot account for the material oddity of the scene. The camera fixed on this bucolic landscape shows something else: the old man's aim is off because the present/absent man in his sights is the man he saw in his dream.

Let us follow the camera in *Bend of the River* as it pans sideways and scans in the night the faces of Cole (Arthur Kennedy) and his companions, who are all listening to the sound of rifle shots fired in the distance, a visible/invisible fulfillment of the promise made by Stewart's/Mac Lyntock's hallucinated face when he, facing us, shouts after a foe who has already turned his back to him: "Some night I'll be there." The man of their dreams is the one who shoots and kills in the darkness, which does not mean *off-camera*, since his absence is, on the contrary, present on all the faces. From inside the saloon in *The Far Country*, we hear the sound of the little bell attached to the saddle relaying in the darkness outside the steps of the horse. How could this B-movie killer not miss his shot after being driven mad by the jingling of that bell? We know that the bell attached to Jeff Webster's saddle had been given to him for the little ranch out in Utah by the dreamer Ben, who dies because he cannot sacrifice the coffee for the trip that was to take him to the house of his dreams. There is no doubt that there'll never be a ranch in Utah for Jeff Webster. And Harry Kemp, in *The Naked Spur*, gives up reclaiming the ranch in Kansas that had sent him out on his bounty hunting journey in the first place. It is this expropriation that accounts for the strength of Mann's heroes as they face the unending army of those who trade the small change of their lost homes, those who think *they belong* (two haunting words) and crave to possess: merchants and prospectors—whether honest or not—whose gold fever brutally illuminates their faces and weighs down their gestures at the decisive moment; professional bandits whose every shot brings them inexorably closer to the most fascinating name and the most fabled of banks, those of an abandoned city where only death awaits them; adventurers captivated by the whims of a star or owners so possessed by the glitter of their possessions that they have gone mad or blind. Although they were once upon a time masters of the game, they will all fall, as the story nears the end, before this man who embodies neither the law, nor the land, nor the paternal image: this man whose whole secret is to know that the door of the house is closed for good and who passes by, coming hither and going thither, tormenting their dreams with the mute jingling of the bell of the expropriated.

That's the point where the moral of the fable and the logic of the narration meet. In the final moment, all must fall before the man they have time and again reduced to impotence, but who alone is capable of accomplishing the *some things* a filmmaker and his hero have to do together. He alone can reach the end together with the audience and signify them by riding away on his horse or wagon with the heroine, even though he has no interest in her or in starting a family. Her role is simply to announce, like those four ritual verses in Euripides, that the expected and the unexpected have changed places, that the artists have held up their end of the contract, and that the audience can now go home.[1] Victory belongs to the one who can crown the action with the words THE END, the one who knows, like the Stoic sage and the Aristotelian poet, that action, tragedy, and life can only be dominated by that measure of time that lends them grandeur and a set number of episodes. The others, the senseless, the bad poets, the "evil" characters and the extras don't know that. They see no reason to put an end to their stories or family romances, or to have done with the law and the father, gold and rifles. The sage is free to leave them to their folly, and Mann's hero sometimes thinks he can play the sage by turning a blind eye to them. The poet, though, is less tolerant than the sage. Tragedy, Aristotle says, must have a beginning, middle, and an end. It is only right for the bad guys to be shot down, or else the Western, missing an end, would never have come into being in the first place—the same is true of tragedy. Meanwhile, for all those who'd rather never have done with anything, providence invented television and the serial, both of which can last as long as the world: all they need to do is announce that tomorrow, like today, nothing will happen either. The time of the cinema is different. It is the time of the tracking shot in *The Naked Spur* that reveals, from the killer's position at the top of the cliff, the body of the old prospector lying peacefully in the sun, a donkey licking his face. Mann leaves it to Ben's indefatigable donkey to provide the commentary on this tender and bucolic image of the common cruelty of the fable and the film: "He's done dreaming the impossible." Ben, played by the anti-Stewart Robert Ryan, may marvel at his knack for telling jokes and for shooting at dead men's boots, but he too will tip over to the other side when his time comes. Following the apex when he believes he's in control of the action, it will be his turn to be caught by a weapon of fortune, the naked spur James Stewart uses to make his way up the rocky face of the mountain.

In short, *to do* and *to have to do* are more complicated acts than it might seem at first, disjointed as they are by the logic of *some things*. It doesn't much matter whether Mann's hero is a man of justice or a reformed criminal, since that is not the source of his quality. His hero belongs to no place, has no social function and no typical Western role: he is not a sheriff, bandit, ranch owner, cowboy, or officer; he doesn't defend or attack the established order, and he does not conquer or defend any land. He acts and that's it, he does some things. With the exception of *The Tin Star*, his actions cannot be identified with any duties towards a group or with the itinerary that reveals that group's values. Outside of the recurring formula—*to have to*—there are no similarities at all in Stewart's paths as a man of justice, an adventurer, and a reformed border raider and that *River of No Return* on which ex-con Robert Mitchum rafts downstream with his son and Marilyn Monroe, who just quit the saloon where she was working as a singer. Preminger's is a family triangle, a *Bildungsroman* about a son who understands, in repeating the gesture, how his father could have shot someone in the back and still have been justified; it is a journey homeward that begins with the trees cut down for building the house and ends on the word *home*. Preminger epitomizes and stylizes the Western's family romance or ballad with a masterly touch. He's like Macpherson, a masterful plagiarist reviving a past moment of art or conscience. Mann, for his part, makes no posthumous Westerns. There can be no doubt that all his Westerns belong to the period of the end of the Western, to that moment when its images were being severed from its beliefs and put to use in a new game. This is a time of moralists and archeologists who invert the values of the Western and ask themselves about the elements and the conditions of possibility of the American *epos*; of psychologists and sadists who never tire of harping on the ambivalence of feelings and relationships, or of tracking down ghosts and exposing violence; of plagiarists who lift from the dictionary of fables and images the elements for posthumous Westerns composed of images more beautiful than natural; of show-offs who try to ally the shock of images to the charms of demystification.

Mann is none of these things. It is true that he opened, with Daves, the way for the rehabilitation of the Indians, and he is more than willing to help himself to that man of wood Victor Mature to sap the moral of the Blue Coats and to sow discord in the barracks and homes of all aspiring Custers. Mann can also compose scenes of violence and cruelty, rituals of humiliation, whose paroxysms, in *Winchester 73*, *The Naked Spur*, *The Man from Laramie*, or *Man of the West*, always exceed what the simple narrative logic of the confrontation calls for. In *Man of the West* he includes a striptease scene whose violence is all the sharper for offering nothing that could come within reach of the censor's scissors. Following the path of pioneers and gold hunters, in *Bend of the River* and *The Far Country*, Mann lends to the romance of these first settlers its most lyrical images, as well as its most picaresque and parodic ones. He glides smoothly from the pranks of the old captain and his black acolyte on the steamboat—both of them straight out of Mark Twain and the legends of the Mississippi—to this unreal, low-angle shot of the ballet of immigrants standing in silhouette on the boat deck, waving goodbye to the curious crowd gathered on the quay and greeting a new world with one and the same gesture. He can type the settler population of the Klondike, or compose the craziest of genre scenes with the syrupy and flowery romances of these three ladies of ripe age and pure morals before brutally interrupting it with the unloading of a corpse, or condense into a few images—an interrupted hanging, an improvised trial on a poker table—the equivalence between law and lawlessness that reigns in Judge Gannon's territory. In contrast to the colorful characters of the first settlers, Mann populates his last Westerns with crepuscular characters—the blind rancher and his half-crazed son, the colonel drunk on vengeance, the old bandit in the midst of his band of degenerates—all of whom take a piece of the legend of the far-West with them to the grave. Mann is not interested in returning to the first settlers of the myth, or in the forms of defecting from it; nor is he interested in psychologizing or aestheticizing. We must not conclude, though, as is sometimes done, that Mann is nothing but a craftsman, a drudge with no sensibility for ideas. Before being a moralist or a craftsman, Mann is an artist, that is, he is first and foremost what Proust understood by an artist: a polite man who doesn't leave price tags on the gifts he gives. He is a classical artist, more interested in genres and their

potential than in legends and their resonances. The classical artist is not
interested in myths or in demystification, but in the very specific operation
whereby a myth is turned into a fable, into a *muthos* in Aristotle's sense—a
representation of men in action, an arrangement of incidents that has, as
Aristotle says, a certain grandeur, a proper measure, a *tempo* that distinguishes
it from the time without beginning, middle, and end of the world.

Some things, then, have to be arranged into a proper time in this autonomous system of actions that does not simulate a curtain opening onto
some episode supposedly taken from the course of a story. This system is
such that it cannot be identified with any time, whether lost or regained,
with a lost childhood, the learning of a value, or with the embodiment of
a dream; it has its own rhythm and follows its own logic as it moves across
these fragments of myths and stories and their aleatory arrangements. No
matter how different Mann's scriptwriters may have been, and some among
them had big names and personalities, the action in his films obeys a few
constant rules in terms of individualization and construction. The first rule
concerns the singularization of the main character. It is very rare for this
character who comes from elsewhere and represents no one but himself not
to be placed from the opening shots of the film at the center of the action
around which everyone will revolve. He bears no insignia that would make
his function clear, his stature is by no means imposing, and yet all he has
to do is enter the frame for the action and the characters to come under his
sway, which means, first of all, under his gaze. He designates with his gaze
the point toward which the action must unfold. "Camp here!" announces
the guide in *Bend of the River* and the conveyor in *The Man from Laramie*, and the
old prospector cannot but acquiesce: "You're the boss." We don't know, any
more than the prospector does, what this *here* is, or whether it is by chance or
design that the hero comes upon these charred planks and tattered uniform
remains. We now see James Stewart, a hat already in his hands, scanning
the rocky mountaintops trying to discern a cause for an effect we don't yet
know. As he lays the hat back down, the camera follows him, dipping down
to the ground where the remains of a blue tunic lie. We intimate that we're
witnessing a funeral rite, though we don't know yet that it actually is one.
With his gaze, then, the hero arranges the action, the places, and the characters that take part in the action. He determines its direction, and introduces
us to it as if we were privileged spectators. The hero, albeit so unheroic in his
stance, displays the constancy of someone who's completely in control of
the action of the film. If he is parsimonious with his words, it is because he
has made his whole body into the narrative voice that gives body to the story.

The hero is alone, set apart from the others from the very first images. The modality of his relationships is that of the encounter, that's the second major rule. Mann's community is formed around the encounter, and not around a place, the family, or an institution. The act that founds this community is always a situation that has to be judged in a glance, a decision taken on the spot. When the camp is set, Stewart/Mac Lyntock goes out reconnoitering and his gaze falls on Kennedy/Cole in the hands of some men who've tied a rope around his neck. A rifle shot and a relation is forged. "The horse, I didn't steal it, if that makes any difference to you," Cole tells him. Evidently, this makes no difference at all to the ex-raider Lyntock, even now that he's reformed. The only differences that actually matter are the differences perceivable in the instant it takes to survey the situation and make the decision. "Strictly a gamble," the man whose neck has just been saved says a little later. The gamble of the community is renewed with each passing instant, and the community often wins. In fact, it goes on winning as long as the pure logic of the snap judgment and the gesture it prompts are playing: a silent chase of the Indians set in the form of a midsummer night's dream; a saloon exit that has become the stuff of anthologies; a crazed stampede across tents in flames; the methodical shooting of the pursuers who fall for the trap of the false camp fire. It only loses in the final moment, when gold fever breaks the seeing and judging machine and when Cole, his whole body undergoing an abrupt conversion, declares himself the leader of those who've just given Mac Lyntock a terrible beating. He takes advantage of a favorable situation to collect the ante, though in so doing he drives the situation to the edge of the oneiric. The camera now frames him grotesquely caressing his chin with his pistol, when what he should actually be doing is putting a few bullets in the man he has just betrayed. From this moment on, Cole is portrayed as the leader of a troop of ghosts decimated by a specter. Between the initial decision and the final usurpation, the time of the film would have been that of the episodes where the gamble of the community is renewed, where new encounters—with the merchant, the gambler, the captain, the gold hunters—increase and complicate the heteroclite community formed by people who are all going in the same direction, or at least claim to be.

Another instance of the same rule is the woman who appears on the deck of the boat where the hero is being chased in *The Far Country*. Here is Jeff (James Stewart) hiding in Ronda's (Ruth Roman) bed, rendered invisible to the eyes of his pursuers by the screen—a bar to vision—made by the show of outrage put on by a woman in nightgown who acts out for us a fake

erotic scene straight out of vaudeville. Much later in the film, this fake scene
will turn into a real sacrifice of love since, in the meantime, the original
group has had to accept into its ranks the villainous representative of the
law, deranged by his thirst for hanging, and the disarming representative of
humanitarian love, who abandons the father for whose studies she had been
slaving away as the char-woman of a saloon. The action, and here is the third
rule, has to be constructed in the minuscule gap between the moral of the
script and the logic of the encounter. The script of *The Far Country* is the
apologue of a selfish man who is as indifferent at first to the entreaties of
the lover of humanity as he is to the spectacle of honest prospectors being
oppressed by a villainous gang of thieves, but who in the end picks up his
gun to avenge his friend and purge the colony of scum. Still, no matter how
satisfying the image of the army of honest people suddenly forming in
close ranks behind Jeff Webster, or how tender the final embrace with the
lover of humanity, the end of the film does not point to any community,
gained or regained. The film ends on the shot of the little bell, a sibling, so
to speak, of the spur and the Winchester. These are all metaphors for the
passage, for the obstacles that chance will always put in the path of the hero
and for the weapon of fortune found to face it. They are the weapons of
the landless man who vanquishes all of those whom the god of gold has
driven mad by the inconstancy of desire he mints, final metonymies for the
logic of the action, for the singular complicity of the action itself. This
lawman's real community is not with these decent people who feed on bear
steak, coo flowery melodies, and dream of having a town with sidewalks,
lampposts, and a church. His community is with all the people that the logic
of chance and of thinking only from one episode to the next has yoked to
his footsteps: the people he encounters in escaping from a hanging or foiling
one, the people he travels with and who are, due to the very needs of the
voyage, only temporary partners—now objects of distrust, now subjects
one has no choice but trust in. It is with all these people who demand his
constant vigilance, his unflagging attention to the signs of what they may
be plotting (*strictly a gamble*) so that he is sure to be in control of the gesture
that foils it. The community of this loner who's been set apart from the
others from the very first shot is not the ethical community of those he
fights for, but that born from his encounters with the people he acts with
and who require him to be always on the lookout for ambiguous signs, to
rub shoulders with dreamers and their potential to distract, to be constantly
looking and always acting, doing each and every time the *some things* that draw
the episodes to a close and drive the action one step further. We see now why

the moral of the fable pushing the hero to identify himself with the ethical community is never realized save in the conventional images of the *happy end,* though without there being materialized in these images either happiness or the end. Mann never allows his hero to forget, in the throes of some communitarian or romantic effusion, the thing he has to do. He has to drive the action itself, his every gaze and gesture have to be pure embodiments of the risk of the action: the risk of the particular task—whether of justice or profit—that the script has entrusted to him, but also the risk of the logic of filmic action itself, whose essence and peril has to be gambled in every episode. For filmic action, once it has been released from the shelter of myth or of the *Bildungsroman,* is left at the mercy of each moment's varying intensity, much as the hero is at the mercy of a hand inching towards a belt or a kiss distracting his vigilance.

The point of conjunction of this double risk shared by every art that "represents men in action" bears an old name that defines an equally old, yet always fresh, problem: identification. Plato laid down the terms of the problem in his discussion of the peculiar pleasure spectators, even those of high birth, derive from shuddering and shedding tears over the ignoble sufferings of characters who are naught but phantoms. This pleasure in suffering is the work of the deceitful passion of identification, which seizes the soul and nurtures its intimate divisions. We are all well acquainted with Aristotle's decisive response to Plato's indictment. Tragic action isn't a portrayal of characters that requires identification, but a construction of incidents that regulates the play of identificatory passions through the grandeur, temporal progression, and cadence of its episodes. The Western is not tragedy. But its art, like every art that represents men in action, is defined by its ability to maintain the separation, even in their conjunction, of the time of aesthetic emotion and the time of anxiety for the danger threatening the character in the fable. The temporal cadence specific to cinema concentrates this question on the construction of the episode, and here Anthony Mann's genius really shines through. Mann works with two major forms of constructing episodes, one of which plays on the different intensities of the episodes, the other on their similarities, one on the continuity between episodes, the other on their proper qualities. To the first type belong those forms of dramatic construction of the pathetic event that can be illustrated with two episodes, one from *The Last Frontier* and the other from *The Tin Star.* I am thinking of the scene in *The Last Frontier* where the old fur-trapper Gus is sent to his death by one of the aspiring Custers. The horseman forges ahead in the glade in alternating long and close shots that suddenly reveal, crouching behind the trees, all the shades watching him. Just then, the camera abruptly goes elsewhere and frames Gus' companion Jed in a thicket seemingly unrelated to the place of the action. He climbs a tree, and it is from his point of view that the camera, taking in the idyllic landscape with an overhead shot, reveals the immense army of Indians lying on the ground awaiting the man on horseback riding amidst the trees in the middle distance. And it is still from Jed's point of view that the camera pans upwards, first to the host of feathered Indians on horseback, and eventually to the Indian who bends his bow at the exact moment that Jed's rifle shot, following the camera, hits him. Old Gus will die, but the spectator will not have confused the emotion of filmic action, which changes spatial relationships and the quality of silence, with the anxious identification with the promised victim. Counter-suspense might not be a bad name for this process that purifies pathos by creating a *decrescendo* at the very heart of the progression of the inexorable. This process reoccurs, albeit differently, in the assassination of the doctor in *The Tin Star*. What makes this scene so peculiar is not that Mann elides the act, but how he manages to arrest all anxiety with the shock of the first shot. The doctor is leaving the house where he was delivering a child when, in the darkness of the forest and the night, a boot and spur shine on the right of the screen while left and back the doctor's carriage starts making its way down the narrow path. Our knowledge that death awaits the doctor produces the relief of the next shot, of the bandit politely asking the doctor to help his wounded brother. It produces the relaxation that gives a purely dramatic interest to the scenes that follow, which culminate in the carriage riding into the festive town, where we learn, through the sudden change of expression in the faces of the townsfolk, that the person in the carriage, the hero of the party, is dead. If we can enjoy this scene, it is because we already know what Mann does not show us, because he manages, with a single shot, to arrest empathic anxiety in order to release aesthetic emotion.

Dazzling as these demonstrations are, it is not in this form that we find Mann's most singular genius, but in the second form, which plays on the equivalent intensity of the episodes, all of them seemingly saturated by the most minute events, by gestures and lines as clear as they are ambiguous, all closed in on themselves and yet invaded by parasite temporalities. Here is Mann's true kingdom, in these moments of rest that are anything but restful, in these nocturnes that punctuate the voyage of the heteroclite community, and not in those required scenes where he excels nonetheless at doing just what has to be done. In the foreground, two characters in profile—

half-turned towards us, half-engulfed in their precarious partnership—are discussing what they have to do the next day and what the night sounds portend. Behind them, the camp fire confusedly lights up the bodies lying down on the ground or the wagon, so that we don't really know who's awake and who's asleep, who's listening and who isn't. James Stewart wraps his hand around a woman's body and she, in the next shot, turns her face and smiles at someone who's no longer there and whose meticulousness she perhaps mistakes for love. As the camera pans sideways to where coffee is being poured, the reflection from a flame casts a glare on a steaming cup and on the conversation that gets going around it, on the stories that remain half-told, and on the memories and dreams just then working their seduction. Now is when a kiss is sometimes surprised by someone looking on, and sometimes benefits someone feigning sleep. This is a moment of the night when a sense, a romance, or a myth insinuates itself and injects its diffused temporalities into the time of the gaze and the decision: the illusion of a past, or a future, or of a legend, of a privileged relationship even in the community of chance. Betrayal is always close on the heels of the seductive appeal of a moment of rest in the past or the future.

The best examples of this are, undoubtedly, the moments of rest and the nocturnes that make up the plot of *The Naked Spur*, the paramount film of the heteroclite community. Howard Kemp sets off after the wanted criminal Ben Vandergroat in the hopes of collecting the five thousand dollar bounty on his head to buy back the ranch he lost. In the course of the journey, Kemp has to take on board an old prospector, a military deserter, and the immaculately coiffed little savage accompanying the runaway Ben. The film's whole story is the common voyage of a group necessarily complicit in their difficulties and constantly threatened by the betrayal that the gallows bird, his hands tied, foments with his incessant talking. The drama, though, revolves less around Ben's (Robert Ryan) loquaciousness and perpetual smirk than around the incessant approximations of bodies whose gestures and speeches suggest both complicity and betrayal. One night on the edge of a river, Lina (Janet Leigh) is wiping dry the sweat on the wounded Kemp's forehead. He's deliriously talking in his sleep to the fiancée who left him, and Lina answers and comforts him in her place. The next morning Lina is shaving Ben to the left of the frame and the old prospector Jesse (Millard Mitchell), lying down next to them on the right, is talking in his sleep about how he squandered away his life on always useless prospections. He is unwittingly telling the murderer, without talking to him, where he can crack the complicity. Kemp, anxious to get his wound bandaged, calls for him from the other side. "I'll do it," says Lina. To James Stewart's eternal question, "Why?" (why did she take care of him the night before? Why bother taking care of someone who never takes care of anybody?), Lina responds with one of the two answers available to a woman, each of them summed up by the two rivals of *The Far Country*. Her answer is not the provocative Ronda's "Should there be a reason?," but the sympathetic Renée's "Somebody had to." True, somebody has to take care of the sick companion—the logic of the present and of the community demands it. But meanwhile, the other logic, of the past and the future, of romance and betrayal, is holding steady on its course as Lina, her face turned towards us, attends to the wounded man lying down in profile and defends the murderer, this man who is not "her" man but who has quite by chance become her guardian and fed her dreams of owning a ranch in California. Robert Ryan takes advantage of the time it takes for the wounded man to get up with a limp to loosen, his gesture barely noticeable, the girth of the saddle on Kemp's horse. The next shot shows the group marching in order towards their common destination. Kemp, chilled to the bone, pays no attention to Ben, who next to him is treating everyone to his family romance while surveying from the corner of his eye the girth sliding along the horse's flank. Suddenly, all dialogue comes to a brutal halt, and by the next image we seem to be watching a silent film: James Stewart falls from his horse and rolls down the side of the hill; everyone looks on in silence while Stewart makes his way back up to the trail and onto his horse; an exchange of glances is the extent of the confrontation between Kemp and Ben. Night has now come to prolong, and alter, the silence of the event. The camp fire lights up Janet Leigh's face. James Stewart is lying down, his head nodding occasionally, Robert Ryan is lurking in the shadows, and Millard Mitchell wakes up with a start and looks around before falling back asleep. Kemp gets up limping at the sound of the cry of an animal. The camera frames Lina lying down, Kemp's gaze, again Lina in close-up, Kemp wrapping his hand round her, Lina turning her dreamy face, and lastly Ben's smirk as he observes the whole thing. Nothing much has happened really, except for some movements: some bodies have been drawn closer and made more complicit and also more apt for betrayal, the one dramatized in the next scene. In the cave where the group of travelers stops to wait out the storm, Ben with one look sends Lina over to Kemp, who is, as always, keeping guard over the cave's entrance, on the border between the outside darkness where the rain resounds and the interior darkness that engulfs the supine bodies. In the next shot, she's kneeling in front of the crouching guard and talking to him about the music of the rain and of guitars on

Sunday dances, of what she'll do in Abilene, the final destination of this voyage, and in California, the final destination of her dreams, of her home, lost and refound, of having a ranch, a family, and neighbors. The indifferent music of her sentimental words backs up the imperious music of the shot reverse-shot, which Mann never abuses, though he's fully cognizant of its powers, of how its rhythm leads men to the paroxysm of anger and a man and a woman to that abandon that culminates in a kiss. Ben, of course, flees during this minute of distraction, only to be immediately denounced by the sound of a rock and recaptured by his guardian's nimble hands. But can anyone say that the scene of complicity was really just a ruse? "It just happened that way," Kemp snaps back sarcastically at Lina. But his irony is a bit excessive. This is how things "happen" in the movies: by a field that narrows down to one body while another exits the frame; by a two-shot that draws bodies closer and the alternating shots that intertwine their dreams; by the rocking to and fro of speech and image, of shot and reverse-shot, of the one real image and the imaginaries that transform it into the ruse of an absent totality; by the rhythm that lulls night watchers to sleep before a sound off-camera awakes them. That's how seduction works and, deep down, James Stewart is wrong to complain about it. Besides, the ones who always get tangled up in the traps of seduction are the wise guys who inanely identify the effect of a voice or of an image with their sorry calculations, the ones who think they know everything about deceit and seduction, and never the one who knows only the present moment and the course to follow.

The hero's success is the success of the film. He alone is synchronous with the time of the action, with its linear direction as well as with the discontinuity of its episodes. All the others are always chasing after the straight line of their dreams, always looking out for the right moment to strike. Their weakness stems from the fact that they are characters of the Western, figures of its mythology, some of them dreamers of the impossible and others simply trigger-happy. But Mann's hero is no longer a figure of the Western. He is simply the representative of this action that moves across their territory, intersecting their paths and dreams. Hence his strange demeanor: this hero in the lead role is already as distant as the passerby. He is someone who knows the gestures and the codes, but can no longer share the dreams and the illusions. More than a character that we love and fear for, he's a straight line stretched between the filmmaker's point of view and the viewer's. Victor Mature's climb in *The Last Frontier* is a metaphor for this, but its actualization is to be found in James Stewart's performances, in the way they ensure the constant occupation of time. The very specific function of this always busy hand that is content for now to clutch a blanket and that knows at the decisive moment to reach for the spur or the pebbles is to maintain the steady progression of the action, to reject the suppleness of dead time, of the time that narrates on its own and generates empathy at bargain prices. We don't have time to fear for Stewart. He's so busy that he makes us too busy to have the time to fear for him. With his constant occupation of time, he affirms the slight distance that separates the representative of the action from the characters of the Western; he makes the character as efficient as any character in Ford (Mann's avowed model), but without taking into the bargain Ford's insistence on embodiment and moral empathy. And there, the moral of the work prevails over the moral of the fable, the doing over the having-to-do. Stewart seems predestined to embody this distance with his gaze, his expression, and his gestures of a displaced man, of someone out of his element in the Western that portrays in their complicity the comedy and the incarnations of the American ideal. The best illustrations of this are *Bend of the River*, *The Naked Spur*, and *The Far Country*, the paradigmatic trilogy of action in Mann. *The Man from Laramie* already obeys a different logic, even though it cannot be denied that Stewart, in this film more than any other, plays the man who comes from elsewhere, the wounded and humiliated hero who ultimately prevails. But the stranger's solitude that Mann's camera and Stewart's performance were used to constructing ever so patiently at the heart of the complicities of the communal voyage is in this film already a feature of the script, and this changes the relationships between bodies and the logic of the action. The passerby has now become an investigator whose investigation turns him into a voyeur spying into other people's affairs, into a decomposing family and a sinking universe. The end of the Western has already imposed its agenda and determined this story that isn't really a Western at all, but a detective melodrama about an investigator whose clues lead him to the heart of a much darker secret than the one he was looking for: the symptoms of the decadence of a tribe and a world, the nightmares of its master as he sinks into darkness, the frenzied gestures of the empty-headed heir, the silent intrigues of the bastard child who manipulates the meaning of the story to make sure he becomes sole heir. In this world consumed by a self-destructive drive, Stewart's fragile invincibility takes on extra-terrestrial powers. It is like a ghost that this man with an arm in a sling orders Dave (Arthur Kennedy) essentially to commit suicide by pushing the wagon loaded with rifles over the cliff in an act that demands from Dave a thousand times more strength than he would have needed to disarm his foe. The triumph of this lawman closes an action that is no longer his. It marks his definite passage to the other side, a ghost with nothing else to do other than leave to its ghostly destiny the by now provincial world of the Western. The final image we have of James Stewart indicates clearly enough that he will not return to get entangled in its games.

With his departure, a certain way of composing the form of the action and the subjectivity of the hero becomes impossible. Mann had to develop a dramaturgy specific to each of the actors—Victor Mature (the Huron), Henry Fonda (the professor), Gary Cooper (the annihilator)—he cast in his subsequent stories of savage intrusion or final return to the land of the Western. He also had to create a specific *mise-en-scène* to go along with, or thwart, these stories that range from the coherent figure of a parody taking the genre to the grave to the contradictory figure of a new beginning that organizes its own end. Parody triumphs in *Man of the West*, where the West has become the workaday world of respectable married people, and where the five thousand dollar bounty and the ranch it was going to buy back in *The Naked Spur* have become a two hundred dollar purse to hire a qualified schoolteacher for the offspring of the honorable citizens of Good Hope. Instead of the headstrong companions played by Arthur Kennedy and Rock Hudson, all Gary Cooper can enlist as a helper is a card sharp without cards, with a pot belly and a bowler hat. The film, with its outmoded story of decadence, takes us on a trip to the land of shadows where we meet a killer and his band, all still held captive to the infantile dream ("We shall be rich") of the fabulous gold of a town that no longer exists. The rants of this killer are those of bad theater, or of the nightmare. And indeed, all we would have to do to turn the whole story into a nightmare would be to add two shots to the film, one of Gary Cooper being lulled to sleep by the jolts of the train and the sight of charming green landscapes, and a second of him waking up with a start at the cries of "Forth Worth, everyone down." But that's not how Mann organizes the relationship between these two worlds, which he does, instead, in the passage from a shot to a reverse-shot. There can be no doubt that the silent house Gary Cooper peeks into through the broken windowpane is abandoned, that all one will find behind the Colt shining alone in the darkness on the other side of the door are ghosts, or the surviving debris of the Western: a crazed old man and his supporting characters, who were given, much too late, a part for which they no longer had the voice, head, or faith; a crazed old man who could only find these supporting roles to relive the spectacle of bygone Westerns. "I've never seen anything like it in my life," he says, gloating over the senseless fight in which Link Jones strips the crazy Coaley of his clothes. And, in fact, the two stripping scenes that punctuate the film have the hallucinated violence of gestures that have lost their dramatic rationality, and in the face of which the moral satisfaction of witnessing Coaley's well-deserved punishment seems almost trivial. Ultimately, it is the cinema that we hear dreaming aloud about the dissociation of the elements of a genre in the strange meditation of the cousin sitting next to Gary Cooper on the wagon. True, it certainly is an absurd enterprise to start again and again the cycle of robbing, killing, and fleeing, and there can certainly be no doubt that the old man—the old actor who likes to think he knows a lot about direction and production—is a little *soft in the head*. And yet, there is no other home or family for the supporting characters of the Western who failed to adjust in time to urban morals and psychoanalytic melodramas. Nothing left to do, then, but go all the way to the end, to the abandoned town where the ghosts and supporting characters of the Western will see justice served, where the representative of the new morals and reality will, as any good accountant should, frisk through the pockets of the cousin who had relieved him of his purse and then cross his arms as if he were laying a corpse out in a casket. The logic of conflictual complicity that joined the representative of the action to the character of the Western comes crumbling down: complicity has become only a ruse, and the common voyage a final visit that buries a world gone by.

Maybe more than in this fiction of collapse, and more even than in *The Last Frontier*, where a disrespectful Victor Mature annihilates Custer's legend well before the respectable Gary Cooper annihilates the legend of Doc Holliday, it is in *The Tin Star*, the film dedicated to that third great character of the Western universe, the sheriff, that the real suspension of Mannian action is most manifest. *The Tin Star* is a fiction of return that seems at every level to oppose these fictions of annihilation. It bears all the traits of a posthumous Western. What could be more exemplary of that than this story of a sheriff who has to impose law and order in the face of the anger of the townsfolk and the cowardice of the town's dignitaries? And what better character and actor to dramatize and give psychological depth to the story than Henry Fonda, in this role of a disenchanted man who rediscovers the reasons symbolized by the star? James Stewart would not have fared so well had he had to portray a similar ethical and psychological radicalization in an episode of *The Far Country*. It would be difficult to picture him giving Anthony Perkins a course in the finer points of being a sheriff that objectifies, in pedagogical *items*, all the traits of his performance, or to imagine him expressing the traces of the past, the dilemmas of the present, and the flame of a rediscovered future with Henry Fonda's flexibility and ease. This *Bildungsroman* that combines the education of the green sheriff, the moral trajectory of the disenchanted man, and a whole nest of other family romances, runs counter to all of Mann's rules about adventure, the encounter, and the decision. Henry Fonda may teach his pupil to take the split second necessary to make sure his shot is good, but he himself seems often to pause a split second too long in his contemplation of the mother and child before him and in recalling the mother and child who've died. However, unlike *Man of the West*, where the direction sometimes follows, and sometimes exceeds, the logic of the fable, in *The Tin Star* the tension between the logic of the script and the logic of Mannian action gives the direction new energy. Mann extracts a lesson in film directing from the heart of this story about shooting and moral lessons. Instead of the visitor who annihilates the ghosts of the Western, here it is the *mise-en-scène* that splits apart the script and organizes a confrontation between two Westerns.

Look at the crazy stampede of the fanatical posse Bogardus leads in pursuit of the assassins. On his orders, they surround the house where the bandits are hiding out, set fire to its four corners, and, for a final touch, send a flaming hay-cart crashing into it, at which point the livestock flees the barn and, in the haze of flame and smoke, gets all mixed up with the horses of the delirious posse. This spectacular *mise-en-scène* is the visual demonstration of its own inefficiency: the two bandits, of course, have fled. And now, in the void it leaves, another film starts: a kid on horseback approaches the still-smoking ruins, sees a dog, and whistles to call back the fleeing animal. Another *mise-en-scène* develops at this point. Much more than a face capable of moving sensitive hearts, the kid's arrival gives this new *mise-en-scène* a rhythm with which to structure the action. Henceforward, the time of the action will be governed by a very specific infantile rhythm: that of nursery rhymes. The strident and booming band disappears and is replaced by the rhythm of nursery rhymes: the sheriff chases the outlaws; the child chases the dog; the dog tries to find its owners; Henry Fonda tries to find the child. Another sort of heteroclite community is formed. The child's insouciant gait, instead of being a source of anxiety and identification, lends a strange serenity to the action, the serenity Fonda shows as he meticulously prepares the small fire with brooms—in every way the opposite of the giant flames of the bad *mise-en-scène*—that smokes the bandits out of their cave. The fates of the characters are settled in the flow of the action and not in the predeterminations of the script. The last episode confirms this lesson: Bogardus' defeat is another holiday granted to the Western character, to the bad actor and the bad director, one that is perhaps more subtle, despite

appearances, than the apologue of *Man of the West*, because it is worked out
from within the tension between the script and the *mise-en-scène*, from within
the logic that relates the doing and the having-to-do.

Maybe the best way to put it would be to say that in the fates of the
vanquisher and the vanquished we have two denouements that don't
coincide. Anthony Mann does not shy away from the shot of the tin star
shining "anew" on the breast of his hero. And, for the first time, the final
image lets us believe that the hero will really return home and start a family.
A classical artist would hardly think of achieving his effects by mocking
conventions; nor would he dream of allowing himself to identify the end
of a story, the fulfillment of a narrative contract, with the metanarrative
argument of the end of an era, a myth, or a genre. Decadence makes for
cheap philosophy. The only good end is the one that contains the action
within its proper limits, the one that leaves open the possibility that the
action may be continued, restarted. This is what's called the risk of art, and
Anthony Mann has always assumed that risk. Before the *remake* of *Cimarron*,
Mann never let the action of any of his films gain its effect by overflowing
into legend or by being identified with this or that place, moment, or figure
of the Western epic. He always constructed singular and self-supporting
Westerns, and never Westerns that traded on some form of recognition.
At the "end of the Western" he even managed to give us many unique
figures: a freeze frame (*The Last Frontier*); an immortalization (*The Tin Star*);
an execution (*Man of the West*). The cemetery keeps its spoils, the treasure
box remains open, and the image could move again. Whether it does or not
depends, it is true, on conditions that go beyond the powers of the classical
artist, who subscribes to genres and to the invention of narrative contracts.
One thing will always elude him: the regime of sight that gives genres their
visibility, the perceptive contracts that the power of merchandize signs with
the public gaze. This is the realm of two other categories: sometimes of
Romantic artists, but more often of non-artists. Anthony Mann is neither,
which is why his films seem so distant to us.[2]

NOTES

1. "Many are the shapes of Heaven's denizens, and many a thing they bring
    to pass contrary to our expectation; that which we thought would be is
    not accomplished, while for the unexpected God finds out a way."

2. I would like to thank Jean-Claude Biette, Bernard Eisenschitz, Alain Faure, Dominique Païni, Sylvie Pierre and George Ulmann, who made it possible for me to see these films again when no theaters ever screened them.

CHAPTER 6

The Missing Shot
The Poetics of Nicholas Ray

I was for a long time haunted by a shot. At the beginning of Nicholas Ray's *They Live by Night*, the escaped convict Bowie is about to enter the garage when there materializes before him a body the likes of which no one had ever seen before: dressed in a mechanic's coveralls, this being who is neither an adult nor a child, masculine nor feminine, who is entirely adapted to the space where it evolved but entirely alien to the people who occupy it, is a being possessed of a singular beauty born from the impossibility of classifying it under any of the genres of beauty known to the cinematographic repertoire. It is as if, all of a sudden, a being removed from resemblance, a real being, had come to exist in the cinema, the evident cause of an unparalleled love. Bowie's all-consuming love for Keechie would then perfectly parallel our love for cinema's power to create a body. And Cathy O'Donnell's downcast eyes and androgynous body, much more than Harriet Anderson's provocative bosom and looks in *Summer with Monika*, would be perfect emblems of the fierce independence characteristic of the auteur cinema celebrated by the Nouvelle Vague. I dreamed for a long time of writing about this amazing shot, a shot that would be, for the cinema, what the apparition of the young girls in flower on the beaches of Balbec was for literature: the construction of a completely novel individuation, of a love object that is one precisely because it has been stripped of the identifiable sexual properties that make it an object of desire.

Reason inevitably won out: the shot does not exist. Bowie and the audience had met Keechie long before the scene in the garage. Still, my having seen it for so long was no trick of memory, and I was not surprised to discover the same error in another commentator, as if we needed this missing shot to contain the impression left by this body. After all, the apparition of this singular body and novel beauty has indeed taken place cinematographically.

I say an apparition, and not the miraculous upsurge of being that a certain phenomenology has taught us to impose on the image, because an apparition is the outcome of numerous appearances and disappearances, additions and subtractions. Cinema isn't the art of visual evidence celebrated by the aesthetes of the 1960s. The young girl with rosy cheeks on the beach in the book was born from a web of metaphors, and Ray needs more than a cinematographic trope to get this body removed from resemblance to materialize before us.

What he needs, first of all, is a synecdoche. At first, there is nothing other than the sound of a car engine and two headlights in the night. In Edward Anderson's novel, Keechie's car drives by but never finds the wounded man it had gone after, Bowie, who is completely lost in his interior monologue. In the film, Bowie slowly extracts himself from under the billboard giving him cover and walks towards the two lights in the night followed by a dog that appears out of nowhere. A glare of light violently illuminates the windshield and rearview mirror, but leaves in the dark this face that seems completely hidden under a hat pulled all the way down over the eyes, so that all we see of it are two unevenly lit up cheeks. This body's center of gravity, it seems, is in the hands tightly clasped around the steering wheel. "Any trouble?" asks the young man standing to the left of the frame and with his back to audience. "Could be," replies a white voice that injects the coded indifference of passwords with double meanings with a hint of something else, a slight insolence, something like a secret shrug of the shoulders: "Could be. Could be something else. Whatever difference that makes."

A few shots and reverse-shots is all it takes for these two people to exchange in the night information about different things that "could be." The young man starts making his way around the car to enter on the passenger side, and it is only now that the face of the young girl at the wheel appears fully in the light, for us, though not for him. The second he enters the car, darkness again descends on the two bodies now sitting side by side. The car has barely left when it reaches its destination. The driver, still in the dark and shot from the back, says she has things to do and points the young man in the direction of the cabin where he'll find his two partners.

The paradox is that for this apparition to materialize, its traits must appear one by one. Like the smile of the cat or Rodrigo's thirty sails,[1] all we have at first are this voice, these cheeks, and these hands floating in the night as if severed from their body. Cinema has to frustrate the natural realism of mechanical reproduction. Indeed, it is through a very specific operation of subtraction that the film distances itself most sharply from the novel it adapts. Here is how, in the novel, Keechie appears to Bowie, who has finally made it to the hide-out: "Bowie now saw the girl standing behind the screened doorway of the store. She was dark and small and her high pointed breasts stretched the blue cotton of her polo shirt."[2] This is an ordinary, a plausible vision of the object of desire, though I don't mean with that to accuse Anderson of being a novelist of ordinary tastes. It is obvious that he wants to capture how this young and coarse runaway stares at this standard image of the feminine body. And I doubt Nicholas Ray had any objections to the image the novelist gives of the ordinary dreams of this rural America during the Depression that he himself traveled through when he was involved in those big cultural projects linked to the agricultural policies of the New Deal. It's just that the cinematographic invention needs another body of desire. The director has already intimated this in the image of the two heads touching that precedes the opening credits: "This boy … and this girl … were never properly introduced to the world we live in." This also means that they cannot be introduced—to us, to each other—as the subjects or objects of the desires of rural America, as a girl with high pointed breasts seen behind a screened doorway. The director separates the images from the very start. The ordinary object of desire, the silhouette of a woman with high pointed breasts, was left behind, up there on the billboard Bowie was using for cover. Venturing forward from the billboard, Bowie heads towards uncharted territory, towards this fragmented body that so far exists only as two cheeks lit up by a glare of light, two hands clasped around the steering wheel, and a white voice.

Something essential happens in the gap between two types of shots, the overhead helicopter shots of the three thieves' escape and the close shots of Bowie and Keechie's first encounter. The film swallows in this gap the form the realist novel uses to develop an intimate connection between social stereotypes and the minute perceptions and sensations of individuals. Between the objectivism of the escape and the subjectivism of the gaze in the night, between the silhouette of the billboard and the half-face in the car, the director has undone the literary form, call it literary cinematographism, through which Bowie was "introduced" to his world and through which Keechie could herself be introduced to it without much ado. Edward Anderson situates his novel on the zone of indecision between objective narration and interior monologue that appropriates everything for itself, the stream of consciousness that collapses every distinction between the events of the world and the hero's perceptions, between the stereotypes of the self and those of society. It makes sense that literature should create this sort of intimacy between the internal and the external monologue and stereotype, as that is how it compensates for the weak sensible powers of its medium, how it puts the flesh of shared experience on the words of the made-up story. Literature creates a continuum between the language of intimate emotions and the neon signs of a highway, and in that continuum we see the story of the individual fates of the characters imprinted on the shared canvas of a society. But the cinematographic invention has to be constructed against the grain of literary cinematographism. Cinema has to put strangeness in the bodies it presents, introduce a distance between those it brings together. The body Bowie meets in the night is totally alien to his "consciousness," he cannot assimilate it to the stream of his perceptions. That body is also, and for the same reasons, resistant [*soustrait*] to our powers of identification. There must be, at first, only a glare of light and an indifferent voice if the intimacy without familiarity of a purely romantic relationship is gradually to come into being.

The initial abstraction that separates Keechie's body from Bowie's stream of consciousness, and with it the cinematographic figure from literary cinematographism, lays the ground for a second operation of subtraction that isolates the two lovers in the thieves' hide-out. In the cabin where Keechie's father is driving a hard bargain for his services to the three thieves, a door opens and we finally see all of Keechie standing in the doorway with her boyish looks, her hair pulled back, the collar of her unisex coveralls upturned, and her arms so laden with bags that the high pointed breasts that stretched the fabric of the polo shirt have disappeared. The brutal reverse angle shot of Bowie's gaze that follows is not enough to create the intimacy between the two young people. Two people exchanging glances is a rather coarse way of indicating a budding love, and Keechie and Bowie spend very little time looking at each other. Keechie especially, since she's always so busy. Keeping herself constantly busy is her way of being fully present to, but also fully absent from, her father's and her uncle's world. Keechie's absent presence cuts right through Deleuze's very neat opposition between the functionality of the action-image and the expressive power of the affection-image. The film captures the different intensities of sensation in the execution of ordinary, daily tasks like fixing a heater, pulling out a jack, changing a car wheel, or massaging a wound. These are actions that two people do together, or that one does while the other looks on, actions whose proper gestures and time are much better suited to indicating the love budding between two people who don't know what love is than any ecstatic exchange of glances or conventional approximation of bodies.

Ray, to develop the drama, has to isolate the two young people even when they're surrounded by those who do not allow them their intimacy. This calls for a new operation that imposes two overlapping yet incompatible spaces onto the homogeneous sensorium created by the "cinematographic" prose of the novel. Everything happens around the way Ray handles an ordinary task, the fixing of the smoking heater, a scene that the novel, true to its realistic logic, constructs as a natural modification of the sensations of the young man: "The voice of the girl, Keechie, made Bowie's veins distend and there was a velvety, fluttering sensation in his spine. She was squatting over there now by the Bunk's kerosene heater, the brown flannel of her skirt stretched tight around her bottom, showing T-Dub how to keep the wick from smoking."[3] The trajectory of the sensation, from the heater in the Bunk to the flutter the voice sends down Bowie's spine, is once again headed towards an ordinary representation of the object of desire: fabric stretched by a body's curves. The novel inscribes the relationship between the two young people in the same sensible logic that governs the complicity of the three fugitives. The director breaks up this continuity by changing the trajectory of the perceptions. In the film, the one in control of the trajectory is Keechie, this body committed to the efficient execution of everyday tasks. A slight disturbance in the order of things attracts her attention while she pretends to be listening to yet another of her Uncle Chicamaw's jokes, and we follow her eyes till they rest on Bowie, who's hopelessly trying to get the heater to stop smoking. Getting the heater to work properly is the business of this authoritarian Cinderella with soot-covered cheeks, who by the very next shot is kneeling in front of it under the gaze of the three thieves and of the camera, which now plunges towards her from the left. The film doesn't give us the time to pay any attention to Chicamaw's jokes about Bowie's inefficiency because by the very next shot both Chicamaw and T-Dub are gone. Even better, it is as if they had never been there, as if there never had been enough space for the two of them in this room. Only Bowie and Keechie are now framed by the camera placed at floor-level on the right. Even this may be saying too much, since all we really see of Bowie are the back of his head, part of his shoulder, and his arm holding out a handkerchief. "Here," he says simply. "Thanks," says the kneeling Keechie as she looks up at him without meeting our gaze. This instant when they are alone doesn't last even five seconds. By the next shot the camera has already moved back to frame Keechie and Bowie squarely between the two other thieves, before it closes in on Keechie one last time for her comeback to the thieves' cracks about the "head" of the gallant Bowie: "His head is alright to me."

Nicholas Ray breaks up the narrative and linguistic continuum of the realist novel by squeezing two spaces and two incompatible relationships into this one crowded and cluttered room. Henceforward, the narrative structure of the film essentially develops the coexistence of the incompatible spaces it constructs against the grain of the faithfully adapted book in six shots that together don't add up to more than thirty seconds. Faithful to the logic of ordinary tasks, Keechie and Bowie seal their initial separation from the others and develop their intimacy in the process of avoiding a police patrol and of changing a car wheel. Let's turn now to the garage scene. An expedient dissolve shows us the young virgin in coveralls getting her drunk father to bed and bringing out the jack for the once upon a time aspiring mechanic to show his talents. Seated on the fender, Keechie observes the repair work and this being, of a kind unknown to this place, who tells her his bleak family history while loosening the screws of the wheel. She gets up, fidgets with the steering wheel and puts on the sententious tone of an older sister to scold this young dreamer for thinking he can get squared up and start his small filling station while running with his partners, for thinking he can want to have both the fast life of the thief and the quiet life of the small business owner. She dominates him from the height of her knowledge, the knowledge of a child who has seen nothing of the world and yet has understood all about it simply by attending to the smoking heater or to her drunk father, by comparing the rectitude of the ordinary tasks required by the daily life of the place with the jumble of tortuous operations that make this place their way-stop. Right at this moment her knowledge reigns supreme, but it does so from the depths of the certainty of a timid child who has come to know the world by cutting herself off from it and by denying its presence through the link between well-executed tasks and sensible words. Keechie may seem ready to share Bowie's hopes for social reintegration, and yet the knowledge that suddenly takes hold of her authoritative, pensive body suggests something different: that there is nothing to hope for outside of this little piece of the night where two kids play at being mechanics. The concluding shot of the scene is a pure moment of utopia. With the repair done and their sentiments clear, Keechie emerges from the depths of the garage like a dream, takes one of the handles of the jack, and helps Bowie drag it back to where it belongs. This pure moment of happiness around a jack surpasses every image of idling under the shade of a coconut tree. But, even before the others invade this space and before their hands touch only to be separated, Keechie's mocking voice denounces the evil corrupting their shared dream, the invincible enemy that has always already wrecked the secretive happiness of knowing children: the puerile desire of being an adult: "You think you're quite a man now, don't you?"

The secret drama of Nicholas Ray's film, one that goes much deeper than that of the law of a pitiless world tightening its noose around two kids, is this conflict between two infancies, the battle, always already lost, of infantile maturity against adult puerility. Only the child who really accepts to be a woman, who renounces the coveralls of the small androgynous worker and the wisdom of the knowing child, can decide to follow this kid who now thinks he's quite the man. This renunciation makes for the simple and stupefying beauty of the scenes of Keechie finding the wounded Bowie, never to leave his side again. We know she has made up her mind the second she gives, without uttering a word, the money Chicamaw gave her to care for his wounded partner to her father, who'll drink it all. She now sits before a mirror that does not show us her face, undoing and brushing her hair, which falls in waves over her shoulders. The next time we see her, when she appears suddenly behind the bed of the wounded Bowie, she is no longer wearing her mechanic's uniform, but the shirt, cardigan sweater, and skirt of a young woman. She'll always be able to use the brazen sentences of the book, to tell Bowie that she doesn't know what most "girls" want, or to inform him, as she scrupulously massages his back, that she would do "the same for a dog." But these insolent remarks are powerless against the admission of her loose and brushed hair, which reveals the reciprocal feelings and the price they exact. Keechie and Bowie earn their love at the price of its cause: the quiet certainty and unclassifiable beauty of this sexless, childish body, this master of well-executed tasks that deny the folly of the world. Accepting the watch he puts on her wrist amounts to accepting from then on to want what he wants, he who wants only to keep on wanting. She accepts to live by the law of those who want, the law of the world they're about to confront and that has, at this very moment, already defeated them. The little deity protecting the place is now thrown on the highway, a creature to protect for him and an ordinary lover for us.

What makes the film so heart-rending, much more than the futile efforts of these two young lovers to elude the thieves and the tragic absurdity of the law's fierce pursuit of "Bowie the Kid," the crazy killer born of their imagination, is that they had been defeated at the outset, when the only one who could resist the law of the world abdicated her powers. Defeat is the other name of their love. In *They Live by Night*, one cannot even plead the injustices of social law and the cruelties of chance, as one can, for instance, in *You Only Live Once*. Bowie and Keechie's decision to run away as

lovers is tantamount to rushing headlong towards death. The two heroes
of Lang's film were the victims of an implacable chain of circumstances
that could have been different: the prejudices of a boss and of a landlord,
neither of whom want an ex-convict in their midst, an exchange of hats, a
hidden car, an absurd defense reflex at the moment of greeting. The trap that
ensnares the two lovers who live by night was not set by this smooth and
logical machinery that perfectly combines the effects of social law and of
chance. That is Fritz Lang's bread and butter. Ray lacks Lang's cruelty, the
pleasure he takes in making the camera lens and the sights of a rifle coincide,
his male-chauvinistic, unwavering contempt for all those well-intentioned
young women who think it their business to redeem society's outlaws with
their love. The beauty of *You Only Live Once* stems from a classical mastery
of the arts, which makes its happiness from the misfortunes of others,
its perfection from how well it can arrange the suffering of its creatures.
Nicholas Ray's Romantic filmmaking has nothing to do with this. But we
must not confuse Romanticism with simple sentimentality towards those
who suffer. It is true that Keechie, the drunkard's daughter, is too close to
the teenager who had to go into the night looking for his father in the bars
of Wisconsin, and too close also to the young wife of the days of misery
and enthusiasm spent in New York, for Raymond Nicholas Kienzle, *alias*
Nicholas Ray, to enjoy seeing her through the sights of a rifle. Ray has for
these lost children the tenderness of someone for whom the intimate rifts
in the American dream were the closest he had come to the war of 1914,
the Weimar Republic, and exile. Romanticism against Classicism is not the
outpouring of feelings against cold rigor, but one beauty against another:
the beauty of a perfectly crafted Aristotelian plot that transforms fortune
into misfortune and ignorance into knowledge against the Baudelairean loss
of that which there was never any point in knowing, the original loss of what
"can never be found again – never!"

It isn't, in other words, Nicholas Ray's kind-hearted nature or fragility
that keeps him from constructing in a carefully planned crescendo the
stages and episodes of the flight, or the calculations of the hunters and
the wanderings of their prey. The defeat is original. Hence Ray's relative
detachment from the scenes of their flight, why it didn't bother him much
to have to cut the bank holdup scenes the censors were so bent against. At
the end of the day, these imposed cuts serve the logic of the film. There is
no reason, then, to waste any time constructing the chase and the flight in
alternating montage, or to belabor on the closing of the trap. All Mattie the
informer has to do to trap Bowie is to play on his well-known weakness: his

ignorance concerning what "women" want. The dice had been cast much earlier, when the two lovers abandoned the kingdom of the night and threw themselves into a world that neither of them had been properly introduced to. Ray is not half as interested in capturing the great confrontation between the fugitives and the social order as he is in capturing the slight clumsiness of these two people who don't quite know what they are doing. The first shot of their flight is of Bowie on the bus holding a crying baby and trying to figure out how to soothe this child whose mother, an expert at doing things, is content to leave crying of hunger so she herself can get some sleep. A little later, the high-angle shot of their backs frames them as if crushed by the width of the street they have to cross to reach the house where they get married. Throughout their flight, our tenderness for their idyllic love and our shared pain for the fate awaiting them are mixed up with the discomfort we feel before people who are clearly out of their element. It's impossible not to see these doomed lovers with the same discomfort we feel when we see country people in their Sunday best disembarking into a world whose customs they know nothing about. Conversely, it is just when they are most adroit that their gestures of people happily in love are most borrowed. Keechie, with her perm and suit, has become a young woman like any other; even her feelings have lost their mystery. The way she purrs like a satisfied cat and her fits of jealousy are both taken from an ordinary repertoire. She's as adrift in her body of a young married woman on honeymoon as in her new clothes, both of them as borrowed as Bowie is in his double-breasted suit. It is, however, this very clumsiness, this defeat, that gives the film its paradoxical power. Our knowledge of the ineluctable gives to the clumsiness of country people and the foolishness of the young newlyweds a mournful beauty, a beauty born from the mourning of another. To create the fragile and slightly awkward body of this doomed lover, Ray had to burn the other Keechie, the invulnerable child of the garage. This burnt icon haunts the face that in the last shot of the film turns towards us while Bowie lies dead on the ground and reads the last words of his letter, the intimate and catch-all "I love you."

Such is the Romantic double law of beauty, exemplarily illustrated in this film. It is a law of composition—an image is made of many images; and it is a law of subtraction—an image is made from the mourning of another image. This can be easily verified in that remake of *They Live by Night* called *Breathless*. We know that Jean Seberg's final stare into the camera transposes the famous "gaze into the camera" of the last shot of *Summer with Monika*. But this composition that adds to the image is indissociable from the composition that subtracts from it. Superimposed onto the composed face of Patricia/Monika is Keechie's pained face. This Keechie has added to her role that of Mattie the informer, and yet what still shines through, beyond every fictional transaction, is the face of an original defeat.

NOTES

1. Rancière is referring to a line from Pierre Corneille's *The Cid*: "This dim light which falls from the stars, at last with the tide causes us to see thirty sails" (Act IV, sc. III). These thirty sails are as common an example of metonymy in the Francophone world as the Crown or the Whitehouse are in the Anglophone.—Trans.

2. Edward Anderson, *Thieves Like Us*, in *Crime Novels: American Noir of the 1930s and 40s*, ed. Robert Polito (New York: The Library of America, 1997) 232.

3. Anderson, *Thieves Like Us*, 237.

Part III

If There is a Cinematographic Modernity

CHAPTER 7

From One Image to Another?
Deleuze and the Ages of Cinema

Let's assume that there is a cinematographic modernity and that it confronted the classical cinema of the link between images for the purposes of narrative continuity and meaning with an autonomous power of the image whose two defining characteristics are its autonomous temporality and the void that separates it from other images. This break between two ages of the image has two model witnesses: Roberto Rossellini, the creator of a cinema of the unexpected that confronts classical narrative with the essential discontinuities and ambiguities of the real, and Orson Welles, who broke with the tradition of narrative montage through the creation of deep focus. And it also has two model thinkers: André Bazin, who in the 1950s, a religious agenda firmly in the background, deployed the arsenal of phenomenology to theorize the artistic advent of the essence of cinema, which he identified with cinema's "realistic" ability to "reveal the hidden meanings in people and things without disturbing the unity natural to them";[1] and Gilles Deleuze, who in the 1980s set about articulating a theory of the break between these two ages based on a rigorous ontology of the cinematographic image. The correct intuitions and theoretical approximations of the occasional philosopher Bazin find their solid foundation in Deleuze's theorization of the difference between two types of images, the movement-image and the time-image. The movement-image, the image organized according to the logic of the sensory-motor schema, is conceived of as being but one element in a natural arrangement with other images within a logic of the set [ensemble] analogous to that of the finalized coordination of our perceptions and actions. The time-image is characterized by a rupture with this logic, by the appearance—in Rossellini—of pure optical and sound situations that are no longer transformed into incidents. From these pure optical and sound situations eventually emerges—in Welles—the crystal-image, the image that no longer links up to another actual image, but only to its own virtual image.

Each image, thus split off from other images, opens itself up to its own infinity. Thenceforward, what creates the link is the absence of the link: the interstice between images commands a re-arrangement from the void and not a sensory-motor arrangement. The time-image founds modern cinema, in opposition to the movement-image that was the heart of classical cinema. Between the two there is a rupture, a crisis of the action-image or a rupture of the "sensory-motor link," which Deleuze ties to the historical rupture brought about by the Second World War, a time that generated situations that no longer fit the available responses.

Clear as its formulation may be, Deleuze's division becomes quite confusing as soon as we look more deeply into the two questions that it raises. First of all, how are we to think the relationship between a break internal to the art of images and the ruptures that affect history in general? And secondly, how are we to recognize, in concrete works, the traces left by this break between two ages of the image and between two types of image? The first question brings up what is fundamentally equivocal in "modernist" thought. In its most general garb, this form of thought identifies the modern revolutions in the arts with each art's manifestation of its proper essence. The novelty of the "modern" is that the essence of the art, though it had always been active in the art's previous manifestations, has now gained its autonomy by breaking free of the chains of *mimesis* that had always fettered it. The new, considered in this light, has always already been prefigured in the old, and the "rupture," in the end, is nothing more than a required episode in the edifying narrative through which each art proves its own artistry by complying with the scenario of a modernist revolution in the arts wherein each art attests to its own perennial essence. For Bazin, Rossellini's and Welles' revolutions do no more than realize cinema's autonomous vocation for realism—which was already manifest in Murnau, Flaherty, or Stroheim—through their opposition to the heteronomous tradition of a cinema of montage illustrated by Griffith's classicism, Eisenstein's dialectic, or the spectacularism of expressionism.

Deleuze's division between a movement-image and a time-image doesn't escape the general circularity of modernist theory. The difference is that in Deleuze the relationship between the classification of images and the historicity of the rupture takes on a much more complex figure and raises a more radical problem. The problem is no longer how to harmonize art history and general history since, strictly speaking, for Deleuze there is no such thing as art history or general history: all history is "natural history." Deleuze raises the "passage" from one type of image to another to the level of a theoretical episode, the "rupture of the sensory-motor link," which he defines from within a natural history of images that is ontological and cosmological in principle. But how are we to think the coincidence of the logic of this natural history, the development of the forms of an art, and the "historical" break marked by a war?

Deleuze himself warns us from the beginning. Although his work discusses films and filmmakers, although it starts on the side of Griffith, Vertov, and Eisenstein and ends on the side of Godard, Straub, and Syberberg, it is not a history of cinema. It is an "attempt at the classification of signs" in the manner of a natural history. What, then, is a sign for Deleuze? He defines it as follows: "signs themselves are the features of expression that compose and combine these images, and constantly re-create them, borne or carted along by matter in movement."[2] Signs are the components of images, their genetic elements. What, then, is an image? It is not what we see, nor is it a double of things formed by our minds. Deleuze develops his reflections as a continuation of the philosophical revolution started by Bergson, so what is the principle of that revolution? It is to abolish the opposition between the physical world of movement and the psychological world of the image. Images are not the doubles of things, but the things themselves, "the set [ensemble] of what appears," that is, the set of what is. Deleuze, quoting Bergson, defines the image as: "'a road by which pass, in every direction, the modifications propagated throughout the immensity of the universe.'"[3]

Images, properly speaking, are the things of the world. It follows logically from this that cinema is not the name of an art: it is the name of the world. The "classification of signs" is a theory of the elements, a natural history of the combinations of beings. This "philosophy of cinema," in other words, takes on a paradoxical turn from the very beginning. Cinema had generally been thought of as an art that invents images and the arrangement between visual images. And along comes this book with its radical thesis. What constitutes the image is not the gaze, the imagination, or this art. In fact, the image need not be constituted at all. It exists in itself. It is not a mental representation, but matter-light in movement. Conversely, the face looking at images and the brain conceiving them are dark screens that interrupt the movement in every direction of images. Matter is the eye, the image is light, light is consciousness.

We might then conclude that Deleuze is not really speaking about the art of cinema, and that his two volumes on images are some sort of philosophy of nature which treat cinematographic images as the events and assemblages of luminous matter. A type of framing, a play of light and shadow, a mode of linking shots would be so many metamorphoses of the elements, or so many "dreams of matter" in Gaston Bachelard's sense. But it isn't that simple. Deleuze presents his natural history of images in movement as the history of a certain number of individualized operations and combinations attributable to filmmakers, schools, epochs. Let's look, for example, at the chapter he devotes to the first major form of the movement-image, the perception-image, and, in that same chapter, at his analysis of Dziga Vertov's theory of the kino-eye. Deleuze writes: "What montage does, according to Vertov, is to carry perception to things, to put perception into matter, so that any point whatsoever in space itself perceives all the points on which it acts, or which act on it, however far these actions and reactions extend."[4] There are two problems with this claim. First, we may ask ourselves if this is really what Vertov was trying to do. It would be easy to object and say instead that Vertov's camera is very careful not to carry perception to things, that it tries, on the contrary, to retain perception as its special privilege and to join all spatial points at the center it constitutes. Second, we could point out that every image in *Man with a Movie Camera* ultimately points back to the persistent representations of the omnipresent cameraman with his machine-eye and of the editor whose operations alone can breath life into images inert in themselves. We could also, alternatively, accept Deleuze's argument. But that only makes the paradox more radical. Vertov, he says, carries "perception to things." But why should he do that? Wasn't Deleuze's starting point that perception has always been in things, that it is things that perceive and are in an infinite relationship with one another? The definition of montage turns out to be paradoxical: montage gives images, the events of matter-light, properties that already belong to them.

This is a problem that requires a two step answer, it seems to me; this duality, incidentally, is in keeping with a tension constantly at work in Deleuze's thought. On the one hand, the perceptive properties of images are only potentialities. Perception is "in things," but in a virtual state, so that it has to be extracted from them, snatched out of the relationships of cause and effect that relate things to one another. Beneath the order of bodily states, of relationships of cause and effect and of the action and reaction that characterize bodily relationships, the artist institutes a plane of immanence where events—incorporeal effects—are separated from bodies and composed in their proper space. Beneath the chronological time of causes acting in bodies, the artist institutes another time to which Deleuze gives the Greek name *aiôn*: the time of pure events. What art in general, and cinematographic montage in particular, does is snatch from bodily states their intensive qualities, the events harbored in them in a potential state. This is precisely what Deleuze, in the chapter on the "affection-image," is working out with his theory of "any-space-whatevers." Filmmakers snatch from narratives and characters an order of pure events, of pure qualities separated from bodily states: in Lulu's killing in Pabst, for instance, there is the light shining on the knife, the gleaming knife blade, Jack's terror, Lulu's "tenderness." Pabst isolates these and composes them in their own proper space, one removed from the orientations and links of the story, and removed, more generally, from the way in which we construct the everyday space of our oriented perceptions and finalized movements.

We now come to the second reason for the paradox, one that brings a different logic into play even though, at the end of the day, it is probably only a different way of saying the same thing. If we must give things a perceptive power they already "had," it must be because they have lost it, and, if they've lost it, it is for a very specific reason. It is because the phosphorescence of images of the world and their movement in every direction were interrupted by this opaque image called the human brain. The brain confiscated the interval between action and reaction for its own benefit and proceeded from this interval to place itself at the center of the world. It proceeded to constitute a world of images for its use, a world of readily available information that it uses to construct its sensory-motor schemas, orient its movements, and make of the physical world an immense machinery of causes and effects that transform it into the means for its ends. Montage has to put perception back in things because its operation is one of restitution. Intentional artistic activity renders unto the events of sensible matter the potentialities the human brain had deprived them of in order to constitute a sensory-motor universe adapted to its needs and subject to its mastery. There is something emblematic in how Deleuze puts Vertov, one of the main representatives of the sweeping Soviet and constructivist desire for a complete reorganization of the material universe in the interest of human goals, to perform, symbolically, the inverse task: to put perception back in things, to constitute an "order" of art that returns the world to its essential disorder. This is how a natural history of images can assume the shape of a history of the art whose operations abstract the pure potentialities of sensible matter. But this history of the art of cinema is just as much a history of redemption. The work of art, in general, undoes the ordinary work of the human brain, of this particular image that placed itself at the center of the universe of images. The proposed "classification" of film images is in fact the history of the restitution of world-images to themselves. It is a history of redemption.

Hence the complexity of Deleuze's notion of image and of this history of cinema that actually isn't one, a complexity that shoots to the surface as soon as we turn our attention to the analyses that sustain Deleuze's thesis and the images he brings forth to illustrate it. Deleuze argues that the time-image is situated on the other side of the rupture of the "sensory-motor schema." But are its properties not discernible already in the constitution of the movement-image, especially in the way the affection-image constitutes an order of pure events by separating intensive qualities from bodily states? The time-image foils traditional narration by banishing all conventional forms of the relationship between narrative situation and emotional expression in order to release the pure potentialities borne by faces and gestures. But this power of the virtual proper to the time-image is already a feature of the affection-image, which is said to release pure qualities and compose what Deleuze calls "any-space-whatevers," spaces that have lost the character of spaces oriented by our will. The very same examples, in other words, can be used to illustrate the constitution of the any-space-whatevers of the affection-image and the constitution of the pure optical and sound situations of the time-image. Consider how Deleuze uses as an example one of the model representatives of cinematographic "modernity," Robert Bresson, himself an admirable theoretician of the autonomy of the art of cinema. Bresson shows up at two key moments of Deleuze's discussion. The chapter on the affection-image contrasts Bresson's way of composing any-space-whatevers with Dreyer's: whereas Dreyer relies on close-ups of Joan of Arc and her judges to release the intensive potentialities of the image, Bresson impregnates space itself with these potentialities in his way of relating spaces, of rearranging the relationship between the optical and the tactile. Deleuze's analysis of Bresson's cinema is ultimately analogous to his analysis of Vertov's: both show that the work of restituting to the image its potentialities is already operative in all the components of the movement-image. The analysis of Bresson in *Cinema 2: The Time-Image*, under the title "Thought and Cinema," for the most part restates what Deleuze has already said about Bresson in connection with the affection-image. The very same images examined in the first book as the components of the movement-image reappear in the second book as the constitutive principles of the time-image. It seems impossible, in other words, to isolate in the model filmmaker of the "time-image" *any* "time-images," any images endowed with properties that would distinguish them from the "movement-image."

We would willingly conclude that movement-image and time-image are by no means two types of images ranged in opposition, but two different points of view on the image. Although it speaks of films and filmmakers, Deleuze's real project in *Cinema 1: The Movement-Image* is to analyze forms of the art of cinema as events of matter-image. And although *Cinema 2: The Time-Image* imports the analyses of *The Movement-Image*, it analyzes these same cinematographic forms as forms of thought-image. The passage from one book to the other would not mark the passage from one age of the cinematographic image to another but the passage to another point of view on the same images. When we pass from the affection-image, the form of the movement-image, to the "opsign," the originary form of the time-image, we're not passing from one family of images to another, but rather from one side to the other of the same images, from image as matter to image as form. In short, we pass from images as elements in a philosophy of nature to images as elements in a philosophy of spirit. As a philosophy of nature, *The Movement-Image* uses specific cinematographic images to introduce us to the chaotic infinity of the metamorphoses of matter-light. As a philosophy of spirit, *The Time-Image* shows us, through the operations of the cinematographic art, how thought deploys a power commensurate with this chaos. The destiny of cinema—and of thought—is not in fact to lose itself, as some simplifying "Dyonisism" would have it, in the infinite inter-expressivity of images-matter-light. Its destiny is to couple this infinity to the order of its own infinity: that of the infinitely small that is equal to the infinitely large. Its exemplary expression is to be found in the "crystal-image," in the crystal of thought-image that links the actual image to the virtual one, and that differentiates them in their very indiscernibility, which is also the indiscernibility of the real and the imaginary. The task of thought is to render unto the whole the power of the interval confiscated by the brain/screen, and, of course, rendering the interval unto the whole means creating another whole from another power of the interval. The interval-screen that arrests the inter-expressivity of images and imposes its laws upon their free movement is set in opposition to the crystal-interval, the seed "impregnating the sea." Put more soberly, the crystal-interval creates a new whole, a whole of intervals, of solitarily expressive crystals born from the void and lapsing back into it. The categories Deleuze claims are specific to the time-image—false relationships, false movement, irrational cuts—wouldn't actually describe the identifiable operations that separate two families of images so much as mark how thought becomes one with the chaos that prompts it. And the "rupture of the sensory-motor link," a process not to be found in this natural history of images, would in fact express this relationship of correspondence between the infinity—chaos—

of matter-image and the infinity—chaos—characteristic of thought-image. The distinction between the two images would be strictly transcendental and would thus not correspond to an identifiable rupture, whether in the natural history of images or in the history of human events or of forms of the art of cinema. The same images—from Dreyer and Bresson, or from Eisenstein and Godard—are equally analyzable in terms of affection-image or opsign, of organic description or crystalline description.

Tenable as this perspective is, Deleuze won't allow it. It is true, he admits, that the movement-image was already an open whole of the image, but it was a whole still governed by a logic of association and attraction between images, still understood on the model of action and reaction. In the time-image, in modern cinema, conversely, each image actually emerges from the void and lapses back into it, so much so, in fact, that it is the interstice, the separation between images, that plays the decisive role in modern cinema. There aren't just two points of view on the same images. There are really two logics of the image that correspond to two ages of the cinema. Between the two, there is an identifiable crisis of the action-image, a rupture of the sensory-motor link. Deleuze ties this crisis to the Second World War, to the concrete appearance, amidst the wreckage of war and the helplessness of the vanquished, of disconnected spaces and of characters who can no longer react to the situations confronting them.

This avowed attempt to historicize obviously brings back the initial paradox: how can a classification among types of signs be split in two by an external historical event? Can "history," taken as a given at the beginning of *The Time-Image*, do anything but sanction a crisis internal to the movement-image, that is, a rupture internal to the movement of images that is in itself wholly indifferent to the tribulations of the times and the horrors of war? It is just such a crisis that Deleuze stages in the last chapter of *The Movement-Image*. The strong point of Deleuze's dramaturgy there is to be found in his analysis of Hitchcock's cinema, which is marshaled in as the privileged example because in many ways it sums up the entire genesis of the movement-image. All of its components find their place in it: the play of light and shadow formed in the school of the perception-image and perfected by German expressionism; the constitution of any-space-whatevers where pure qualities (for example, the whiteness of the glass of milk in *Suspicion* or of the snowfield in *Spellbound*) compose a plane of events; the immersion of these any-space-whatevers in determined situations; the constitution of an overarching action scheme based on the formula action/situation/action. The integration of all these elements defines what Deleuze calls "mental-images": Hitchcock, he says, films relations. The real object of his cinema are these games of equilibrium and disequilibrium developed around a few paradigmatic relationships: the relationship innocent/guilty, for example, or the dramaturgy of the exchange of crimes. Hitchcock's cinema marks the end of the constitution of the movement-image, an integration of all its elements. According to the logic of artistic activity, this completion should mean the end of the movement, which had always been operative in each of these types of cinematographic images, of restituting to matter-image its intensive potentialities. Deleuze, however, presents this completion as an exhaustion. The crowning moment of the movement-image is likewise its moment of crisis, the moment when the schema linking situation and reaction cracks and we're thrown into a world of pure optical and sound situations. But, we may ask, what are the signs by which we recognize this rupture, this crack? We recognize it in situations of paralysis, of motor inhibition, Deleuze answers. In *Rear Window*, the chaser of images Jeff, played by James Stewart, is struck with motor paralysis: his leg in a cast, all he can do is look at what his neighbors across the courtyard are doing. In *Vertigo*, the detective, Scottie, also played by James Stewart, is paralyzed by vertigo and cannot chase the thief over the rooftops or climb to the top of the bell-tower where the murder disguised as suicide is committed. In *The Wrong Man*, the wife of the wrong man, played by Vera Miles, sinks into madness. The neat mechanics of the action-image culminates in these situations of sensory-motor rupture that throw the logic of the movement-image into crisis.[5]

This analysis is at first sight a bit strange. The "paralysis" of each of these characters is actually only an aspect of the plot, a feature of the narrative situation. It is hard to see in what ways the characters' motor or psychomotor problems hinder the linear arrangement of the images and the action from moving forward. Hitchcock's camera is not paralyzed by Scottie's vertigo, but turns his vertigo into the opportunity to create the spectacular effect that shows James Stewart hanging from a gutter over a vertiginous abyss. Deleuze contends that the image has lost its "motor extension." But the motor extension of the image of Scottie hanging over the void is not an image of Scottie recovering and mounting back onto the rooftop. It is the image that links this event to its fictional continuation: to the subsequent shot where we see that Scottie survived the whole ordeal, and, more importantly, to the huge narrative and visual machination that his revealed handicap sets in motion. Scottie will be manipulated in the preparation of a suicide that is really a murder. His vertigo doesn't hinder in the least, but rather favors,

the play of mental relations and of "sensory-motor" situations that develop
around these questions: who is the woman Scottie has been asked to follow?
Who is the woman who falls from the bell-tower? How does she fall, murder
or suicide? The logic of the movement-image is not at all paralyzed by the
fictional situation. The only remaining alternative is to consider the paralysis
symbolic, to say that Deleuze treats these fictional situations of paralysis
as simple allegories emblematic of the rupture in the action-image and its
principle: the rupture of the sensory-motor link. However, if Deleuze has
to allegorize this rupture by means of emblems taken from the stories, isn't
it because it cannot be identified as an actual difference between types of
images? Isn't it because the theoretician of the cinema must find a visible
incarnation for a purely ideal rupture? The movement-image is "in crisis"
because the thinker needs it to be.

Why does he need that? Because the passage from the infinity of matter-
image to the infinity of thought-image is also a history of redemption, of
an always thwarted redemption. The filmmaker takes perception to images
by snatching them from bodily states and placing them on a plane of pure
events; in so doing, the filmmaker gives images an arrangement-in-thought.
But this arrangement-in-thought is always also the re-imposition of the
logic of the opaque screen, of the central image that arrests the movement in
every direction of other images to reorder them from itself. The gesture of
restitution is always also a new gesture of capture. This is why Deleuze wants
to "paralyze" the logic of the mental arrangement of images, even if to do
that he's forced to give an autonomous existence to the fictive properties of the
characters in the stories. It is not at all surprising that Deleuze should apply
this treatment to the manipulating filmmaker par excellence, to the creator
for whom a film is a rigorous assemblage of images organized so as to orient
and disorient the affects of the viewer. Deleuze turns against Hitchcock the
fictional paralysis that the manipulative thought of the director had imposed
on his characters for his own expressive ends. Turning this paralysis against
Hitchcock amounts to transforming it, conceptually, into a real paralysis.
Significantly, Godard performs the very same operation on the images of
the same Hitchcock in *Histoire(s) du cinéma*, where he isolates shots of objects
from their dramatic function: the glass of milk in *Suspicion*, the bottles of
wine in *Notorious*, the glasses in *Strangers on a Train*. Godard turns these into
still-lives, into self-sufficient icons. Albeit by different paths, Deleuze and
Godard apply themselves to the same task: to paralyze Hitchcock's cinema,
to isolate its images, to transform the dramatic progression of his cinema
into moments of passivity. And, through Hitchcock, it is more globally

the cinema, in some ways, that they try to make "passive," to free from the despotism of the director in order to render it, in Deleuze, to the chaos of matter-image and, in Godard, to the impressions left by things on a screen that has been transformed into the veil of Veronica.

This brings us to the heart of Deleuze's singular relationship to cinema, which is, more profoundly, the heart of the problem cinema poses for thought given the particular place it occupies in what is generally called artistic modernity, and which I prefer to call the aesthetic regime of art. What distinguishes the latter from the classical, representative regime is a different conception of art, a different idea of how to think about art. The representative regime understands artistic activity on the model of an active form that imposes itself upon inert matter and subjects it to its representational ends. The aesthetic regime of art rejects the idea of form willfully imposing itself on matter and instead identifies the power of the work with the identity of contraries: the identity of active and passive, of thought and non-thought, of intentional and unintentional. I suggested earlier on that the most abrupt formulation of this idea is to be found in Flaubert, who set out to write a book that depended on nothing external and was held together solely by the strength of its style. This book, thus stripped of all subject and all matter, would affirm only the now absolute power of style. But what must this sovereign style produce? A book that bears no traces of the author's intervention and displays instead only the absolute indifference and passivity of things with neither will nor meaning. More than an artistic ideology, what is expressed here is a whole regime of how to think about art that expresses also an idea of thought. Thought is no longer understood as the faculty of impressing its will upon its objects, but as the faculty of becoming one with its contrary. Hegel's time saw this equality of contraries as the Apollonian power of the idea emerging from itself to become the light of a painting or the smile of a stone god. From Nietzsche to Deleuze, it became the inverse, the Dionysian power through which thought abdicates the attributes of will and loses itself in stone, in color, in language, and equals its active manifestation to the chaos of things.

We have already mentioned the paradox cinema poses for this idea of art and thought. Cinema, due to its technical apparatus, literally embodies this unity of contraries in the union of the passive and automatic eye of the camera and the conscious eye of the director. In the 1920s, theoreticians mined this unity to make the new art of images identical to a proper language, one that was at once natural and constructed. But they overlooked the fact that the automatism of cinematographic passivity confounded the aesthetic equation. Unlike novelists and painters, who are themselves the agents of their becoming-passive, the camera cannot but be passive. In the cinema, the identity of contraries is there at the outset, and hence lost from the outset. The filmmaker who directs the mechanic eye with his eye has already consigned his "work" to the state of inert pieces of celluloid that can only be brought to life by the work of montage. Deleuze theorizes this double mastery in the idea of the sensory-motor schema: as a result of the mechanical apparatus of the cinema, the identity of active and passive reverts back to the omnipotence of the mind coordinating the work with a sovereign eye and hand. The old logic of form fashioning matter reinstates itself anew. In limit cases, the eye of the filmmaker need not even look through the eye of the camera. One filmmaker to have achieved this was Hitchcock, who boasted that he never looked through the eye of a camera because the film was "in his head." The pure affects extracted from the state of things were initially conceived as functional affects designed to incite wonder or anxiety in the audience. Hitchcock embodies a certain logic in which cinema reverses the aesthetic identity of passive and active and rehabilitates the sovereignty of the central intelligence. That is why Deleuze brings him onto center stage at the end of *The Movement-Image*, where he describes Hitchcock as a demiurge vanquished by the automata he had himself created, as afflicted in his turn by the paralysis he had conferred on them.

The rupture of the "sensory-motor schema" has not taken place as a process that can be identified by specific characteristics either in the composition of the shot or in the relationship between two shots. The gesture that frees the potentialities remains, as always, the gesture that chains them up again. The rupture is always still to come, like a supplement of intervention that is simultaneously a supplement of disappropriation. One of Deleuze's first examples of the crystal-image, taken from Tod Browning's *The Unknown*, is significant in this regard.[6] It is very difficult to specify, in the shots themselves or in their sequential arrangement, the traits by which we would recognize the rupture of the sensory-motor link, the infinitization of the interval, and the crystallization of the virtual and the actual. That is why Deleuze's whole analysis has to rely on the allegorical content of the fable. The hero of *The Unknown* is an armless man with a circus routine—he throws knives with his feet—whose physical disability ingratiates him to his assistant, who cannot stand the hands of men. The problem, we learn soon enough, is that his disability is feigned: he has taken on this identity in order to hide from the police. Afraid that his assistant might discover his disguise and leave him, he takes a radical decision and has his arms amputated for real. Things end badly for him since, meanwhile, the circus strongman has squeezed the assistant's prejudices out of her in his embrace. What interests us, though, are not the misfortunes of the hero, but how Deleuze turns them into an allegory for the radical form of the "rupture of the sensory-motor link." If *The Unknown* is an emblem of the crystal-image, the exemplary figure of the time-image, it is not because of properties specific to the shots and their assemblage, but because the film allegorizes the idea that artistic activity is a surgery of thought: the thought that creates must always self-mutilate, amputate its arms, in order to thwart the logic by which it invariably takes back from the images of the world the freedom that it restitutes to them. Amputating the arms means undoing the coordination between the eye that has all the visible at its disposal and the hand that coordinates the visibilities under the power of a brain that imposes its centralizing logic. Deleuze subverts the old parable of the blind and the paralytic: the filmmaker's gaze must become tactile, must become like the gaze of the blind who coordinate the elements of the visible world by groping. And, conversely, the coordinating hand must be the hand of a paralytic. It must be seized by the paralysis of the gaze, which can only touch things from afar, but never grasp them.

The rupture that structures the opposition between the movement-image and the time-image is a fictive rupture, so that we may do better to describe their relationship not as an opposition, but as an infinite spiral. Artistic activity must always be turned into passivity, find itself in this passivity, and be thwarted anew. If we find Bresson both in the analysis of the affection-image and among the heroes of the time-image, it is because Bresson's cinema embodies, more than any other, the dialectic at the heart of Deleuze's two volumes, because his cinema embodies a radical form of the cinematographic paradox. His whole cinema is made of the double encounter of active and passive, voluntary and involuntary. The first encounter joins the sovereign will of the director to these filmed bodies that Bresson preferred to call models so as to distinguish them from the tradition of the actor. The model seems, at first, to be a body entirely subjected to the will of the auteur, who demands that the model reproduce the lines and gestures he provides without ever playing, without ever embodying the "character" as traditional actors do. The model is to behave like an automaton and to reproduce in a uniform tone the lines taught by the auteur. But there the logic of the automaton capsizes: the model's mechanical, unconscious reproduction of the lines and gestures dictated by the director infuses them with its own

interior truth, invests them with a truth that it is not cognizant of. The
director is even less cognizant of it than the model, so that the lines and
gestures he tyrannically imposes upon the model produce a film he could not
have foreseen and that may even run counter to everything he had planned.
The automaton, says Deleuze, manifests what is unthinkable in thought: in
thought in general, but mainly in its own thought, as well as, and above all, in
the thought of the director. To this first encounter between will and chance
we must add a second: the truth the model makes manifest, which neither
it nor the director were cognizant of, again escapes it, because it is not in
the image it offers the camera, but in the way those images are subsequently
arranged during montage. The model only gives the film its "substance."
It is the film's raw material, somewhat like the spectacle of the visible that
unfolds before the painter. It is not by chance that Bresson calls the models
"pieces of nature." The task of art is to arrange these pieces of nature in a
way that expresses their truth and that brings them back to life again like
flowers in water.[7]

The gap between what the mechanical eye should capture and what it
has captured is cast off and seems to get lost in the indifferent equality
of the "pieces of nature" the artist must assemble. Doesn't this reproduce,
once more, the old tyranny of intentional form impressing itself on passive
matter? This question underlies Deleuze's whole analysis of Bresson. Deleuze
puts the "hand," as an emblem of the work of montage, at the heart of his
analysis because his main concern is with the relationship between the will
of the artist and the autonomous movement of images. He suggests that
Bresson constructs a "haptic" space, a space where touch has been freed
from the imperialism of the optical, a fragmented space whose parts are
connected "manually," by groping. Montage is the work of a hand that
touches, not of a hand that seizes. Deleuze gives another example, again
allegorical: the scene in *Pickpocket* where space is constructed by the hands
of the pickpockets passing around the stolen money. These hands, Deleuze
points out, don't seize, they just touch, they just stroke the stolen object.[8]
These pickpockets who don't seize what they steal and are content just
with touching it to connect a disoriented space are evidently kin to the man
whose false disability is transformed into a real amputation. Still, the best
illustration of this dialectic is no doubt to be found in *Au hasard, Balthazar*,
a film that is really a long story of hands. The story starts with the first
shot, the hand of the young woman touching the donkey, and continues by
transforming her hand into the hands of the two young boys seizing and
pulling the donkey they want to make into their toy. The story goes from

there to the hands of the child that baptize the donkey, then on to the hands that load, strike, and whip the donkey. The donkey is first of all a symbol of passivity, the animal that suffers the blows. And indeed that is all Balthazar will do until he is shot dead at the end of the film as a result of a smuggling deal gone wrong. In the meantime, another play of hands has set in: the play of desire of the roguish Gérard, who wants the young Marie just as the two boys want the donkey, and who conducts his chase with perfect hand and eye coordination. His hand takes advantage of the night to hold Marie's hand resting on a bench in the garden. Later on, this same hand disconnects the cables of the young woman's car, immobilizing it and making her feel the power of the gaze that subjects her even before the hand reaches for her bosom and around her neck. Later on there'll be the slapping hand that forces a revolted Marie to recognize her master, and then the hand the miller rests on top of Marie's to indicate anew her dependence.

The whole film is the story of two preys, the donkey and the young girl, at the mercy of those who assert their power in the coordination of gaze and hand. How can we not see it as an allegory à la Deleuze? The roguish Gérard is basically the perfect Hitchcockian director. Like Hitchcock, Gérard spends all his time setting traps: provoking accidents by spilling oil on the road; bringing Marie's car to a stop by using Balthazar as bait; transforming the vagabond Arsène into a murderer by giving him a gun and convincing him that the police are coming to arrest him. He is constantly arranging, with his hands and his words, the specific visibility that will produce the movements he's after and hence allow for new gestures of capture. Gérard is an allegory of the "bad" filmmaker who imposes the law of his desire on the visible. The paradox, evidently, is that this bad filmmaker is uncannily like the good one. When her mother asks Marie what good she can possibly see in Gérard, she replies: "Who knows why one loves? He says to me: *come.* I come. *Do that!* And I do it." But the uniform tone with which the "model," Anne Wiazemsky, delivers these lines betrays the kinship between the power of the hunter Gérard and of the director Bresson. He also tells his models: *say that*, and they say it; *do that*, and they do it. The difference, some might say, is that in doing what Bresson wants, Anne Wiazemsky also does something other than what he wants, she produces an unexpected truth that thwarts his intentions. But it is the way Bresson directs the traps set by the director Gérard that must make the difference between the two "*mise-en-scènes.*" This difference, though, always gets played out at the very limits of the indiscernible. This indiscernibility is of course related to the play of hands. Deleuze's claim that Bresson constructs "haptic" and manually connected spaces is his way of talking about the fragmentation of shots characteristic of Bresson's cinema. Deleuze claims that this fragmentation reveals the power of the interval that separates the shots and puts emptiness between them, instead of the power of the linear progression of the "sensory-motor" links. But, in practice, this opposition between two opposing logics is almost indiscernible. Bresson's visually fragmented shots and connections amount to an ellipsis. He's more than willing to show us only parts of bodies: hands touching a donkey's stomach, arms baptizing it, a hand pouring a can of oil, the same hand moving in the darkness towards a hand resting in the light. But the fragmentation of bodies and shots is itself an ambivalent procedure. Deleuze sees in it the infinitization of the interval that disorients the spaces and separates the images. But we could also see the fragmentation as doing the inverse, as intensifying the coordination between the visual and the dramatic: we seize with our hands, no need then to represent the whole body; we walk with our feet, no need to show our heads. The fragmented shot is also an economic means of bringing into sharp focus what is essential in the action, what classical theories of painting used to call the pregnant moment of the story. Gérard's hand may have been reduced to a minuscule black shadow that touches Marie's hand, or, if you prefer, the white spot to which her hand has been reduced. But this fragmentation only accentuates all the more the "implacable" coordination between Gérard's hunt and the film that directs it. The whole film proceeds thus according to an almost indiscernible difference between the voluntary *mise-en-scène* of the hunter and the involuntary one of the director. Coming back to Deleuze, this means the near-total indiscernibility between the logic of the movement-image and the logic of the time-image, between the montage that orients spaces according to the "sensory-motor" schema and that which disorients it so as to render the products of conscious thought equal in power to the free deployment of the potentialities of world-images. Bresson's cinematography and Deleuze's theory both bring to the fore the dialectic constitutive of the cinema. Cinema is the art that realizes the original identity of thought and non-thought that defines the modern image of art and thought. And it is also the art that overturns this identity and rehabilitates the claims of the human brain to its place at the center of the world, from where it can put everything at its disposal. This dialectic jeopardizes from the outset any attempt to distinguish two images by means of specific traits, and so to fix a border separating a classical from a modern cinema.

NOTES

1. André Bazin, "The Evolution of the Language of Cinema," in *What is Cinema?*, vol. 1, trans. Hugh Gray (Berkeley: University of California Press, 1967) 38.

2. Gilles Deleuze, *Cinema 2: The Time-Image*, trans. Hugh Tomlinson and Robert Galeta (London: The Athlone Press, 1989) 33.

3. Gilles Deleuze, *Cinema 1: The Movement-Image*, trans. Hugh Tomlinson and Barbara Habberjam (London: The Athlone Press, 1986) 58.

4. Deleuze, *Cinema 1*, 81.

5. Cf. Deleuze, *Cinema 1*, 200–5.

6. Deleuze, *Cinema 2*, 72.

7. Robert Bresson, *Notes on the Cinematographer*, trans. Jonathan Griffin (Copenhagen: Green Integer, 1997) 23.

8. Deleuze, *Cinema 2*, 12–13.

CHAPTER 8

Falling Bodies
Rossellini's Physics

Morning in Rome. Pina. "The beginning is more than half the whole," says Aristotle. For Rossellini the beginning, this more than half the whole, is entitled *Rome, Open City*. It is of course not his first film, and there's no shortage of critics who never miss an opportunity to bring up Rossellini's earlier films, devoted, as it were, to the war efforts of Fascist Italy. It was *Rome, Open City*, however, that established whatever precarious consensus there was between a predominantly Italian Marxist gaze, attuned to the worthiness of representing the anti-Fascist struggle, and a predominantly French phenomenological gaze, attuned to how major political themes are rooted in the restitution of the intimate truth of ordinary bodies. *Rome, Open City*, in other words, is both the great film about the Italian resistance and the manifesto of neorealism, an epic about people who die without talking anchored in the representation of everyday life and using only the gestures and intonations of real people. It is impossible not to praise the way it dovetails political content and artistic form, the historical struggle of the people and the struggle to achieve a real representation of the people. Years later, nostalgic critics will pit this perfect adequation against the poorly worked out stories, the awkward links, and the Catholic sermons of *Stromboli* and *Voyage to Italy*. It is odd, though, to note the extent to which these same critics seem to have completely overlooked both the improbabilities that abound in this realist manifesto and the lightness that characterizes these model fighters of the resistance. The leader of the resistance is having an affair with a cabaret dancer who makes her living from the liberality of the occupying officers. When his place is tipped off, he seeks refuge with his companion at arms Francesco, who lives in a building where a group of kids assiduously apply themselves to preparing and handling explosives. He makes sure to send word of his move to another "artist" of the same ilk as his girlfriend. The priest who provides him with false documents is also sheltering a Wehrmacht deserter. There has never been, one would say,

such a singularly strange representation of the resistance. Still, it is not the
recklessness and political impatience of these characters that make them
seem so unfit for the clandestine life of the resistance. It is, rather, the
director who seems radically unsuited or indifferent to the representation
of the resistance. The impatience with which these characters, so eminently
reasonable and measured in thought and action, throw themselves into harm's
way doesn't just fly in the face of the notion that this is a model political
film. It also jars with Bazin's image of Rossellini's cinema as a patient search
for the secret of beings and things, and with Deleuze's characterization
of it as a cinema of disconnected spaces and of pure optical and sound
situations. Their rush to hurl themselves into the trap is as far away from
Marxist political conscience as from the patience of Bazin's phenomenology
and of Deleuze's sensoriality. Their impetuosity translates the director's
desire to get as quickly as possible to the only thing that really interests him:
the meeting of antagonistic elements, the pure collision of extremes.

We will not find the best illustration of the purity of this meeting, of
this fall that is also an accomplishment, in the heroic martyrdom of the
communist and the priest. Rossellini once said he was more than willing
to make a whole film for the sake of a scene, a shot, sometimes just for
the sake of a gesture: Edmund wandering the streets of Berlin, the tin cans
that come tumbling down the village steps in *Miracle*, the two Anglo-Saxon
"trees" who fall prisoner to the mass of Neapolitan microbes at the end
of *Voyage to Italy*. There is no doubt that Rossellini conceived all of *Rome,
Open City* for the scene of Pina's death, a scene, incidentally, that is also
highly improbable. In order to dash after the truck driving away her fiancé,
Francesco, Pina has to force her way through a barrage of soldiers and
tear herself free from arms that should *visibly* have been able to stop her.
This doesn't sit too well with the incapacity to respond to a situation that
Deleuze describes. Nor does it have anything to do with the strength of
despair or the healthy vigor traditionally accorded to women of the people.
Pina is a creature who breaks her chains, takes a step to the side, and goes
there where her maker bids her go. She tears herself away from the swarm
of German soldiers and tenement dwellers and finds herself all alone in
the middle of the street, a black silhouette on an enormous white stretch,
comical almost as she dashes towards us, towards the camera and the rifles,
her exaggerated gestures reminiscent of those of a woman running after
a bus that left without waiting for its passenger. We're reminded of those
comedies where the delayed bride and groom have to run off to church half-
clad. And, indeed, Pina and Francesco were supposed to meet at the altar

later that morning. Very few directors would have resisted the temptation of prolonging—and thus of losing—this marvelous suspension of image and meaning with the use of slow motion or the freeze frame. Rossellini never displays such lack of courage in his art. For his camera and for the rifles, it's time to put an end to this suspension. Pina now crashes on the white street like a great bird. The crying boy, and the priest trying to console his pain, who swoop down on her one after the other are themselves like two birds outlined by the hand of a painter, and both equally unstoppable for the soldiers. Never have the weight of a falling body and the lightness of grace been better joined than in this body whose gentle curve vanquishes from the outset all pain and disorder. This line that closes in on itself (it wasn't so long ago that Jacques Rivette turned to Matisse, the painter of swooping birds, to talk about arabesques) is the happiness of this image that condenses the relationships and tensions of the film without symbolizing them, without identifying them with something other than the interplay of black and white that defines the filmic image. This isn't to say that the painter of the underground movement in Italy works only for "aesthetic" pleasure, for the thrill of the beautiful shot that loops the tragic death of a mother and of a woman of the people into a gracious arabesque. For Rossellini, there is no beautiful shot that is not a moment of grace in the strongest, Pauline sense of the term; no beautiful shot that does not give its absolute consent to the encounter with the thing or person it was not searching for. In this instance, it marks the exact concordance of an ethical upsurge and an aesthetic trace. Beyond every political determination, the priest and the communist engineer both die without talking for the sake of this pure original élan, for the absolute gratuity or generosity of this liberty. We never hear Pina talking about the glorious future, though she is the one who rushes headlong towards the rifles and the camera and outlines the exact curve of this liberty. All the gentleness amassed in her fall is expressed again in the infinitely gentle gesture of Don Pietro, who holds in his hands the head of the dead Manfredi and with his thumbs closes the eyelids that Manfredi's torturers had left open. In a long scene from another film, *The Flowers of St. Francis*, it will again fall to the same actor, Aldo Fabrizi, to unfold, albeit differently, the meaning of this same gesture. Fabrizi, playing the tyrant Nicolai, holds in his hands the equally beat up face of Fra Ginepro, whom his men had tortured, until he concedes defeat, until he is disarmed by the absolute enigma of this fearless face, by the incomprehensible power that is the strength of the weak, the invincible strength of those who have consented to the most radical abandon, to absolute weakness.

But let's not anticipate. Even if he grants Pina's and Don Pietro's gestures the power to represent the cause Manfredi dies for, the director of *Rome, Open City* no doubt agrees with Manfredi—and with his critics—that Franciscan kindness alone is not enough to defeat the Nazi torturers. What he knows already, however, is that he hastens his heroes to the headquarters of the Gestapo because this place where the people fighting for freedom come face to face with their torturers is the site for a clash between two types of *mise-en-scène*. There are two film directors at the Gestapo headquarters, one who uses for a set the torture chambers where resistance fighters scream loudly but say little, and the other the lounge fitted with all the elements of a Hollywood set for a film about Lili Marlene's Berlin—mirrors, paintings, and a piano. This is how Bergmann, the head of the Gestapo, and his associate Ingrid have divided their respective sides and roles. In the room on the left, Bergmann traces lines on the location map, arranges the shooting schedule, and gives his instructions to his sound engineers—that is, his torturers. Ingrid is responsible for the actresses and for arranging the images that will produce, in the adjoining set, the sought-after confession speech. Her art is to use the image, the drug of the mirror, to trap all these "actresses" who see their art as the art of putting makeup on their reflection in the dressing room mirror, the same mirror that reflects Ingrid's eyes contemplating their prey and that holds the snapshot of Marina and Manfredi, the static shot of Ingrid's *mise-en-scène*, the little trap inside the big trap. Rossellini clearly doesn't want to dwell too long on the act of denunciation nor on what Marina's motivations might be. The drug she receives as payment is only the small change of her petty desire, of her great fear of the Unknown. When Marina picks up the phone to denounce her lover, her idiotic friend, Lauretta, tells her with the lucidity of those still half-asleep: "Maybe they're right, maybe we're the idiots." This "maybe" haunts the actress of the bad cinema: the vertigo of having to act differently, of having to leave the dressing room and its mirrors to throw oneself headlong onto the street, the void, liberty. Marina's betrayal is her refusal to change *mise-en-scènes*. But, contrary to what Ingrid's image might have led Marina's image in the mirror to believe in the room on the right, the *mise-en-scène* in the room on the left has failed. This Hollywood-style use of the image as trap can do nothing to make the men of freedom talk. When she sees her dead lover, Marina collapses like a soulless mass, a mannequin, and Ingrid bends down to remove her costume, the fur coat, for the next extra to use.

"It isn't hard to die well," says Don Pietro to the priest trying to comfort him with superfluous words of encouragement, "the hard thing is to live

well." This perfectly formulated antithesis will be answered by the voice of
another Christian, Simone Weil, who was herself involved in the resistance
and whose figure will inspire the director of *Europe 51*: "Death is the most
precious thing which has been given to men. That is why the supreme
impiety is to make bad use of it. To die amiss. To kill amiss."[1] Rossellini's
mise-en-scène presupposes the exact identification of spiritual and material,
political and artistic, so that we would do better, in his case, to formulate
the problem in terms of falling well or badly. Under the subheading of
the meeting of the film director and the philosopher, we might add Weil's
definition of the spiritual physics of art: "A double movement of descent:
to do again, out of love, what gravity does. Is not the double movement
of descent the key to all art?"[2] There are two ways of falling, and they are
separated by a bare nothing that in art can only be called the soul: not a
part of the representation, but an almost imperceptible difference in the
light that shines on it. The exact measure of Rossellini's "realism" is in the
precision with which he traces the gesture that sums up the trajectory of
liberty, in his determined identification of the believer's spiritualism and the
artist's materialism: the so-called soaring soul perfectly circumscribed by the
curve of the falling body. "Genius of Christianity," say Rohmer and Rivette
in pages that have since become famous. We should mention, though, that
this genius[3] was from the very beginning split in two. Death and life in
Christ, the crucifixion of the flesh after His example and glorification of the
body by the light of the Word made flesh. Centuries of Christian polemic,
dating from the Desert Fathers all the way to the Reformation and the
Counter-Reformation, have sedimented this duality around two poles: the
thought of incarnation, of bodies transfigured by the presence of the Savior,
that at its limit borders on idolatry; and the thought of renunciation, of
mortified flesh and of the denunciation of images, that at its limit borders
on becoming another paganism—the paganism of philosophers, the
Platonism of the soul lamenting its fall and longing to be separated from
the body. Rossellini's heroes, his heroines especially, are always traveling
between these two poles, between asceticism and idolatry: the renunciation
of the images in the mirror, of Pharisaic values and of the security of one's
home culminates in Irene's absolute asceticism in *Europe 51*; contact with
the proliferating Madonnas, the cult of the dead, the programmed miracles,
and the quasi-pagan excesses of Neapolitan Christianity culminates in
Katherine's critique of "pure ascetic images" in *Voyage to Italy*. The scandal
that gives the fabric to Rossellini's films is always somehow related to an
ambiguity at the point where renunciation and incarnation meet. But we

should say that Rossellini's particular genius is that he can bring these diverging roads together in the conciliation of the image, that he can fix the indiscernible presence of the incorporeal in the corporeal in the movement of an ascending, descending, or falling body; in a gaze that is fixed, lost, or turned to the side; in the way a head tilts towards another head, an arm extends towards another arm, and in how hands receive a pensive brow; in the murmur of an invocation that is both prayer and blasphemy.

Morning in Berlin. Edmund. To unravel the arabesque of Pina's falling Rossellini turns it into the plot of another film, *Germany Year Zero*, a film about the ruins of a city where a boy plays, wanders, and jumps into the void. Rossellini constructed this film for those final scenes where Edmund, who has just killed his father, plays all those ancestral games for which kids the world over turn cities into playgrounds. He balances himself on the very edge of the sidewalk and of a public fountain, and he hopscotches from one side of the broken sidewalk to the other; he kicks a ball, or anything that might pass for one, around in the street, and he picks up a make-believe gun to shoot at squares of light; he slides down ramps used for construction materials, and he walks, runs, comes to a full stop to think, about what we shall never know, then sets out again resolutely towards an unknown destination... The insouciance of childhood, is it beautiful or monstrous? And, anyway, why assume that Edmund, the intelligent child and family breadwinner, is any more insouciant than Pina's son, Marcello, who lectures Don Pietro on the need for the historical bloc between two experiments with explosive chemicals? Or maybe it is enough to do as the text in the opening credits invites us to do and see in his insouciance the innocence of childhood perverted by the force of ideologies, Edmund led to parricide by what his old Nazi teacher had to say about the necessary elimination of the weak? The problem is that everything we see in the film denies this causal law. Our unease as we watch Edmund in action goes beyond all our fears and concerns regarding the moral consequences attendant on the troubles of the time and ideological inculcation. It seems hardly necessary to note that the schoolmaster delivers his speech very offhandedly, less attentive to what he is saying than to what is happening behind his back—his landlord groping at the young boy he had left on the steps of the building. Nor is there any need to stress that the father himself is distraught at being only another useless mouth to feed, that he deplores his cowardice in the face of the only desirable way out. It is enough to see Edmund grab the flask at the hospital while his father deplores his own weakness. It is enough to see Edmund, now back at home, rise slowly from the table while his father curses his past cowardice and the present cowardice of his oldest son, walk behind his older brother who's sitting with his head buried in his hands, and step resolutely into the adjoining room where he prepares, unflinching, the fatal tea while the voice off-screen goes on talking. It's enough to see the tea ball glimmer like a circle of light before the father picks up the cup. Edmund isn't just a child who does what others tell him to do; his act is a silent protest against this disorder of voices and gestures that never coincide. The whole film is here, in the relationship between Edmund's meticulous gesture and the voice off-camera. Edmund acts while all the others talk, undaunted at the idea of turning words into deeds. This is the source of our profound unease before this gesture that joins cold-blooded cruelty and supreme tenderness. Edmund brings to his act of parricide the same courage that the companions of St. Francis of Assisi bring to their commitment to a literal application of the words of the Gospel. He sets about the task of "eliminating the weak" with that humble devotion that is precisely the strength of the weak. There is no gesture of love more moving than Edmund placing his hand on his father's arm to dissuade him from sharing with the others a drink prepared specially for him. All ideologies and all explanations that appeal to the dangers of ideology are disarmed by this coincidence of opposites, by the perfection of this quiet gesture of love and death. These explanations will never be able to explain that there is nothing more on Edmund's silent face than in his meticulous gestures; nor that this "nothing more" that manifests itself in the unwavering decision to murder and in the moving tenderness of its execution is nothing less than liberty. Edmund is spurred to action by his vertiginous discovery of the pure ability to do, or not do, what others say, the discovery that he alone is responsible for his act, the sole agent of its coming into being. The film would be infinitely reassuring if all it did was urge us to condemn dangerous words and protect a child who is being crushed under the weight of a world in ruins. But all that really weighs on Edmund is the crushing weight of the liberty of the year zero. The Nazi catechism cannot produce the act, and remorse cannot drive him to suicide. There is no cause in either case, but only vertigo, the attraction exerted by the void of unlimited possibility: the gaping window of the bombed out building, the window that is also the source of the light that forms the white squares Edmund pretends to shoot at with his imaginary pistol.

Surely everyone must feel the profound kinship in this impassioned improvisation in black and white between the games—the hopscotch from one black splotch to another—Edmund plays with as much concentration as he puts into killing his father and that other vertigo, the white page and the jump into the void of the film. Edmund composes this page that is already saturated with Pina's fall with masterful improvisation, until he too throws himself before his true father, his creator, before this revolutionary filmmaker who always refused to work with a detailed script and instead improvised from day to day, basing his decisions on the capacity of his actors and on his own ability to guide them to the source of every action and every representation. Nor can we separate the complicity between the camera and Edmund's games from something else we know: the film is dedicated to another child, the young Romano Rossellini, who was himself playing the games Edmund plays in the film on the eve of its making, but who had died before shooting started. Still, this perfect complicity between biography and fiction cannot account for the unbearable lightness of Edmund's fall. The fall that closes the child's improvisations—the equal cruelty and tenderness with which the artist leads his son back to death, or reconstructs his death as play—must know its profound kinship with the absolute generosity or violence of the creator who freely reclaims what He has freely given. The call of the void to which the parricide child surrenders must reveal its proximity to the call presented by St. Francis of Assisi, God's Juggler, who teaches his brothers that the way to decide where they must go preach is to spin round and round, as kids do, until vertigo throws them on the ground and points them in the direction of the call.

The old Claudel must have felt something of this sort when he was asked to give his opinion about Rossellini's production of *Joan of Arc at the Stake*, which Claudel had only wanted to see represented as an oratorio because the sound of Joan's chains breaking had given him the idea for it in the first place. The story goes that at the conclusion of his own text, which read "God is strongest," the old master blasphemously scribbled, as if in agreement with Rossellini: "It's Ingrid who's strongest." Rather than celebrating a new divinity of the artist, the story points to a more profound complicity between divine liberty and the power of this improviser who breaks the chains of his characters by hurling them into the void and who, in so doing, redefines *mise-en-scène* as something other than the illustration of a story, as the trace of a fall, an arabesque within which the sound generating the work still vibrates, but differently.

The improviser had paved the way for this in *Miracle*, a film made entirely for the pleasure of shooting the scene of the tin cans that come tumbling down the village steps, as well as in the most improvised of all his films, *Voyage to Italy*, which he constructed around a sound we cannot hear, the sound of the pebbles Katherine Joyce tells her husband about in the sun-drenched terrace of Uncle Homer's villa. These pebbles had been thrown at her misty, rain-splashed window by a young man, barely more than a child, who was later found chilled to the bone in the garden: Charles, the consumptive poet of "pure ascetic images" who had come to bid Katherine a final goodbye before his premature death. Ingrid Bergman listens for the sound of the pebbles thrown by this Tom Thumb behind so many windows, their noise makes her go up and down so many steps, and yet we shall never hear their sound, for the simple reason that neither she nor we have ever heard it. They are paper pebbles. Rossellini the improviser was not above borrowing, and he borrowed these pebbles from a story by a namesake of Katherine's, James Joyce. They come from what he remembered of Joyce's story about the impossible and immaterial love that the model wife of "The Dead" reveals to her husband as the snow that drowns out every noise descends softly upon all of Dublin. The call of these absences resounds in the analogy of the work's arabesques.

The two paths. Michele and Irene. In *Europe 51* we encounter another falling child, Michele, a rich kid with no problems of conscience who also succumbs to the call of the void. It is clear that he does not fall because his mother wastes socializing all the time he would have wanted her to spend on him. Nor does he jump because of the troubles of the time and the disturbances of conscience, as Andrea, the loquacious heir of the quiet Manfredi, suggests. Michele himself tells his mother the reason when she asks what's got into him that he insists on sullenly pacing up and down the apartment in total boredom: nothing, *niente*. He jumps into the emptiness in the middle of the stairwell for nothing. Or rather, he jumps to get his mother to abandon her home and exchange every possession and every consideration for the satisfaction of a single quest: to find out what he said, what he might have said, to the hospital doctor or the communist journalist in explanation of his act. Irene's quest is of course futile: like Pina, like Edmund, Michele has simply thrown himself before his creator by jumping into the void that annuls every cause and good cause, beginning with that of realism. He jumps down for nothing, other than to mark the milestones along the path that his mother will have to retrace, but backwards. If Rossellini elides Michele's act, if he doesn't show us the fall that would have tarnished the beauty of this bourgeois stairwell, it is because the thread of events is spun backwards. All we have of the fall is the absent voice calling Irene to retrace the path of the act. Thenceforward, it is Irene who sticks out like a sore thumb in these bourgeois surroundings as she tries to rewind the trajectory of the fall. So she goes to look elsewhere. Her first destination is the working-class apartment blocks on the outskirts of town where she goes escorted by her scandalous communist cousin, Andrea, who thinks the trip will take her mind off of her useless quest and place her squarely in a solid universe of causes. She goes with Andrea to the land of the people and there she sees their profound suffering: that of a child whose life is hanging on the money needed for his treatment, and that of the people, whose miserable condition can be explained by easily identifiable causes. But in the course of her visit, Irene loses her way. A glance to the side carries her steps from these apartment blocks where factory workers live to the vacant lots on the edge of the river where the sub-proletariat live in huts. She enters a universe where the reference points normally used to classify sufferings, their causes, and their remedies no longer apply. We might be tempted to see here the Deleuzean universe of "optical and sound situations" that break the continuity of the "sensory-motor schema." The problem, though, is that Irene's disorientation, like Pina's dash, is not an impossibility to react brought about by the troubles of the time. They are both movements dictated from behind the camera by the imperious voice of the director. Rossellini's *mise-en-scène* is, point for point, the active refutation of this simple scenario of a world in ruins and disturbed consciences that the communist journalist tries so hard to impose. This is why Irene only keeps going further and further off, further and further to the side. From the huts where Passerotto lives with her fatherless children, Irene goes to the cement factory and fills in for her, becoming a worker for a day; as she is leaving, she encounters a consumptive prostitute and becomes her nurse. Irene's wanderings are her attempt to respond to a call not heard, an absent voice. She surrenders, like Edmund and St. Francis' companions, to the call of chance and finds herself on an unpredictable trajectory whose progression is extremely rigorous nonetheless: every step she takes only estranges her further from the system of explanations and motivations that holds together the rules of good conduct, of mental hygiene, and of all things social. She rejoins the point where the child fell at the bottom of the spiral, that is to say, she rejoins it up there, standing behind the barred windows where those who no longer believe in causes or can no longer serve any are locked up. There, in a furtive gesture that sums up the entire trajectory of the film, the entire path she had retraced until coming to the point where the fall had called her, the madwoman—the saint—blesses the crowd that has gathered to bid her a last goodbye. The road up and the road down are one and the same.[4]

A hillside. Nannina. Up and down, the identity of paths (*su* and *giù*, as Italian succinctly puts it), such is the topography of *Miracle*, a film that hangs from a hillside, held aloft between four shots: of the sea, barely visible below, of the village projecting from the face of the hill, of the flatland where goats graze, and of the monastery at the top of the hill. The film hangs, also, on the indiscernibility between truth and falsehood, between the miraculous and the blasphemous. Here, again, we must be careful to distinguish what someone may tell us about the film and what the film shows. An unfortunate simpleton imagines she's pregnant with the Savior after being raped by a vagabond she thought was St. Joseph... It would all be very simple if that is what we saw. But on the screen, standing in front of Nannina and then next to her, all we see is a pure apparition that says nothing in reply to this woman who pretends to find its voice familiar. He sits next to her in the square where she tells him to meet her (*"La! su!"*), pours her a drink, and she sinks into a contented sleep. The apparition has disappeared by the time she awakes from her torpor, and nothing besides her ravishment has taken place. These are the sorts of scenes that tend to be marked by a discrete transition, like the ellipsis novelists used long ago, or the wood burning in the fireplace of Hollywood films. But parentheses of this sort have no place in Rossellini's cinema. It isn't a matter of prudishness, it's just that a director so attuned to the power of a single glance, so skilled at capturing with a single shot a body's tiniest movement towards another, can do without suggestion and exhibition both. Which one of those entangled and exposed limbs that so repeatedly grace our screens will ever attain the quiet shamelessness of Ingrid Bergman, the provocative power of her face as she approaches, but does not touch, the face of the priest in *Stromboli?* Prudishness has nothing to do with it. Rossellini's camera resists representing anything that takes place, or should take place, in the shadows: a political conspiracy, a sexual encounter, or even a sentiment whose expression cannot be shown in the perceptible relationship between a glance and whatever attracts or troubles it. A Rossellini film is a surface of inscriptions that does not tolerate the least trace of dissimulation, the presence of something that must remain latent, a truth hidden behind the appearance, or a scandal concealed behind the smooth surface of things. The force of scandal, here, has to do with the fact that nothing is or could be dissimulated. No matter how intensely Rossellini scrutinizes faces, he never allows his microscope to discover something that the attentive onlooker would not have perceived on his own. We discuss below the difficulties Rossellini encounters in *Fear*, where he brings to the screen an idea that, as a moralist, he has no issues with: the liberating power of confession. But what could Nannina confess? Her folly or blasphemy is entirely dependent on this space oriented only by the path leading up or down, on this image that time and again tells everything worth knowing, everything that is part of the event, this image that undermines all the solid structures that tolerate a distinction between the appearance of things and their hidden reason, deceit and truth, the delinquency of a vagabond and the intervention of a transcendent power: the structures that partition the space of perception and of social relationships into surfaces comprised of above and below, front or back. What is so unbearable about this rounded belly and obtuse brow is that nothing anywhere makes it possible for one to discern what it is they're carrying. Their secret is the absence of a secret, it is that they've forsaken the codes of visibility and interpretation that ordinarily stitch the seams of the social. The pure ravishment of this meeting with the unknown leaves no other trace in reality than this child that nothing can determine whether he's a gift of divine grace or the offspring of a bad encounter.

This does not mean that the director conspires with his idiot to advance a beatified fideism, to turn the disappearance of the cause into the blank check that allows us to read anything we want into the image and to substantiate every theory. We should not take the disappearance of the cause somewhere up there, in the direction of the other church that hangs over the village of exegetes and scandalmongers packed tightly around the parish church, as an indication of Rossellini's surrender to pure fideism, but as an indication of a different idea, one that demands more from interpretation, namely the courage of the person entrusted with delivering the meaning or the child. The courage of the actor [*interprète*],[5] and the attention of the spectator together determine the meaning of the encounter. Plato had already told us this: we see in Ion's gaze whether his song is an artificial fabrication or a divine gift. We must then look more attentively at Anna Magnani (Nannina), to whose art the film is dedicated. It falls to the mother, to the actress, to give birth to this fatherless child, to impress her own quest upon the child's face. This is why the wretched Nannina, the daughter of the land, has to trace the same path of renunciation as Irene, the respectable mother, the bourgeois woman from the North who is brought face to face with the radicality of her status as a foreigner by her search for what her son had told her and by her obstinate determination to know nothing of society save for what she sees. Nannina, too, has to leave her "home," the pitiful place the village idiot and grotesque god of the parish church square, Consinello, had given her and now takes away. She must endure the insults of the enlightened youth, hear the sound of the tin cans thrown from the church square onto the steps of the village, and, when chased by a pack of old bigots and young skeptics, gather her miserable rags and run up the long path to the high church. She must run up there, even though she'll find that the church is closed and that there is no place up there for the sacrilegious birth during which this backward simpleton holds on to the iron rings on the wall as if she were on a cross or on a delivery bed, and invokes the name of God as a breathing technique for a painless delivery. And, even though all she gives birth to is a human being, nothing more than the fruit of her own labor and improvisation, she exclaims nonetheless in the presence of the child we cannot see, but only hear: "*Creatura mia.*" Rossellini needs two words and one image to sum up the whole uncertainty of the film and of two centuries of discussion about the human fabrication of the gods. He confronts the clever man's suspicions that everything has a false bottom with this demonstration of the identity of contraries: the humble confession that nothing here requires celestial intervention and the quiet affirmation of the miraculous power to create. We should perhaps circle back from Anna Magnani's last words to the first written words of the film, dedicating it to her art. It may just be that the Catholic hierarchy did not react so much against the doubt cast upon its mysteries and miracles as against the quiet pride of this humility, at the excess of this final reversal that transforms St. Paul's empowering of the weak into an assault on the monopoly of creation.

Home of the fisherman. Karin. Up and down, in and out, obedience to the call and the trap of the mirror: these are the categories that structure how Rossellini stages the huge conflict between North and South. We must start out again from the Gestapo headquarters in Rome, where the couple Bergmann and Ingrid shoot all their scenes either in the lounge all fitted with mirrors or in the confession chambers. The war didn't end with the defeat of the officers of the "master race"; it goes on, but under different guises. It falls to Ingrid Bergman, the Swedish actress who came to Rossellini via Hollywood and who joins in her name and surname the diabolic duo of directors, to wage a vertiginous double combat and carry out the double execution that consumes the pride of the master race from the North and of the *mise-en-scène*—the art of reflection and drugs, scripts and frames— erected by conquering Hollywood in the effort to protect its studios and drawing rooms from every call of the unknown and every vertigo of liberty. Under different names and characters—Karin in *Stromboli*, Irene in *Europe 51*, Katherine in *Voyage to Italy*—Ingrid Bergman always acts out the same scenario of power being consumed in the flame of liberty. This consumption is not reducible to what the hurried viewer of *Voyage to Italy* gets to see: the haughty Northerners who arrive with their *Bildungsroman* only to see their script turned inside out and utterly derailed by the pagan-Christian excesses of the set and of the Neapolitan figurations—the shameless, gigantic proportions of ancient statues and the obscene proliferation of rounded bellies before the altars of the Madonna; the Christian veneration of skulls thrown together in a heap and the embracing bodies of pagan lovers just discovered under the lava of the volcano; the vapors of the Solfatare and the delirium of the processions, this "panicked sense of nature" whose whirlwind whisks Alex and Katherine away only to return them to one another. The point isn't to make the proud confess their weakness, or to get them to know the barbarous heart and simple customs of civilization, or to make them feel at home on the other side of the mirror. After all, this capacity to feel at home in foreign lands is an old directorial trick, something the conqueror has always taken pride in. Precisely this temptation is illustrated on the little black island of Stromboli by Karin, the displaced woman, the daughter of the North who once had an affair with an officer of the master race and now thinks she can put all of that behind her by following this fisherman whose voice promises the romance and sun of Southern isles. Is it ignorance, or is it a ploy to get Karin to touch the depths of her hardships, that leads the local priest to suggest, apparently to dissuade her from leaving, that she fix up her conjugal home? With the help she gets from masons recently returned from Brooklyn, where they no doubt acquired plenty of experience fixing up restaurants called *Napoli* or *Vesuvius*, it doesn't take Karin long to arrange the set for her *mise-en-scène* and then to set about consciously perverting the relationships of in and out, here and elsewhere. She removes Madonnas and family photos and decorates the walls with tufts and nets, bedecks the tables with vases, lets a prickly fig tree into the home, and paints Northern flowers on the whitewashed walls.

Karin makes the place feel like home by transforming the fisherman's home into one of those "fishermen houses" that distinguished ladies from the North in their conquest of the Southern isles will soon be buying and fixing up for their Mediterranean holidays. The fisherman's family thinks his house lacks modesty and refuse to enter it. The director, for his part, has no intention of letting Ingrid's little sister frame all her dreams of escape within this set worthy of the amateur filmmaker at best. He turns her out of doors with the child and question she's carrying and sets her on the road up, though here it does not abut on a church but on the fire-spewing crater.

He relieves her of her meager baggage and leads her into the presence of the divinity that shows the desire to escape and the illusion of a home in their common vanity. The modesty that Karin—like Irene the bourgeois but also like Nanni the simpleton—must learn in the confrontation with the God-volcano is certainly not the strength to resign herself to her domestic duties, but the courage to leave behind every home in answer to the call of this dead child or to the question of the child about to be born. Rossellini doesn't ask the woman who came from the land of the conquerors to familiarize herself with the mores of her new land: he makes her touch the depths of her condition as a foreigner in order to bear witness to a condition we all share.

Undoubtedly, Rossellini has already intuited a different problem: Karin can very well leave her home to meet this God of lava and fire, and Ingrid can very well consume her entire craft, her whole career as a Hollywood star, in the flame of this passion, but the war is lost. The relationship between the two worlds that structures Rossellini's *mise-en-scène* will soon take a sudden turn, and even the furthermost isle will be tipped over to the side of the Northerners, to the side of these directors and architects who open all the houses to the outside, let trees infiltrate them, and tame the place's pagan-Christian barbarism with the whitewashed walls of their civilization. In contrast to the final conversion of *Voyage to Italy* or *Stromboli*, it is the atheism of the Protestant North that ultimately gains the upper hand over the Christian paganism of the South, over its preference for closed spaces, its neat divisions between what's honorable and what shameful, its submission to the God of fire, its cult of the dead, and its obstinate habit of rebuilding and recultivating anew in the exact same way what the lava of the volcano will in time bury again. If we regret this loss, it is not because we long for the closed morals of the village, for the black women of Stromboli who look down at the distractions of the foreigner, or for the refrains the men of the island sing in the ears of the *cornuto* [cuckold]. We long for what was possible to wrest from them as violence of scandal and grace of liberty. The architect and tour guide will soon rearrange the relationship between in and out, freedom and necessity, and trace a new and level path for the scandal-less audacity of a sterilized liberty to parade against the backdrop of the yellow sun, the whitewashed walls, and the blue Mediterranean. The first to suffer the consequences of this will be young French enthusiasts eager to make French cinema breath the air of Rossellini's liberty and walk to the unpredictable rhythm of Edmund's steps. But the liberty these young filmmakers hope will vibrate in their images has lost the point of gravity or scandal that gives to the performances of the improviser the immaterial weight of courage. The secret force of Edmund's hopscotch is there, in Karin and Nanni panting as they climb their mountain, in Irene's painful journey. The sense of scandal and of miracle was locked up behind bars with Irene, and with this imprisonment Edmund's lightness was lost, his arabesques effaced by the whitewashed walls of Karin's inheritors. It is in vain that these young Rossellinis try to revive it by dint of sliding on the snow, of surprise starts in reverse gear, of cycling exercises inside an apartment, of mad races through fields and dunes; or by dint of disconcerting encounters, false continuities, and discrepancies between sound and image. There is nothing to the subversion of codes once the sense of the fall—the jump into the unknown and the confrontation with scandal—has been lost. Ferdinand-Pierrot stresses, albeit ironically, this very point at the beginning of *Pierrot le fou*: liberty and scandal have joined hands to sing the praises of the singular comfort, and invisibility, of women's underwear. This liberty he wants to flee from, however, is already down the path of his flight. Together, they travel south at the speed of stolen cars towards Mediterranean shores without any volcanoes to climb, morals to violate, or village gossips to endure. This new liberty plays on the permanent subversion of codes to render scandal impossible, no matter how determined one is to find it. No doubt Godard's singular greatness is that he picks up the wager of this impossible and chases to the edge of silence and the void these images and words fleeing from the derisory liberty that incessantly catches up with them.

Home. Irene II. Some have seen in *Fear* a Hitchcock script mistakenly entrusted to Rossellini; others have stressed the continuity between this story of confession and *Rome, Open City*. Maybe both sides are right, and wrong. In *Rome, Open City*, the *mise-en-scène* of confession was the work of others, their bad film foiled by the courage of the members of the resistance and the liberty of the director. It was a film within a film. It may very well be the case that the script of *Fear* signals a rapprochement by transposing a story originally set in Vienna in the 1920s to post-1945 Germany, and by turning into an experimental biologist the husband who traps his wife with the aid of an intermediary, the actress disguised as a blackmailer. But the film is still missing the *mise-en-scène* that encompasses, and defeats, the machinations designed to induce confession. The closest we have to this in *Fear* is, possibly, the internal reversal by which Irene, in her turn, traps the one trying to trap her and makes her confess to what she really is: a washed up cabaret actress being manipulated by a director of the old school. But this reversal in the mechanism of confession is still part of the scenario of confession. It is not strong enough to break free of its constraints, to beat into the ground these side blows that confront a being with the truth about herself by inducing her to confess the only thing worth confessing: her weakness. And indeed, nothing could prevail upon that, not these machines for confession that hold, or assume the other to be holding, some hidden knowledge, nor any of these experiments that organize the other's weakness. There where liberty is not open to the chance of the encounter and where bodies have nothing to reveal, no soul can appear.

Should we see in all of this an unprecedented powerlessness on the part of the director? Or should we see Rossellini deliberately and clearly marking the end of the line? *Fear* is like the last episode of a cycle that starts in Rome occupied by the officers from the North and ends in this Bavarian chalet for blond Gretchens and Colonel Blimps. The conquerors have gone back home. The film adapts a story by Stefan Zweig, an exiled Jew who killed himself at the other end of the earth, in which the conquerors are settling their family affairs: the lies of the children and the adulterous affairs of the wives; the punishment of the daughters and the anxiety of the mothers, confession and forgiveness. The war is over. The machine designed to make people talk has returned to its normal regime. The Italians may change the title of the film and its ending to make it seem that Irene is only walking into a summer house on a movie set. But that only brings into greater focus the sense that the film is a return home. Irene II returns to the home Irene I had left as if no child had ever fallen into the void and no mother had ever lost her way. Rossellini had wanted his dramaturgy to fan the flames of a new liberty from Europe's wound. In *Fear*, this wound has closed. The cycle of the foreigner comes to an end, bringing to a close this pirating project where Rossellini turned one of Hollywood's model children against its cinema. Let's hear the sound of a last fall, the deafening echo of the imperceptible noise of the pebbles. Irene has come to her husband's lab to kill herself with some of the liquid he injects into his guinea pigs when the sound of a flask smashing on the ground, amplified by the music of Renzo Rossellini, brings the mother and the actress back to reality. At this moment, Rossellini returns to the cinema of others what he had taken from it. The crazy project of consumption ends. He takes Ingrid back home, back to the scripts and sets that were hers not long before this and will be hers again shortly hereafter. For her, Rossellini dismantles the *mise-en-scène* he had mounted for her. The light that shines in this film and that passes for one last time over Ingrid Bergman's face is like the flash of a final love gesture, the flame of this inverse consumption. A little further away, in Bayreuth, Brunhilde's pyre is burning again. On the ashes of hope, the Gods resume their ordinary twilight.

NOTES

1. Simone Weil, *Gravity and Grace*, trans. Gustav Thibon (London: Ark Paperbacks, 1987) 77.
2. Weil, *Gravity and Grace*, 137.
3. Like Rohmer and Rivette before him, Rancière is alluding to Chateaubriand's *The Genius of Christianity*.—Trans.
4. For a longer discussion of Irene's voyage, please see the third part ("A Child Kills Himself") of my *Short Voyages to the Land of the People*, trans. James B. Swenson (California: Stanford University Press, 2003) 107–34.
5. "Interprète" is one of the words for actor in French. Rancière's claim that the idea demands "more from interpretation" plays on both meanings of the term: it demands more from us, the interpreters, and from Anna Magnani, the actor, the interpreter.—Trans.

CHAPTER 9

The Red of La Chinoise
Godard's Politics

How should we understand the politics Godard puts into play with his cinematographic practice in *La Chinoise*? The opinions on the matter have more or less followed the fluxes and refluxes of the left. Accused when first released of being just a caricature, and not a serious representation, of real militant Maoists, the film was later praised as a brilliant anticipation of the events of May 1968, and as a lucid look both at the passing infatuation with Maoism by bourgeois youngsters and at the outcomes of that infatuation: the return to order and terrorism. The question of whether or not the film or its characters are actually good Marxists is not only not interesting, but also misguided, since we're bound to get nowhere with such relationships of subordination: it is the coordination that we must look at instead. Godard doesn't film "Marxists" or things whose meaning would be Marxism. He makes cinema with Marxism. "A film in the making," he says, and we must understand this in many ways. *La Chinoise* invites us onto the set, it makes us feel like we're watching the shooting of the film. And it also makes us feel like we're watching Marxism, a certain Marxism anyway, in the process of making itself into cinema, of play-acting. As we watch this play-acting in *La Chinoise*, we see also what *mise-en-scène* means in the cinema. It is the intertwining of these two that we must look at more closely.

We might start with the following formulation: Godard puts "cinema" between two Marxisms—Marxism as the matter of representation, and Marxism as the principle of representation. The Marxism represented is a certain Marxism, Chinese Maoism as it figured in the Western imaginary at the time, which the film represents from the angle that renders the stereotypes of its rhetoric and gestures complicit with Godard's method of the object lesson and classroom exercises.[1] Maoism here is a catalogue of images, a panoply of objects, a repertoire of phrases, a program of actions: courses, recitals, slogans, gym exercises. The montage of all these elements brings into play another complicity. The method of the "object lesson" happens to align perfectly with the specific Marxism that serves as the principle of representation, namely Althusserian Marxism, which, in 1967, was essentially a doctrine that held that Marxism for the most part still had to be invented, and that inventing it was like relearning the sense of the most elementary actions. Godard, as is his wont, treats Althusser in bits and pieces that he takes, for the most part, from prefaces and conclusions. He composes with these bits and pieces the speech of the militant Omar and the peroration of the actor Guillaume. And he is likely to have read this sentence, which could well sum up his whole method as a filmmaker, in the preface to *Reading Capital*: "I venture to suggest that our age threatens one day to appear in the history of human culture as marked by the most dramatic and difficult trial of all, the discovery and training in the meaning of the 'simplest' acts of existence: seeing, listening, speaking, reading—the acts which relate men to their works, and to those works thrown in their faces, the 'absences of work.'"[2]

Althusser's project of knowing what "seeing, listening, speaking, reading" mean is exactly what Godard puts into play in *La Chinoise*. At the center of the film there are two red objects, the *Little Red Book* and the *Cahiers marxistes-leninistes*: linked by their color, these two objects stand in a relationship of solidarity and contradiction. The *Little Red Book* compiles the detached maxims that all those who took part in the Cultural Revolution either learned by heart or simply brandished as rallying calls. The *Cahiers marxistes-leninistes* is the Marxist journal of the students of the École Normale Supérieure, the sophisticated militant journal that lends to the chosen bits and pieces learned by the Red Guard their theoretical foundation as well as their practical acceptability. This journal transforms the Althusserian project of relearning to see, speak, and read into Maoist rhetoric and gestures. Godard's method is to split up the terms of this operation, to break up the evidence, by making Althusserian pedagogy the principle for the *mise-en-scène* of Maoist rhetoric and gestures. The film, then, is about learning to see, hear, speak, or read these phrases from the *Little Red Book* or from the *Pékin Information*. But it is also about learning to read with them, as if these phrases were just another example, and in essence no different from the stories and examples that illustrate the workbooks pupils use when learning to read and write in elementary school. *La Chinoise* is an exercise on Marxism with Marxism as much as it is an exercise on film with film.

"To give vague ideas a clear image." To understand the formula that is like an epigraph for the film, we have to feel that the tension weighing down on the relationship between word and image is strictly parallel to the tension that fueled—in the China of the time and in the Western Maoist imaginary—the fight between two conceptions of the dialectic. "One is split in two," the formula reclaimed by Maoists; "two are joined in one," the formula stigmatized as "revisionist." The strength of the film is that it brings together cinema and Marxism by treating those two formulas as two different conceptions of art in general, and hence also of Marxist cinema.

What does a Marxist film, a film that proposes Marxism as the meaning of the fiction it puts on the screen, ordinarily do? How do the waves of progressive fictions that flourished on the heels of *La Chinoise* work? Basically through a mixture of beautiful images and painful speeches, of fictional affects and realist references, that when combined compose a symphony on which Marxism imposes itself as the theme or melody necessarily being sought by the mass orchestration. As such, these films remain tied to the everyday functioning of communication. They join two in one in the image of the everyday *chassé croisé* of words and images. Words make images. They make us see. A sentence gives a quasi-visible that never attains the clarity of the image. Images, in their turn, constitute a discourse. We hear in them a quasi-language not subject to the rules of speech. The problem, however, is that when we "see" a word, we no longer hear it. And likewise with the image: when we hear it, we no longer see it. This is the dialectic of the "two in one" instituted by the principle of reality.[3] It is identical in every way to the rhetorical-poetical principle of the metaphor. The metaphor, more than a means of making an abstract idea concrete by linking it to an image, is this *chassé croisé* of words that hide by becoming visible and of images made invisible by becoming audible. One *quasi* entails the other. One refers to the other, lasts only as long as is needed to do the other's work and to link its powers of disappearance to that of the other. The result is this melodic line that is like the music of the world.

We might call this, after one of the episodes of the film, the bowl-and-toast principle. Look at Henri drink his café au lait and butter his toast in front of his water heater as he itemizes all his reasons for going back to the Communist Party. The realistic weight of his words is entirely dependent upon these accessories. Had he delivered it with a blackboard behind him and a professor's desk before him in the apartment of his old comrades, the same speech would lose 80 per cent of the force and conviction it receives from the "popular" *gestus* of this "popular" kitchen, which changes even the connotation of his student cap: here it is the cap of the son of the prole and not the cap of the student who plays at being a prole. The interview with the maid Yvonne is another demonstration of the same genre. The speech in which this daughter of the people evokes the hardships of growing up in the country immediately generates an image. No need, then, to show us the countryside, we see it in her words. It would be clumsy to show it, even perverse. And Godard's perversity is to insert at this point not the quintessential countryside Yvonne's words make visible, but a silly countryside that he sums up in two images: chickens in front of the wall of a farmhouse, and cows in a field of apple trees. The common work of art and politics is to interrupt this parading, this incessant substitution of words that make us see and of images that speak which imposes belief as the music of the world. The point is to split in two the One of representative magma: to separate words and images, to get words to be heard in their strangeness and images to be seen in their silliness.

There are two possible ways of achieving this dissociation. Jean-Pierre Léaud announces the first one in the film: would that we were blind, he says, then we would really listen to each other, really understand each other. This dream of seizing the radical experience of hearing or seeing at its origins invariably takes us back to the experiences that made these two senses so dear to the eighteenth century. Diderot's *Letter on the Blind* and *Letter on the Deaf and Dumb* are never very far from Godard, nor is Rousseau's *Discourse on the Origin of Language*. At its limits, the method of the "object lesson" always tends towards two renowned utopias, the *tabula rasa* and fictional Robinsonades. Godard leaves it to Henri, the "revisionist," to wax ironic about these fictive experiences by recalling the story of Psammetichos, King of Egypt, who tried to discover the original language of humankind by raising two of his children in complete isolation. When he heard them speak, they spoke in the only "language" they were able to learn, that of the sheep whose pen adjoined their retreat. The Robinsonade is how the characters express the experimental situation Godard puts them in. But the principle of the *mise-en-scène* is different. If Godard really wants us to hear the words—and Marxism, like any theory, is first and foremost an assemblage of words—and see the reality they describe and project—and reality is, first and foremost, an assemblage of images—he cannot treat them separately. He must reorganize their liaison, which doesn't mean separating the words of Marxism from every image in order to make us hear them, but the reverse: Godard must really make us see them, he must replace their obscure image-making with a brute image of what they say. He has to put these words in bodies that treat them as the most basic utterances, bodies that try to speak them in various ways as well as to turn them into gestures.

Godard then sets about elaborating an apparatus of separation that makes words audible by making them visible. Here is where Godard gives cinematographic meaning to this representation, at first attacked and then praised for its lucidity, of "petit bourgeois youngsters cut off from the masses and talking non-stop in the isolation of their bourgeois apartment." Godard is fond of the method of enclosing his characters within the four white walls of an apartment where they struggle to put meat on the bones of a few great ideas. The "Althusserianism" of *La Chinoise* is its actualization of Althusser's Diderot-inspired practices. The difference is that in the film the "political" principle of isolation is the condition for the artistic understanding of what a political discourse says. The task of art is to separate, to transform the continuum of image-meaning into a series of fragments, postcards, lessons. The bourgeois apartment is the frame of representation wherein Godard arranges the necessary and sufficient elements for the *mise-en-scène* of the question: what does Marxism, this Marxism, say? How does it speak? How does it turn itself into film? In the pictorial and theatrical frame, words and images can be rearranged in order to undo the metaphorical play that makes sense of reality by transforming images into quasi-words and words into quasi-images.

There are two major forms of representation that work against the metaphor. The first is surrealism, which essentially literalizes the metaphor. Logicians have been pointing out since antiquity that when we utter the word "chariot," no such vehicle issues from our mouths. As a general rule, though, these same logicians have paid less attention to the fact that though the chariot doesn't issue from our mouths, it doesn't for all that fail to dance confusedly before the eyes of our interlocutors. Surrealists then represent the chariot issuing from the mouth. Magritte's paintings are the best illustration of this pictorial method, which, in literature, is at the root of Lewis Carroll's *nonsense*, though it had already served other masters before him, such as Rabelais and Sterne. Godard rarely does without it. He makes his use of it explicit in the scene of Jean-Pierre Léaud throwing rubber-tipped darts at images of the representatives of bourgeois culture as an illustration of the idea that Marxism is the arrow trained on the target of the class enemy. And he uses it directly, as in the scene where Juliet Berto illustrates the idea that the *Little Red Book* is the rampart of the masses against imperialism by standing in front of a wall of red books, or when she visualizes the principle that Mao's thought is the weapon of these same masses by turning the radio that broadcasts Mao's thought through the voice of Radio-Peking into a submachine gun.

The surrealist method is itself subordinate to the dialectical method, which replaces the figure of the metaphor with the figure of comparison. Comparison dissociates what the metaphor joins. Instead of telling us, as the slogans of the period did, that Mao's thought is our red sun, comparison makes us see and hear this thought next to the sun. Comparison foils the metaphor's power to join together: it gets us to hear words and see images in their dissociation, though not via some sort of utopian separation, but by keeping them together in their problematic relationship in one and the same frame. It then becomes a matter of showing this: the revolutionary struggle might resemble such an image; a group "armed with the thought of Mao Tse Tung" might resemble the arrangement of such a sequence of discourses and gestures. To interpret Maoist discourse—to understand what it tells us—we must try to perform [*interpréter*] it—to represent it—this way.[4] We have to help ourselves to the bodies of actors, to a set, and to all the elements of representation in order to figure out how to perform/interpret these words, how to make them audible by making them visible.

Godard structures all of this with his remarkable use of color in the film. He distributes on the white background of a canvas or projection screen three pure colors that he never allows to intermix: red, blue, and yellow. These three colors are first of all emblematic of the objects represented: the red of Mao's flag and thought, the blue uniforms of Chinese workers, the yellow of the race. And they are also the three primary colors, the three straightforward colors that oppose the gradation, nuances, and confusion of "reality," that is to say, of the metaphor. They function as the table of categories that Deleuze claims Godard is always creating. The "simple things" to be relearned are determined and reflected in the categorial grid formed by these pure colors. This use of color, even though a constant in Godard, is at its most powerful when the issue at hand is one of color, like the red-white-blue Godard had already used to structure the political fable *Made in USA*. *La Chinoise*, a film about red as the color of a line of thought, is entirely structured by this chromatic apparatus, which structures not only what goes on between the white walls of the apartment, but also the relationship between inside and outside. The outside is the real, the referent of their discourses. It is the green countryside inserted into Juliet Berto's speech. It is the vacant suburban lots and the University of Nanterre barely visible beyond them that Godard uses, once he has them rendered equivalent with a panoramic shot, to illustrate Juliet Berto's speech, to show what her speech about the three inequalities and about the worker–student link looks like. Finally, the real is the alternating scenery of countryside landscape and suburban houses that flies by behind the window of the train where Anne Wiazemsky talks to Francis Jeanson, and that strengthens with its discreet evidence Jeanson's words by showing this rural France, grassy and punctuated by homes, so utterly foreign to the discourse of the aspiring terrorist.

Godard was accused of giving the upper hand to the "realist" discourse of Francis Jeanson, the once upon a time assistant to the FLN,[5] over the discourse of the student extremist who fidgets nervously with the handle on the train window. But Godard doesn't take sides. All he does is place the tension of the two discourses in the tension of the visual sets. He puts in question the evidence provided by the rural France that speaks through Jeanson's mouth by accentuating in him, to the point of caricature, the *habitus* of the professor who's having a little fun at the student's expense: "Yes, but", "And then?", "So?", "What do you conclude from that?," "Ah, I see," "And you're the one who'll do all that?" But mainly, it is the pure colors and forms of the closed off apartment that filter the play of reality and keep it from appearing in a good light. Time and time again, these pure colors and forms refer reality to its mixed character, this mixture of mutually dissembling colors and metaphors that ignites, on the other side of the train window, the reality that proves itself in the perennial referral of its mixed tones—a testament to the infinite complexity of the real—to their dominant tonality: green, the color of life in its essential originality, color of the countryside and authenticity. Green is the mixed color that passes itself off for a primary color. It is also, by convention, the anti-red: green for go, red for stop, the color of the market and not the color of communism. "Green prices, since the Reds have seen their day," ran an ad in the 1990s where debunked Red heroes urged everyone not to miss the bargain prices at FNAC.[6] *La Chinoise* is certainly a film from the red epoch, the epoch of straightforward colors and simple ideas. Not simplistic ideas, but the idea of trying to see what simple ideas look like. The green epoch is the epoch of the mixed colors of reality—supposedly recalcitrant to ideas—that ultimately lead to the green monochrome of life, which is, we're told, simple and to be savored in its simplicity.

Inside the frame structured by the three primary colors, Godard organizes the *mise-en-scène* of the different modes of discourse within which the Maoist text can be spoken. There are three such modes: the interview, the lecture, and the theater. Godard's task is to examine and modify the value of truth and illusion normally accorded to each of these three modes. As a general rule, the lecture is thought to portray the situation of authority commanded by big words divorced from reality. The apparatus of the lecture—table, blackboard, and lecturer standing in front of an audience seated on the floor and answering their questions—seems to accentuate the image of the authority wielded by big words. The interview, on the other hand, is generally thought to sound the voice of the real with the small and slightly awkward words that anyone at all—preferably a woman—uses to describe the personal experiences that have led her to entrust her life to these big words. The image can occasionally lend a supplementary authenticity to all of this. The big eyes and pursed lips of Yvonne, the daughter of the people who seems startled by what she dares to say; the bowl-and-toast of Henri, the realist who knows what he's talking about; the vacant lots that authenticate Véronique's discourse. The authenticity increases when the voice of the interviewer is muted or annulled in order to transform the solicited response into a gush of spontaneity. The *mise-en-scène* calls this truth hierarchy into question. The insertion of a stupid shot, the voice of the interviewer that we hear without being able to make out the words, the performances of the naïve and the canny, these are all ways in which the *mise-en-scène* invites us to see—and hence to hear—that the regime of "authentic" speech is, just like the lecture, the regime of an already-said, of a recited text. It is how the *mise-en-scène* invites us to ask ourselves, instead, if the situation of authenticity isn't actually just like that of the blackboard on which one ventures to write down sentences to be able to look at them and see what they're saying, or like the position of authority held by the amateur professor, who ventures to let these sentences escape his mouth and to hear their echo.

Beyond the professor and the interviewee is a third character, the actor, who takes their two performances back to their common origin, the art of acting. In the confrontation with the student Véronique, it isn't the professor and politician Francis who has the last word, but Guillaume, the actor thus named as a tribute to his ancestor, Goethe's Wilhelm Meister. If Jean-Pierre Léaud's words evoke the *Letter on the Blind*, it is certainly a new version of the *Paradox of the Actor* that he illustrates in the famous demonstration he mimes: a Chinese student covered in bandages has come to show the wounds inflicted upon him by "revisionist" policemen, but what he shows us, as he removes the last bandage, is a face free of any wounds. The political militant and the actor are alike: their work is to show us not visible horrors, but what cannot be seen.

The actor becomes, in the same gesture, the elementary school teacher who returns the speeches and gestures of the naïve interviewee and of the learned professor to their first elements. The actor teaches the militant that it is possible to understand a text by lending one's voice and body to it, just as he teaches all of them how to spell out words and to vocalize and visualize ideas. That's what Jean-Pierre Léaud's work illustrates when he shouts, as a warrant officer would, the "Why?" that is always falsely inquisitive in the professor, or when he mimes the meaning of what he says by changing tones, "we need sincerity ... AND VIOLENCE." Spelling out the sentences of the *Little Red Book* and scanning them with physical exercises, this is to study stereotypes with stereotypy. It doesn't make a chariot issue from the mouth, but at least it makes it weigh on the tongue.

When the naïve country girl asks the amateur professor "What is an analysis?," it is the actor who answers, who shows her in the strictest sense what an analysis is. He decomposes the assembly of gestures and images and returns them to their basic elements. The universality of his art is that it establishes the most basic elements, and assemblies thereof, that make a discourse and a practice intelligible by making them comparable to other discourses and practices, by, for instance, making a political discourse and union comparable to a declaration of love and a love affair. This is what we see in the opening shots of the film, which show the fragmented speeches and intertwining hands of Jean-Pierre Léaud, who still seems to be acting in *Masculine Feminine*, and Anne Wiazemsky, who's still speaking the Bresson of *Au hasard, Balthazar*. It is what Wiazemsky teaches Léaud when she makes the utterances "Do you love me?" and "No, I don't love you anymore" as problematic as political utterances. If we prefer a visual over a dialectical demonstration, there is one in that superb shot of Yvonne, her posture straight out of a maid in Manet, looking out the window in the scene when Henri is being expelled: the image renders her scansion of the word "re-vi-sio-nist" identical to the scansion of "I-don't-love-you-anymore."

Godard shows us what the words and gestures of politics looks like by translating them into the attitudes of being in and out of love. His translation isolates the simple elements of a political speech that resurface not only in the lover's discourse, but also in the glib tongue of the street vendor peddling his wares and in the smooth talking of the market vendor. The final episodes of the film are not an illustration of moral relativism, of the equivalence of all things: the militant's speech as he lays out his copies of the *Little Red Book* the same as the street vendor selling his heads of lettuce. We would do better to recall the Brecht who conceived the episodes of *Jungle of Cities* as the rounds of a boxing match. Like Brecht's variations, the film brings to light all those elements in the job of the actor that are also present in every meaningful action and effective speech. Godard inverts the logic of *Wilhelm Meister*, a book he is always reading and rereading. Goethe's hero starts in love with the theater and ends by finding certainty in collective knowledge. Godard's hero moves in the opposite direction and leads collective knowledge back to the elements of the art of the theater. Politics resembles art in one essential point. Like art, politics also cuts into that great metaphor where words and images are continuously sliding in and out of each other to produce the sensory evidence of a world in order. And, like art, it constructs novel combinations of words and actions, it shows words borne by bodies in movement to make them audible, to produce another articulation of the visible and the sayable.

Theater Year Zero is the title Godard gives to the theatrical adventures of Guillaume Meister, and his allusion to Rossellini's *Germany Year Zero* is nominal as well as visual. Jean-Pierre Léaud roams the same ruined landscape and ventures into underground spaces similar to those visited by the young Edmund, though not to experience there the law of a world in ruins, but to relearn the meaning of the three blows of the theater. Rossellini wanted his title to evoke a world that had been wiped out and to serve as an epitaph to a child victimized by a murderous ideology. Godard's subtitle, in turn, speaks about what Rossellini's film shows: a kid playing hopscotch against the backdrop of a world in ruins. Ultimately, the moral of the film emerges from the opposition between the actor Guillaume and the terrorist Véronique: there is no zero situation, no world in ruins or to be ruined. There is only a curtain that rises and a child, an actor who plays with so much lightness the role of a child whose shoulders have to bear the double weight of a devastated world and of a world about to be born. Anyone determined to think the separation between the games of the child actor and the wanderings that end with the death of the child in the fiction, or between theatrical work and revolutionary work, must also think their community. That is what we see in this cinema between two Marxisms that concludes as a meditation on the theater.

NOTES

I.   "Leçons des choses" and "travaux practiques" are indissociable pedagogical methods that started being used in French schools towards the end of the nineteenth century. The basic idea is to organize exercises where the students learn, literally, from things. I render the first term by "object lesson" and the second by "classroom exercises" or simply by "exercises."—Trans.

2.   Louis Althusser and Étienne Balibar, *Reading Capital*, trans. Ben Brewster (London: NLB, 1970) 15–6.

3.   Not Freud's reality principle! The principle of reality is the principle of the metaphor, as Rancière indicates in the next sentence.—Trans.

4.   Rancière is playing on the word "interpréter," which means to interpret, and also to act out, perform ("interprète" being one of the words for actor in French).—Trans.

5.   The *Front de Libération Nationale*, or National Liberation Front, the ruling party of Algeria through the battle of independence to today.— Trans.

6.   FNAC is a French (now European) chain of megastores selling books, CDs, DVDs, cameras, computers, and so on. The closest equivalent in the Anglophone world might be Borders or Barnes & Noble.—Trans.

Part IV

Fables of the Cinema, (Hi)stories of a Century

CHAPTER 10

Documentary Fiction
Marker and the Fiction of Memory

The Last Bolshevik is the title of the film Chris Marker dedicates to the memory of Alexander Medvekin, the Soviet filmmaker who was born with his century and who died during the Perestroika. To speak of "memory" is to raise the paradox of the film at the outset. Marker's film cannot very well hope to preserve the memory of a filmmaker whose films we have not seen and whose name was, until quite recently, unfamiliar to most of us. Nor is this situation much different with Medvekin's compatriots, who are as likely to know his films as we are. The point, then, isn't to preserve Medvekin's memory, but to create it. The enigma buried in the title[1] raises the problem of the nature of a cinematographic genre, the so-called "documentary," and allows us, via a vertiginous shortcut, to link two questions: What is memory? What is the documentary as a genre of fiction?

Let's take as our starting point some self-evident claims that nonetheless still seem paradoxical to some. Memory is not the store of recollections of a particular consciousness, else the very notion of a collective memory would be devoid of sense. Memory is an orderly collection, a certain arrangement of signs, traces, and monuments. The Great Pyramid, the tomb par excellence, doesn't keep Cheop's memory. It is that memory. There are some who will no doubt claim that there are two regimes of memory separated by an ocean: there is that of the powerful sovereigns of long ago whose reality, in some cases, today boils down to the material and the ornamentation of their tombs; and there is that of the contemporary world, diligently keeping the records that attest to the most commonplace lives and the most ordinary events. It would seem a foregone conclusion that an abundance of information equals an overabundance of memory. And yet, everything in our present denies that. Information isn't memory, and it does not accumulate and store for memory's sake. It works exclusively for its own profit, which depends on the prompt forgetfulness of everything clearing the way for the sole, and abstract, truth of the present to assert itself and for information to cement its claim to being alone adequate to that truth. As the abundance of facts grows, so grows the sense of their indifferent equivalence and the capacity to make of their interminable juxtaposition the impossibility of ever reaching a conclusion, of ever being able to read, in the facts and their juxtaposition, the meaning of *one* story. Negationists have already shown that to deny what has happened, it isn't necessary to deny fact after fact: denying the links that run through them and give them the weight of history is enough. The reign of the informational-present rejects as outside reality everything it cannot assimilate to the homogeneous and indifferent process of its self-presentation. Not satisfied with rejecting out of hand everything as already in the past, it doubts the past itself.

Memory must be created against the overabundance of information as well as against its absence. It has to be constructed as the liaison that connects the account of events and the traces of actions, much like that σύστημα τῶν πραγματῶν, that "arrangement of incidents," that Aristotle talks about in the *Poetics* and that he calls *muthos*: not, as it were, a "myth" that refers us back to some sort of collective unconscious, but a fable or fiction. Memory is the work [*oeuvre*] of fiction. Good historical conscience can denounce this as paradoxical and pit its patient search for the truth against the fictions of collective memory that underpin power in general and totalitarian power in particular. But, in general, "fiction" is not a pretty story or evil lie, the flipside of reality that people try to pass off for it. Originally, *fingere* doesn't mean "to feign" but "to forge." Fiction means using the means of art to construct a "system" of represented actions, assembled forms, and internally coherent signs. We cannot think of "documentary" film as the polar opposite of "fiction" film simply because the former works with images from real daily life and archive documents about events that obviously happened, and the latter with actors who act out an invented story. The real difference between them isn't that the documentary sides with the real against the inventions of fiction, it's just that the documentary instead of treating the real as an effect to be produced, treats it as a fact to be understood. Documentary film can isolate the artistic work of fiction simply by dissociating that work from its most common use: the imaginary production of verisimilitude, of effects of the real. It can take that artistic work back to its essence, to a way of cutting a story into sequences, of assembling shots into a story, of joining and disjoining voices and bodies, sounds and images, of lengthening and tightening time. "The story starts in the present at Chelmno": Claude Lanzmann's provocative opening sentence in *Shoah* sums up this idea of fiction quite well. The forgotten, the denied, or the ignored that these fictions of memory want to bear witness to are set in opposition to the "real of fiction" that ensures the mirror recognition between the audience in the theaters and the figures on the screen, and between the figures on the screen and those of the social imaginary. In contrast to this tendentious reduction of the fictional invention to the stereotypes of the social imaginary, the fiction of memory sets its roots in the gap that separates the construction of meaning, the referential real, and the "heterogeneity" of its documents. "Documentary" cinema is a mode of fiction at once more homogeneous and more complex: more homogeneous because the person who conceives the idea is also the person who makes it; more complex because it is much more likely to arrange or interlace a series of heterogeneous images. Marker composes *The Last Bolshevik* with scenes filmed in Russia today, the accounts offered by the people he interviews, yesterday's news items, and with film clips from different time periods and by directors with varying agendas, ranging from *Battleship Potemkin* all the way to Stalinist propaganda films, with incursions, of course, into the films of Alexander Medvekin himself, all of which Marker reinserts into a different plot and binds together with virtual images.

Marker makes with the real documents he has amassed and treated with an eye to the truth a work whose fictional or poetic tenor is—beyond every value judgment—incomparably superior to that of the most spectacular action movie. Alexander's tomb is not the gravestone laid over the body of Alexander Medvekin. Nor is it a simple metaphor designating an appraisal of the life of a militant filmmaker that is, simultaneously, an appraisal of the Soviet dream and nightmare. The metonymical value of Alexander's tomb is that it speaks to us about another tomb symbolic of buried hope, Lenin's mausoleum. It is certainly a "fictional" choice on Marker's part not to represent Lenin except through metonymy: this demoralized head that the militants who joined forces against the communist putsch in the summer of 1991 gathered around in celebration, and on which kids can now be seen playing lightheartedly. The colossal, Pharaonic head with enormous inquisitive eyes of Felix Djerzinski, the man, it was said till recently, whom Lenin had appointed head of the political police because he was a Pole who had so often suffered in his own body the horrors of the Tsarist police that he would never build a police force in that image...

A tomb isn't a gravestone or a metaphor. It is a poem such as those that used to be written in the Renaissance and whose tradition resurfaces in Mallarmé. Or it is a musical piece in honor of another musician, like the ones written in the era of Couperin and Marin Marais, and more recently by Ravel. *The Last Bolshevik* is a document about the Russia of our century because it is a tomb in this poetical or musical sense, an artistic homage to a fellow artist. It is also a poem aligned to a specific poetics. There are two major traditions in poetics, both of which are susceptible to being further subdivided or entangled. Classical, Aristotelian poetics is a poetics of action and representation that sees the core of the poem as the "representation of men in action," as the performance by one or more actors of the speeches that describe or mime the incidents that befall the characters, and whose arrangement abides by the logic that the progression of the action must coincide with a change in the characters' fortune and knowledge. Romantic poetics abandoned this poetics of action, character, and discourse in favor of a poetics of signs. Here, the backbone of the story is not the causal continuity of the action "according to necessity and verisimilitude" theorized by Aristotle, but the variable signifying power of signs and assemblies of signs that forms the tissue of the work. This power is, first of all, the power of expression whereby a sentence, an episode, or an impression can, even in isolation, represent the sense, or nonsense, of the whole; secondly, it is the power of correspondence that puts signs from different regimes in resonant or dissonant relationships; thirdly, it is the power of metamorphoses by which a combination of signs solidifies into an opaque object or deploys itself in a signifying, living form; and, finally, it is the power of reflection that gives a particular combination the power to interpret another combination, or, alternatively, let itself be interpreted by it. Schlegel formulated the ideal union of all these powers in his idea of the "poem of the poem," the poem that claims to raise to a higher power a poetic power already present in the life of language, in the spirit of a community, and even in the folds and ridges of minerals. Romantic poetics deploys itself around two poles: it affirms the power of speech inherent to every silent thing in the same breath that it affirms the infinite power of the poem to multiply itself by multiplying its modes of speech and levels of meaning.

This poetics complicates, in the same gesture, the regime of truth of the work. Classical poetics is based on the construction of a plot whose truth-value depends on a system of affinities and verisimilitudes that presupposes the objectification of the space-time specific to the fiction. The preeminent Romantic hero, Don Quixote, ruins the objectivity of fiction when he smashes to smithereens Master Peter's puppets. Don Quixote rejects the separation of serious activities and leisure activities with his insistence on the coincidence of the Book and the world, an insistance that bespeaks less the folly of a reader of chivalric romances than the folly of the Christian cross. Romantic poetics replaces the space made objective by fiction with an indeterminate space of writing: this space is, on the one hand, indistinguishable from a "reality" composed of "things" and impressions that are also signs that speak for themselves; and it is also, on the other hand, the opposite of this, a space undergoing an infinite construction that fashions, with its scaffoldings, labyrinths, and slants, an equivalent of this forever mute reality.

Cinema, the preeminently modern art, experiences more than any other art the conflict of these two poetics, though it is, by the same token, the art that most attempts to combine them. Cinema is the combination of the gaze of the artist who decides and the mechanical gaze that records, of constructed images and chance images. Even if it normally uses this double power as a simple instrument of illustration for the service of the succedaneum to classical poetics, cinema is nevertheless the art that can raise to the highest power the double resource of the mute impressions that speak for themselves and the montage that calculates their signifying force and truth-value. Documentary cinema is not bound to the "real" sought after by the classical norms of affinities and verisimilitude that exert so much force on so-called fiction cinema. This gives the documentary much greater leverage to play around with the consonance and dissonance between narrative voices, or with the series of period images with different provenances and signifying power. It can join the power of the impression, the power of speech born from the meeting of the mutism of the machine and the silence of things, to the power of montage, in the broad, non-technical sense of the term, as that which constructs a story and a meaning by its self-proclaimed right to combine meanings freely, to re-view images, to arrange them differently, and to diminish or increase their capacity for expression and for generating meaning. Cinéma-vérité and dialectical cinema—Dziga Vertov's train charging a cameraman lying level with the tracks, and the stroller descending with implacable slowness the famous Odessa steps in *Battleship Potemkin*—are two faces of the same poetics. Marker, poet of the cinematographic poem, organizes them into a new *mise-en-scène*. He alternates shots from the massacre on the Odessa steps in *Battleship Potemkin* with shots of pedestrians walking down the same steps today to make us feel the extraordinary artifice of Eisenstein's "slow-motion," his seven-minute dramatization of people running for their lives down these steps that a pedestrian walking at a leisurely pace can walk down in ninety seconds at most. In the same gesture, Marker also shows the infinite gap separating the

artifice by which art punctuates a historical moment from the artifices of
propaganda: the film where a lookalike of the friendly Stalin sticks his nose
into the broken-down engine of a tractor. The slow-motion Eisenstein uses
to film this hurried flight becomes part of a whole series of operations with
space and time, large and small, high and low, commonplace and singular; it
becomes part of the system of figures that constructs the space-times of the
Revolution. Eisenstein's fiction is a history making fiction, whereas Stalin's
lookalike is only Stalin's lookalike, nothing more than a fiction of power.

From the midst of the present-day images, the fictions of Soviet art,
and the fictions of Stalinist power, there emerges the dialogue of shadows
Chris Marker organizes with the six "letters" he writes today to the already
dead Alexander Medvekin. Sometimes Marker inserts yesterday's images
into today's prose, as in the re-staging of the emblematic scene of the
Revolution's emblematic film; and sometimes he moves in the opposite
direction, going from this or that "thing seen" today to the history of a
people's imaginary. In a church in Moscow, his camera lingers on images that
"speak for themselves": a religious celebration alike in every way to those
of long ago, full of ornamental and ceremonial pomp, burning incense, and
the devotion of the perennial babushkas. It also lingers awhile on the face
of an elderly gentleman who looks just like any other, though he is in fact
not your ordinary devout elderly gentleman. In the congregation there is
this man who, like Alexander Medvekin, is as old as his century and whose
name, Ivan Kozlovzki, also "says" nothing to the Western viewer. This long
take of a face we shall not see again does two things at once: it puts the
communist past and the post-communist present into the fabric of an older
history, the one performed in the great operas of the national repertory, and
it gives Medvekin a double, it furtively sketches the diptych essential to the
elaboration of "Alexander's fiction."

These two figures could not be more opposed. Medvekin spent his life,
his century, working to make the century and the Soviet territory the time
and place for the incarnation of the word of Marx. He spent his years
making communist films devoted to the regime and its heads, though these
heads never allowed the people to see his films. He invented the film-train
to be able to go into kolkhozes, miners' compounds, and so on, in order to
film the work, the living conditions of the workers, and the debates of their
representatives. He had a lab installed in one of the cars of the train to be
able to process the film on the spot and show it to the people he had filmed,
to submit to their eyes, posthaste, this document about their successes and
shortcomings. He succeeded, too well it seems: his implacable images of

desolate groups of huts, of courtyards full of dead trees, of the meetings of pen-pushers, were all assigned a quiet resting place in the archives where only now researchers are uncovering them. He then went on to put the comic and surrealist verve of *Happiness* at the service of the policies for agrarian reform, but the fun it pokes at dignitaries, Orthodox priests, and kulaks is by all accounts far in excess of what the depiction of any "line" calls for, so the film got no distribution. This didn't keep Medvekin from celebrating the official urban planning in *The New Moscow*, but what possessed him to have some fun at the architects' expense by showing, backwards, the new buildings being destroyed and the Savior's Cathedral being reconstructed? The film was immediately shelved along with the others. He was eventually obliged to renounce his own films and to resign himself to making other people's films, films that anybody could have directed illustrating the official line of the moment, celebrating the pageants in honor of Stalin's glory, denouncing Chinese communism, or vaunting Soviet concern for the environment shortly before Chernobyl.

This is not how Ivan Kozlovzki lived his life and century. He sang Tchaikovsky, loved by the Tsars and preferred by Stalin to the musicians of the communist avant-garde. He also sang Rimsky-Korsakov and Mussorgsky, especially his *Boris Godunov*, an opera based on the work of the foremost Russian poet, who was also much loved under the Soviets, Alexander, family name Pushkin. In this emblematic story of an assassinated tsarevich and of a bloody usurper whose plans are foiled by another impostor, Ivan Kozlovzki played Simpleton, who in the final and prophetic scene cries over the impenetrable night, pain, and hunger awaiting the Russian people. He spent his life and century performing these nineteenth-century fables that portray every revolution as doomed from the outset and singing the suffering of a people eternally condemned to subjection and deceit. And he did so to an audience of communist officials who always preferred these stories and this music to the works of the communist avant-garde. The camera, lingering thus on his silent face, does more than just release the furtive counter-image of another life lived in the Soviet century. It inscribes that face in a fiction of memory that is the combat between two legacies: one twentieth century inherited from the nineteenth century against another. These two "centuries" of course intersect, they both deploy their own metamorphoses, contradictions, and reversals. And so it is that, between two images of the singer, between the old gentleman praying in the cathedral and Simpleton's lamentation on the stage of the Bolshoi, Marker inserts another story of popes—the ferociously anticlerical scenes of *Happiness*—as well as another meeting of centuries, men, and "religions": Medvekin's recollections of the Red Cavalry, where he served in the Cossack ranks under Boudienny with the later to be executed Jew Isaac Babel.

The fictional identification of the life of a communist filmmaker and the life of communism's land and century doesn't produce a linear narrative, and that in spite of the fact that Marker's six "letters" to Alexander Medvekin adhere, formally at least, to a chronological order. The first letter is about Tsarist Russia; the second about the first years of the Soviet Union; the third about the agitprop activities Medvekin stirred up with the epic of the film-train; the fourth about the triumph of Stalinism by way of the misadventures of *The New Moscow*; the fifth about Medvekin's death during the Perestroika and the end of the Soviet Union. But this neat chronology is confounded already in the first letter, which piles together all these ages. The first letter, in fact, organizes a different story of life and death, though this will only become explicit in the sixth letter, where we see images of Alexander Medvekin's real death, his living death while filming, in 1939, the enormous pageants in celebration of Stalin for a film entitled *Blossoming Youth*. Marker constructs his film in the interval between two deaths, one real, the other symbolic. Each episode, as Marker intimates with his polysemic title, is really a carefully constructed mixture of times, a pluralization of memory and fiction. There are, in the end, at least four Alexanders grouped under the one of the title. The visit to Medvekin's tomb is sidetracked by the scene of a crowd hurrying in the mud of the late-winter thaw to cover with flowers the tomb of a more illustrious Alexander, Tsar Alexander III. These images, like the images of the religious processions in Moscow and Kiev, are not simply the visual equivalent of Rimbaud's line "Society, and everything, is restored." The kinship between these two tombs is more than simply a synonym for buried hope and for the vindication of the old world. It determines, from the start, the entire narrative structure of the film. Marker doesn't try to show a linear transition from Tsarist Russia to the Revolution, and from its collapse to the restoration of old values. Rather, he throws three Russias into one present: the Russia of Nicolas II, of the Soviets, and of today. These three Russias are likewise three ages of the image: Tsarist Russia the age of photography and of the rich who parade without compunction before the poor; Soviet Russia the age of cinema and of the war of images; contemporary Russia the age of video and television.

Marker has already suggested all of this in one of the first images of the film, that of an officer in St. Petersburg in 1913 ordering the people with his imperious gestures to take off their hats and bow before the passing nobles.

We must make sure we don't misunderstand what Marker means when he says he wants us to remember this "fat man who orders the poor to bow to the rich." It's not that he want us, metaphorically, to store this image of oppression that yesterday legitimated and today might "excuse" the Soviet Revolution. He wants us, literally, not to forget it, he wants us to pair this image of the great parading before the small with its counter-image: the enormous Soviet pageants that the small now declared great—gymnasts, children, kolkhozniks—put on for their "comrades" in the official gallery. Marker, however, is not just having a little fun by confounding those well-established temporal systems, the simple chronological order or the classical narrative told in flashback. He is working out a narrative structure that creates a memory in the present as the intertwining of two histories of the century. This becomes explicit when we meet, in the image of Ivan Kozlovzki singing the part of Simpleton, the third Alexander: Alexander Sergueivitch Pushkin. But Alexander is, first and foremost, the name of the greatest of conquerors, the name of the Macedonian prince who ensured that history wouldn't forget him by subjugating ancient Greece and extending its borders to the furthest reaches of the known world. And it is the name of the illustrious corpse whose tomb explorers have been trying to find for millennia: it is, in other words, one "name of Alexander" that makes this learned history of homonyms incomplete, that refers the tomb-poem to the missing tomb that, perhaps, it always allegorizes.

That is how the "classical" story of fortune and misfortune, of ignorance and knowledge, that ties one man's life to the Soviet epic and catastrophe assumes the "Romantic" form of this narrative that inverts the "black soil of time," just as do those poems Osip Mandelstam wrote on the eve of the Revolution. Mandelstam had wanted to free our "century of clay" from the evil spells of the previous one and to give it a historical skeleton, and this explains the narrative structure of those poems where he interlaces the Soviet present and Greek mythology, the sacking of the Winter Palace and the sacking of Troy.[2] If the structure of Marker's "tomb" has become more complex, it is not because the means of signification of cinema are different from those of poetry, but because of the historicity of cinema itself. Cinema was born as an art out of Romantic poetics, was pre-shaped by it: as an art, it seems almost to have been designed for the metamorphoses of signifying forms that make it possible to construct memory as the interlacing of uneven temporalities and of heterogeneous regimes of the image. Cinema is also, in its artistic, technical, and social nature, a living metaphor of modern times. An inheritance from the nineteenth century and a relationship between the twentieth and the nineteenth centuries, cinema combines our century's dual relationship to the previous century, the two legacies I alluded to above: Marx's century in Lenin's; Pushkin's and Dostoevsky's century in Stalin's. It is an art form whose principle, the union of conscious thought and unconscious perception, had been worked out in the final chapter of Schelling's *System of Transcendental Idealism,* a good hundred years before the first public screenings. And it is also the crowning product of a century of scientific and technical research into how to effect the transition from the science of amusing illusions to the ability to use light to record movements hidden to the human eye. In Étienne Marey's day, cinema was still regarded as an instrument useful to the human sciences and to the search for scientific truth, both of which were contemporaneous with the age of scientific socialism. And although it might have seemed, when Alexander Medvekin was born, that cinema had reached its final destination in the new industry of illusion and public entertainment, by the time he had grown of age, the powers of science and the powers of the image had joined hands once more, much as had the power of the new man, the communist and electric man: communist because electric, and electric because communist. In one fell swoop, writing with light became a practical instrument and the ideal metaphor for the union of the powers of illusion, of science, and of the people.

Cinema was the communist art, the art of the identity of science and utopia. In the 1920s, it wasn't only in the revolutionary Moscow of Vertov and Eisenstein, of Medvekin and Dovchenko, that the combinations of light and movement were chasing the attitudes and thoughts of the old-fashioned man; the same was happening in the aestheticized Paris of Canudo, Delluc, and Epstein. Cinema, the crowning product of the nineteenth century, became the basis for the definitive break between that century and theirs. It was the kingdom of shadows destined to become a kingdom of light, a writing of movement that, like the railway and *with* it, could not but merge into the very movement of the revolution. In *The Last Bolshevik,* Marker tells the cinematographic history of cinema's double relationship to Sovietism. He suggests that it is possible to tell the history of the Soviet century through the fates of Soviet filmmakers, through the films they made, those they didn't make, and those they were obliged to make, because all of these attest to the common destiny of cinema and Sovietism. But there is also a more profound reason: the art of cinema is the metaphor, indeed the very cipher, for an idea of the century and of history that found its political incarnation in Sovietism. Marker's project, in its own way, mirrors Godard's in *Histoire(s) du cinéma*, where Godard proposes to read the history of our century not by looking at its history, but by looking at the *stories*, or some of the *stories*, of the cinema, since cinema is not only contemporaneous with the century, but an integral part of its very "idea." Godard portrays the Soviet and the Hollywood dream factories as mirror images, he sees in State Marxism and industrialized cinema the same conflict between the two legacies inherited by the century. Of course, Godard's method and Marker's are quite different. Godard produces another form of the "poem of the poem" by using the resources of videographic writing to render the power of the blackboard and the power of pictorial montage identical on the screen. He sends the machine devoted to information into shock with his method of saturating images or zigzagging through them; he superimposes in the same "audio-visual" unit an image from one film, an image from a second film, the music from a third, a voice from a fourth, and words from a fifth; he complicates this intertwining further by using images from painting and by punctuating the whole thing with a commentary in the present. Each of his images and conjunctions of images is a treasure hunt: they open onto multiple paths and create a virtual space of indefinite connections and resonances. Marker favors a dialectical method instead. He composes a series of images (interviews, archival documents, clips from the classics of Soviet cinema and from propaganda films, scenes from the opera, virtual images, etc.) that he arranges, always in strict adherence to the cinematographic principles of montage, in order to define very specific moments in the relationship between the cinematographic "kingdom of shadows" and the "shadows of the [utopian] kingdom." While Godard gives us a smooth plane, Marker creates a memory we can scan. And yet he falls prey, like Godard but even more so, to an obvious paradox: he feels compelled to punctuate all these "images that speak for themselves," as well as the interlacing of series of images that make cinema into a meta-language and into a "poem of the poem," with an imperious voice-over commentary that tells us what it is that they "say."

Here we have, in a nutshell, the problem of documentary fiction in particular and of cinematographic fiction in general. Cinema's first utopia was that it was a language—syntax, architecture, symphony—better equipped than the language of words to embrace bodies in movement. This utopia has always had to confront, during the silent and talking eras, the limits of its capacity to speak and all the returns of the "old" language. "Documentary" cinema in particular has always been caught between the ambiguities of cinéma-vérité, the dialectical turns of montage, and the imperialism of the voice of the master, usually *off*, that either lines the unfolding of heterogeneous images with its melodic continuity, or gives a step by step explanation of the meaning of the images' silent presence or elegant arabesques. Marker, the dialectical pedagogue, rarely fails to underline for us the evidence that the image "itself" provides of what our memory tends to forget and our thought resists conceptualizing, or to stress the insignificance or ambivalence of the image when left to its own devices and the concomitant need of making all of its possible readings explicit. *The Last Bolshevik* is a fiction of memory, of the interwoven memory of communism and cinema. Marker, however, cannot resist the temptation of making the fiction of memory he constructs with artistic means into a "lesson on memory" and on the duties of memory. That is what this voice is constantly spelling out for the audience: don't forget this image, be sure to connect it to this other image, look at that image a little closer, reread what there is to read in this image. The director's visual demonstration of Eisenstein's artifice, the alternating montage of clips from *Battleship Potemkin* and shots of pedestrians today who descend those steps more slowly *and* faster at the same time, has been anticipated and made redundant by the professor's explanation. And yet, it would be difficult to read it without the commentary. The "documentary" always plays with how the images and their montage, which should speak all by themselves, have to be referred to the authority of a voice that secures meaning at the price of weakening the images. Undoubtedly, this tension is at its peak in the case of a historical and documentary fiction that is at the same time a cinematographic film about cinema's historical powers. As for the fiction of the "letter" addressed to the dead director, it is the means of ensuring the undivided authority of this voice.

The issues raised here go beyond the already difficult relationship between pedagogy and art and touch the heart of the Romantic poetics that cinema belongs to as the conjunction of the power of speech accorded to mute things and the power of self-reflection accorded to the work. We all know that Hegel radically contested this claim in his lectures on aesthetics. As he sees it, the power of the form, the "thought-outside-itself" of the work, and the power of self-reflection, the "thought-in-itself" of conceptual thought, are mutually opposed. The drive to identify them results either in the work being reduced to the demonstration of a specific virtuosity, an individual signature, or in its being caught in the endless symbolist game between form and meaning where one side is never more than the other's echo. When cinema presents itself as a cinema of cinema and identifies this cinema of cinema

with the reading of a century, it runs the same risk: it finds itself caught
between the infinite referral of images and sounds, of forms and meaning,
characteristic of Godard's style, and the power of the commentator's voice
in Marker. Marker's latest films show his awareness of this aporia and his
attempts to break free from it. *Level Five* is a particularly good example in this
respect. The film deliberately breaks with the equilibrium characteristic of a
documentary in its construction of a fiction of memory around the battle
of Okinawa and around the bone-chilling, collective suicide the conquering
Japanese officers imposed upon the colonized of Okinawa, forcing them
to ape Japanese codes of honor. With a computer, Marker generates the
images of the past in the form of a video game; then, using the dialectical
principles of montage, he confronts the computer-generated images with
present-day images and with the voices of the people interviewed. Marker
has made of this computer a fictional character: memory, tomb, and game
board that allow Marker to combine the resources of video game with the
strategy of Japanese generals and of the game go. As it happens, the game
go is the emblem of another film, *Last Year at Marienbad*, by Alan Resnais, who
also directed the "documentary" *Night and Fog*, and the "fiction" *Hiroshima,
mon amour*. *Level Five* is a sort of computer-age version of *Hiroshima, mon
amour* in which the two lovers have been substituted by a singular couple:
the computer and the woman who uses it to talk to her beloved who's gone
missing. We must not miss the very particular status of this fictional lover.
She is, essentially, the fictionalization of a poetic function—that of the
voice of the commentator. Marker represents this voice in *Level Five*, where
it is not *off*, masculine, and imperious, but fictional and feminine. But he
does so under a very specific mode: the "heroine" herself, Laura, has to step
out of the cinematographic fiction, much like her namesake, the heroine of
Preminger's film, who steps out of the painting to become a living being.
Nor should we forget that *Laura*'s fame is closely associated with the opening
sentence of the film, "I'll never forget the afternoon Laura died," a sentence
that turns out to be spoken by a dead man about a living being.

Thus is the fiction of memory redoubled to infinity and the documentary
revealed to be, more than ever, the actualization of the Romantic poetics
that rejects every aporia of the "end of art." *Level Five* identifies the memory
of one of the most monstrous crimes of the century and of history with
a fiction about the fiction of fiction. But the fictional reduction of sense
in *Level Five* is matched by the material impoverishment of the image. The
aura-less unreality of the computer-generated image rubs off on the images
of various origins Marker assembles in the film. The reduction of levels of

fiction and sense complements the platitude of videographic space. The tension between the "images that speak for themselves" and the words that make them speak is, when all is said and done, the tension between the idea of the image and imaged matter. The real issue has nothing to do with the technical apparatus, but is still a matter of poetics. Godard too turns to video, but he achieves the inverse end: he leads the joyous disorder of words and images back to the glory of the icon. By assembling fragments from the fictions of an entire century, Godard eternizes the spiritual as well as plastic kingdom of cinematographic shadows, the heirs of pictorial figures. With Marker, and here he shows his kinship with installation artists, it is instead the image as an operation of assembling and splitting asunder that affirms itself to the detriment of the material splendor of the kingdom of shadows. At a time when the balance sheets of the century and of the revolutions in image-making technique are being weighed, the "poem of the poem" finds two figures so close together, and yet so radically opposed. One tomb against another, one poem against another.[3]

NOTES

1. The French title is *Le Tombeau d'Alexandre* [*Alexander's Tomb*], which explains why Rancière plays throughout the chapter on the word "tomb" and the name "Alexander."—Trans.
2. Cf. Jacques Rancière, "From Wordsworth to Mandelstam: The Transports of Liberty," in *The Flesh of Words: The Politics of Writing*, trans. Charlotte Mandell (California: Stanford University Press, 2004).
3. I would like to thank Sylvie Astric for drawing my attention to this film and to documentary fiction in general during a program of the BPI (Biliothèque publique d'information) she organized at the Pompidou Center.

CHAPTER I I

A Fable without a Moral
Godard, Cinema, (Hi)stories

Histoire(s) du cinéma: Godard's title, with its double meaning and variable reach, perfectly sums up the complex artistic apparatus he develops to present the following thesis: the history of cinema is that of a missed date with the history of its century. Cinema missed the date because it misunderstood its own historicity, the history it had already announced in virtual images. This misunderstanding is rooted in the fact that cinema misunderstood the power of its images, its inheritance from the pictorial tradition, which it agreed to subject to scripted "stories," heirs of the literary tradition of plot and characters. The thesis thus counterposes two types of "(hi)stories": the stories the film industry illustrated with images with an eye to cashing in on the collective imaginary, and the virtual history told by these same images. The style of montage Godard develops for *Histoire(s) du cinéma* is designed to show the history announced by a century of films, but whose power slipped through the fingers of their filmmakers, who subjected the "life" of images to the immanent "death" of the text. Godard takes the films these filmmakers made and makes with them the films they didn't make. This calls for a two-step process: the first recaptures the images from their subjection to the stories they were used to tell, and the second rearranges them into other stories. The project, simple as its description may sound, requires a set of operations that singularly complicate our notions of image and history, operations that ultimately invert the thesis that cinema betrayed itself and its century and demonstrate, instead, the radical innocence of the art of moving images.

Let's start at the beginning. Not of Godard's series, but of his intervention, which is to say, let's turn directly to the section entitled *The Control of the Universe*, particularly to that part of it offset by the subheading "Introduction to the Method of Alfred Hitchcock," a homage to Paul Valéry's *Introduction to the Method of Leonardo da Vinci*. This entire episode is devoted to an illustration

of the primacy of images over plot. Godard suggests: "We've forgotten why
Joan Fontaine leans over the edge of the cliff and what exactly Joel McCrea
went to do in Holland. We've forgotten what Montgomery Clift's eternal
silence keeps and why Janet Leigh stops at the Bates Motel and why Teresa
Wright is still crazy about her Uncle Charlie. We've forgotten what it is
that Henry Fonda is not exactly guilty of and to what end the American
government hired Ingrid Bergman. But we do remember a purse, a bus in the
desert, a glass of milk, the sails of a windmill, a hairbrush. We remember a
row of bottles, a pair of glasses, a musical score, a bunch of keys, because
with and through these Alfred Hitchcock succeeds where Alexander, Julius
Caesar, and Napoleon had all failed: he takes control of the universe."[1]

Hitchcock's cinema, Godard is saying, is made of images whose power
is indifferent to the stories into which they've been arranged. We remember
the glass of milk Cary Grant takes to Joan Fontaine in *Suspicion*, but not the
financial problems the character thinks he might solve by coming into his
wife's life insurance; we remember the hairbrush the wife who goes mad in *The
Wrong Man*, Vera Miles, brandishes frantically, but not the confusion that led
to the arrest of her husband, Henry Fonda; we remember the close-up shots
of the bottle of Pommard falling in *Notorious* and the sails of the windmill
spinning against the wind in *The Secret Agent*, but not the stories of anti-Nazi
espionage that the characters played by Cary Grant, Ingrid Bergman and Joel
McCrea are involved in.[2] This argument, as such, is easily refuted. Godard
clearly makes his point by dissociating things that are indissociable. We don't
remember the bottles of Pommard in *Notorious* because of their pictorial
qualities but because of the emotional charge that the narrative situation
has invested in them. The bottle that wobbles and falls interests us because
it contains the uranium Alicia (Ingrid Bergman) and Devlin (Cary Grant)
are looking for; because we know that while they're searching the wine cellar,
the champagne at the reception upstairs is running out and Alicia's husband
Sebastian (Claude Rains), a Nazi agent, will presently step down to the
cellar with his butler to fetch some more, hear the bottle falling, and notice
that his key to the cellar is missing because Alicia has taken it. The same goes
for all the images Godard evokes: in every case, it is the narrative situation
that lends importance to the objects. It is easy, then, to refute Godard's
argument. The problem, though, is that Godard doesn't oppose arguments,
he opposes images. What we see running parallel with this discourse are
other images made from Hitchcock's images. The glass of milk, the keys, the
glasses, and the bottles all reappear in Godard, but separated by blacked-out
screens, so that they seem like so many icons, so many faces of things, akin

in many ways to the apples in Cézanne mentioned in passing in the voice-over commentary: so many testimonies to the (re)birth of all things under the light of pictorial presence.

Separating the images from their narrative arrangement is only the first part of Godard's project. The second, and more important part, entails transforming their nature as images. Let's look again at the glass of milk in *Suspicion*, which Hitchcock uses in the film to condense two contradictory affects. It is the object of Lina's (Joan Fontaine) anxiety because she has just learned of her husband's murderous intentions. The mien of the young woman we've just seen in her bedroom, the insert of the dial of a clock appointing the hour of the crime, and the arrow of white light formed by a door opened onto a darkened hallway, all conspire to make us share the intensity of her anxiety. But for us the glass of milk is also something else. Its appearance is like a little visual puzzle: a luminous white spot that shines on the tall and slender body of Cary Grant, and that slowly grows in size as he makes his way up the stairs, the field of vision narrowing with each one of his steps until the glass takes up the whole screen. This small white spot inscribes itself into the play of white, grey, and black surfaces formed by the lights on the walls and the railing of the stairwell. Cary Grant mounts the stairs with habitual impassiveness, as if to the rhythm of a very slow waltz. An image, properly speaking, is exactly this apparatus that produces a double effect: on the one hand, it materializes the anxiety that it makes us share with the heroine by aligning visual and fictional tensions; on the other hand, it separates them: Cary Grant calmly making his way up the stairwell and the abstract play of light and shadow transform the visual enigma. It answers the spectator who's wondering, with the heroine, if there is poison in the glass, with another question that pacifies anxiety by turning it into curiosity: *You're no doubt asking yourself if there's poison in the glass, no? Do you really think there is?* It includes the viewer in the play of the author by distancing him from the affect of the heroine. The name of this double effect, although it is often applied a bit indiscriminately to every situation, fits this scene perfectly. It has been called, since Aristotle, the purification of the passions, and here it is the purification of the dramatic passion par excellence, fear. Fear is aroused simultaneously in its identificatory and purified modes, it is alleviated by a play of knowledge that moves through anxiety and frees itself from it. A Hitchcock image is an element in an Aristotelian dramaturgy. It is the cause of anxiety and the instrument that purifies the anxiety it has aroused. His films are model examples of the representative tradition, a construction of visual incidents that acts on the sensibilities of the viewer by playing with the shifting relations of pleasure and pain through the relationship between ignorance and knowledge.

The images in these films are operations, units that partake in the channeling of hypotheses and the manipulation of affects. In the soundtrack, we hear Hitchcock's voice talking about this manipulation of the viewer's affects until his voice is drowned out and another voice comes to inhabit these images, Godard's. The "Method of Alfred Hitchcock" transforms his images into their contraries: visual units wherein the face of things impresses itself like the face of the Savior on Veronica's veil. Godard has turned them into units caught up in a double relationship—with all the things that have left their impression on them, and with all the other images with which they compose a specific sensorium, a world of inter-expressivity. Transforming images into their contraries requires more than just separating them from their narrative context and arranging them differently. It is a well-known fact that since Dziga Vertov cutting and pasting have generally been used to produce the inverse effect, to show that cinematographic images on their own are just inert pieces of celluloid that can only be brought to life by the operation of montage that arranges them. The montage that transforms Hitchcock's affect-bearing images into icons of the originary presence of things must really be an anti-montage, a fusional montage that inverts the artificialist logic of fragmentation. Four operations make up this anti-montage. In the first, the images are separated by blacked-out screens and thus isolated from one another, which is to say, more importantly, that they have been isolated together in *their* world, a *netherworld* of images whence each image seems to emerge in its turn as if to bear witness to it. Then there is the discrepancy between speech and image that, likewise, works against its normal uses. The text discusses a film while we watch the images of a different film. Godard does not exploit this discrepancy to create critical disjunction, as is most commonly done, but to seal the global co-belonging of text and film to the same world of images. The voice, for its part, gives homogeneity and depth to this world. Lastly, video-editing, characterized by its overexposures, its images that appear, flicker and disappear, or that are superimposed or merged into one another, completes the representation of an originary sensorium, of a world of images whence the images emerge when summoned by the director, like the souls Homer imagines in Hades gathering around Odysseus after having been summoned there by the sound of his call and the smell of blood. In a spectacular moment, Hitchcock's mummified icon returns from the realm of the dead to inhabit the world of "his" images, to replace James Stewart at Kim Novak's side in the sequoia forest of *Vertigo*. The substitution is of course emblematic. By recalling the title of the novel that the film adapts, *From among the Dead*, it inverts the manipulation in the film's diabolical script, where the theme of the woman summoned by her ancestor to the kingdom of the dead serves as a ruse for the criminal manipulations that dupe the detective Scottie (James Stewart). This perfectly measured counter-manipulation transforms the characters and their director into shadows literally emerging from the realm of the dead. The video image uncouples the cinematographic image from the script and places it in this realm in order to make cinema itself the interiority of this realm.

Godard removes these visual fragments from the continuum of a film as a means of changing their nature. He transforms them into units that no longer belong to the narrative/affective strategies of the representative mode, but belong instead to an originary sensorium. There, Hitchcock's images become event-worlds that coexist with the infinity of other event-worlds that belong not only to all other films but also to all other forms of illustration of the century; they become susceptible to striking an infinite number of relationships amongst themselves as well as with all the events of the century. Godard gives us the impression that he hasn't cut up Hitchcock's images, but that it was Hitchcock who assembled all these images that already lived a life of their own in a world of generalized inter-expressivity; all Godard really did was look for them again in his films and assemble them differently, in a way that was truer to their nature.

What is this nature, exactly? This is what we learn presently. Godard follows the Hitchcock episode of *Histoire(s) du cinéma* with a homage to cinema whose composition is a perfect illustration of his method. Godard now parades before our eyes visual fragments taken for the most part from the expressionist and fantastic traditions, represented here by a handful of their most illustrious films: *Nosferatu*, *The Phantom of the Opera*, *Faust*, *Metropolis*, *Son of Frankenstein*, etc. The voice commenting on these terrifying images of monsters transforms them into their exact opposites: whether in the image of Frankenstein presented as Saint Christopher carrying the child-king (*Son of Frankenstein*) or of Brigitte Helm covering the children under the mantle of the Virgin Mary (*Metropolis*), every one of these films seems to boil down to a demonstration of a few of humanity's daily gestures and archetypal poses. They illustrate the major ages and essential moments of life, and cinema, as commented on by the voice-over of Alain Cluny, becomes the encyclopedia of these essential gestures: "From insouciance to disquietude, from the impassioned and truculent first efforts to the hesitant but essential forms of the last, it is the same central force that governs the cinema. One follows it within cinema from form to form, with the shadow and the ray of light which circle around, illuminating one thing, hiding another, causing a shoulder to jut forth, or a face, or a raised finger, an open book, a forehead, or a little child in a manger. That which plunges into the light is the reverberation of that which night submerges. That which the night submerges prolongs into the visible that which plunges into the light. Thought, vision, words, and action unite this forehead, that eye, this mouth, that hand, with the volumes scarcely perceived in the shadow: heads and bodies bending over a birth, a death struggle or death itself [...] the headlight of a car, a sleeping face, darkness becoming animated, some beings leaning over a cradle on which all the light falls, a man executed in front of a dirty wall, a miry road running alongside the sea, a street corner, an obscure sky, a ray of light over some meadow land, the empire of the wind discovered in a flying cloud. Here are nothing but black strokes crossing one another on a glowing canvas, and the tragedy of space and the tragedy of life make the screen writhe in their fire [...] It is there when the cradle is illuminated. It is there when the young girl appears to us leaning on the windowsill, with eyes that do not know and a pearl between her breasts. It is there when we have disrobed her, when her hard torso trembles to the throbbing of our fever. It is there when she has aged, when her furrowed face is surrounded with a cap and when her bony hands cross at her waist to signify that she has no resentment against life for having dealt hard with her."[3]

The reading of this text, which stretches the length of these images of life's archetypal gestures, defines what cinema alone may do, what it alone saw. The text, though, is not Godard's, nor is it a text about cinema. Save for a couple of minor alterations, Godard took the whole of it from the pages Élie Faure dedicates to Rembrandt in his *History of Art*. Even if textual collage is as essential to Godard's method as visual collage, we cannot overlook the fact that this rerouting of Faure's text takes on a very specific meaning. It claims for cinema the legacy of the pictorial tradition. But, more importantly, it claims for it the legacy of a genre of painting that has regarded Rembrandt as its flagship since the beginning of the nineteenth century. Rembrandt became, from that time onwards, the retrospective hero of a "new" kind of painting, one that breaks with the traditional hierarchy of subjects and division of genres that had always structured the opposition between noble history painting and vulgar genre painting. This new painting uses the quasi-abstract play of light and shadow to capture the essential gestures and emotions of everyday life that succeed the pomp that normally surrounded exalted subject matters and memorable exploits. Rembrandt, the hero of a new "history painting" that is in every sense the polar opposite of the old, is thus the hero of a "new history." Not the history of princes and conquerors, but of the intertwined multiplicity of epochs, gestures, objects, and symbols of ordinary human life, of the different ages of life and of the handing down of its forms. This is the new history that critics like Goncourt, assisted by some Hegelian-inspired philosophers, read on the canvases of Rembrandt, Rubens, and Chardin, the new history that was brought to the world of the novel in the prose of Balzac and Hugo and that found its model historian in Michelet and its archetypal art historian in the person of Élie Faure, the theoretician/poet of the "forms," a term that encompasses both artistic forms and the cyclical forms of life in this universe. For Élie Faure, the "spirit of the forms" is the "central fire" that welds them, the universal energy of collective life that does and undoes its forms. In this history, Rembrandt is the exemplary figure of the artist who seizes the spirit/fire at its source, in the elementary gestures of life.

We can now explain the precise nature of this "rerouting" of Élie Faure's text, which Godard uses to transform these cinematographic fables of monsters into the golden book of the essential moments of human life. Godard, in a very phenomenological fashion, conceives the truth of this originary world of images as being none other than this "spirit of the forms" that the nineteenth century had learned to read as the interiority of works of art. This interiority links artistic forms to shared forms of life, it allows all these forms to be associated and inter-expressed in an indefinite number of combinations, and it also ensures that every one of these combinations can express the collective life that threads together every fact, ordinary object, elementary gesture, speech, and image, whether banal or extraordinary. This particular co-belonging of forms and experience has, since those days, gone by the very specific name of *history*. It's over two centuries now since history has designated not the narrative of things past, but a mode of co-presence, a way of thinking and experiencing the co-belonging of experiences and the inter-expressivity of the forms and signs that give them shape. The young woman leaning on the windowsill, the headlight of a car in the night, the miry road, the street corner—but also the sails of the windmill, the glass of milk, the wobbling bottle of wine and the crime reflected in the victim's glasses—all of these have belonged to art since *history* became the name for the co-belonging of individual experiences, whether glorious or mundane, the name for what puts the forms of canvases and the sentences of novels—but also the graffiti and the lizards on a wall, the wear and tear of clothes or the flakes peeling from a façade—into a relationship of inter-expressivity. History is this mode of shared experience where all experiences are equivalent and where the signs of any one experience are capable of expressing all the others. Novalis succinctly summed up the poetics of the age of history in his famous dictum: "everything speaks." This means that every sensible form is a tissue of more or less obscure signs, a presence capable of signifying the power of the collective experience that brings the sensible form into presence. It also means that each one of these signifying forms is open to striking new relationships with all other forms, generating thereby new signifying arrangements. It is as a result of this regime of meaning where everything speaks twice—as pure presence and as the infinity of its virtual connections—that experiences are communicated and a common world created.

Godard relies on this history and poetics of history to transform Hitchcock's affect-bearing images into icons of pure presence, or to use Élie Faure's text on Rembrandt to transform shots from *Fantômas* or *Son of Frankenstein* into images of the elementary gestures of human life. The image-operations of the storytellers of the cinema can become phenomenological icons of beings being born to presence because the "images" of the age of history, the images of the aesthetic regime of art, lend their metamorphic qualities to this operation. The fact is that they belong to a more fundamental poetics that ensures the interchangeability of the functional sequences of representative narrative and the icons of phenomenological religion. Friedrich Schlegel sums up this poetics in the notion of a "progressive universal poetry": a poetry of metamorphoses that not only transforms the elements of ancient poems into fragments that can be combined into new poems, but also ensures that the speeches and images of art are interchangeable with the speeches and images of common experience. The visual fragments taken from Hitchcock and others belong to this aesthetic regime of images, they are metamorphic elements that can always be divorced from their narrative arrangement, or transformed from within, or coupled and reassembled with any of the other images that belong to this great continuum of forms. Each element in this regime is at once an image-material susceptible to infinite transformations and combinations, and an image-sign capable of designating and interpreting every other. This reserve historicity sustains the poetics of *Histoire(s) du cinéma*, this poetics that makes every sentence and image an element that can be associated with every other element to tell the truth about a century of history and of cinema, even if that means changing their nature and meaning. Godard digs into this reserve to construct the real plot of *Histoire(s) du cinéma*: cinema, although it never ceased bearing witness to the century, consistently misunderstood its own testimony.

Godard's *Histoire(s) du cinéma* is the most stunning contemporary manifestation of the Romantic poetics of *everything speaks* and of the original tension that inhabits that poetics. There are essentially two major methods of hearing things speak, that is, two major ways of making things speak the language of their mutism. In the first we place ourselves before things and free them from their subjection to the words and determinations of the plot in order to be able to hear their intimate murmurings. We have to let them impress the imprints of their presence on their own. Things are there and that's all; getting them to speak means refraining from manipulating them. The second amounts to the inverse. Because all things and all meanings inter-express, we have to manipulate them to make them speak, we have to uproot them and put them in touch with all the things, forms, signs and ways of doing that are their co-presents. We have to multiply the short-circuits that produce, with flashes of Romantic *Witz*, the éclat of sense that illuminates common experience.

Histoire(s) du cinéma is governed by the play of these two polarities. Its discourse seems, at first, to come down decidedly on the side of the first method. Cinema is "an art without a future," Godard tells us, an "infant art" whose vocation is to the present and to presence. Cinema is not a "camera-pen," it is just a screen stretched across the globe for things to impress themselves on it. And yet, both the *mise-en-scène* of this discourse and the presentation of the pure presences it reclaims oblige Godard to resort to the second method, which makes every image an element in a discourse in which it either interprets another image or is interpreted by it. This has been the case from the very beginning. Cyd Charisse dancing in *The Band Wagon* isn't just an expression of the immanence of choreographic movement to the moving image, but is presented also as an illustration of Hollywood's pact with the devil, symbolized by Mephisto's appearance in Murnau's *Faust*. Mephisto himself is a double symbol, a figure for Hollywood grabbing this infant art with a mighty hand, and for this art itself, the art of Murnau, who became in his turn the victim of the pact he brought to the screen. This dramaturgy sums up, in some ways, the double dialectic at work in *Histoire(s) du cinéma*: the dialectic that gives it its plot, and the one that makes the construction of that plot possible. In *Histoire(s) du cinéma*, Godard announces a poetics—that of pure presence—that it accuses the cinema of having betrayed. But in order to mount the accusation, Godard has to apply a different poetics—that of metaphorical montage—which obliges him to conclude that cinema was indeed present to its century, though on the metaphorical level, as the way to prove that it was not present to this presence.

Godard organizes his demonstration around a double failure: cinema failed its century because it had already failed itself. The first failure revolves around cinema's impotence before the disasters of 1939–45, and particularly around the fact that it failed to see and show the death camps. The second concerns the pact Hollywood signed with the devil of the dream industry and of commercialized plots. The whole structure of *Histoire(s) du cinéma* is determined by an imperious teleology in which Nazism and the Second World War serve as cinema's truth test. This same teleology limits the plot of *Histoire(s) du cinéma* to the destiny of European cinema and its double undoing: at the hands of the American industry and of the Nazi horror. It also explains why Japanese cinema is so noticeably absent from Godard's encyclopedia. It isn't that the Second World War didn't implicate Japan and mark its cinema, but that by definition neither of these can be incorporated into the schema about the "destiny of European culture," inspired by Valéry and Heidegger, that governs Godard's dramaturgy. The core of the demonstration evidently touches on cinema's relationship to the death camps. If the "flame of cinema went out at Auschwitz," it is for Godard for a completely different reason than for Adorno. Cinema is not guilty of wanting to continue making art after Auschwitz, but guilty of not having been there, of not having seen and shown the images from Auschwitz. Godard's argument is obviously indifferent to all empirical considerations about how exactly cinema could have been there to film at all. In Godard, as in Rousseau, facts prove nothing. Cinema should have been present at Auschwitz because its essence is to be present. There are images wherever something happens—birth or death, banality or atrocity—and cinema's duty is to record those images. Cinema's betrayal, that it made itself incapable of being there to record those images, is rooted in the fact that it had already betrayed itself long before. It had sold its soul to the devil. It had sold itself to that "insignificant little mafia bookkeeper" known as the inventor of the script. It had already surrendered the power of its mute speech to the tyranny of words and the power of its images to the huge industry of fiction, the industry of sex and death that substitutes for our gaze a world illusorily in accord with our desires. Already back then cinema had agreed to reduce the infinite murmuring and speaking forms of the world to these standardized dream stories that can so easily be aligned with the dreams of all the men in the darkened rooms just by parading before their eyes those two great objects of desire, women and guns.

Godard shows all of this through a series of displacements and superimpositions, de-figurations and de-nominations. We see, for instance,
images from Griffith's *Broken Blossoms* and from the rabbit hunt in Renoir's
The Rules of the Game being crushed by Hollywood's Babylonian-like power,
captured in the images of Babylon from *Intolerance* and in the image of the
race on the backs of men in Fritz Lang's *Rancho Notorious*. Godard, as we
can see, makes double use of the same elements. Babylon in *Intolerance* is the
Hollywood empire and also Griffith's cinema, killed by this empire. The
rabbit hunt of *The Rules of the Game* is French cinema destined to be destroyed
by American help (Lesley Caron and Gene Kelly dancing in *An American in
Paris* is the metaphor for this) and an expression of the foreboding that
inhabits the cinema: a foreboding of its own death and of the extermination
to come, both pre-figured in the dance of death performed by the characters
in the film. *Rancho Notorious* is an American film made for an émigré German
actress, Marlene Dietrich, by an émigré German director, Fritz Lang, who
had already given us—in the *Nibenlungen Saga*, *Metropolis*, and *Mabuse*—images
of reality being seized by a murderous fiction and hence had, him too,
announced cinema's decline and the Nazi crimes.

Godard's demonstration depends on his use of cinema's "historical"
power, that is, cinema's power to put every image into associative and inter-
expressive relationships with all other images, or to make every image an
image of something else, a commentary that transforms another image,
either by revealing its hidden truth or by demonstrating its powers to foretell.
But we also learn, in the course of Godard's retrospection, that this "infant
art" never stopped giving itself a totally different power, a dialogical power
of association and metaphor. This art so soon killed off never stopped
announcing its own death, it never stopped taking revenge on the empire of
fiction that was strangling it to death by depicting it time and again as a folly
that was itself headed for destruction. And in so doing, it turns out that the
cinema had also denounced well in advance the histrionics of dictators with
a theatrical bent, which it had depicted in its own way. From the lighting
effects at Nuremberg that, according to Godard, Murnau and Karl Freund
had "set long beforehand," to its culminating point in Charlie Chaplin's *The
Great Dictator*, cinema dramatized time and again the delirium of fiction in
power and the revenge of the real on the fictive. But this very anticipation
spells out a new guilt: cinema failed to recognize the catastrophe it itself
announced, it failed to see what its images foretold.

The argument, left to its inherent merits, is once more not very convincing.
It is always possible to see the rabbit hunt in *The Rules of the Game*, or any other

scene of carnage for that matter, as prefiguring genocide. Conversely, the rather debonair camp the barber and his accomplice escape from without much ado in *The Great Dictator* shows that even Nazism's most acerbic critic was miles away from anticipating the reality of the death camps. Chaplin's artistic procedure in *The Great Dictator* succeeds in brilliantly parodying and perverting Hitler's gestures and in reclaiming them by those means for the common stock of the cinema and political resistance. It does not for all that prefigure the death camps. In contrast, Godard's historical procedure in *Histoire(s)* mobilizes the power of association that connects Chaplin's images—or those of Renoir—with all those images that are their virtual co-presents, all those images that inter-belong in this regime of sense and experience called History. Godard mines this reserved power of meaning for his project. It allows him, on one level, to see in the films of Renoir, Chaplin, Griffith, Lang, and Murnau the figures that announced the realities of the War and extermination to come, and, on a second level, to denounce cinema's incapacity, its failure to recognize its own dialogic and prophetic powers. Godard's accusation, although based entirely on the dialogic poetics of association and metaphor for its formulation, paradoxically confirms the discourse of presence and gives a new twist to the spiraling apparatus of *Histoire(s)*. Godard wants to show that cinema betrayed its own ability to prophesy the future because it had already betrayed its presence to the present. Like Peter who denies the Word made flesh, cinema betrayed the loyalty it owed to this word made flesh called the image. Cinema failed to recognize the redemptive power of the image, the nature the cinematographic screen shares, through Goya's or Picasso's painting, with the religious image, with the natural image of the Son impressed on the veil of Veronica.

Godard's film is about this redemption. Cinema, like Peter at the third crow of the cock, can recognize its guilt because this power of the Image still speaks in it, because something in the Image resists all betrayal. In the time of catastrophes and horrors, it was the "pitiable cinema of news and current events" that preserved the image's power to save. True, it was not in the camps to film the extermination, but it "was there" in general. Cameramen placed their cameras before the things they filmed, before all the destruction and suffering, and allowed them to speak without pretending to make art with what they filmed. The documentary spirit of Flaherty and Jean Epstein lived on in the newsreel, which is why it was able to save the essence of cinema, to allow it to be reborn from the ashes of this global catastrophe and atone for its faults. The two episodes that best illustrate the rebirth of cinema are worth reviewing, not least for the way they expose Godard's

method. In the first, devoted to the year zero of the rebirth, Godard presents
the last scenes of *Germany Year Zero* as a symbol of Italian cinema being born
from escaping "American occupation." Godard's treatment of these scenes
is diametrically opposed to his treatment of the fragments from Hitchcock's
films, which he had uncoupled from their narrative context and transformed
into so many testimonies to pure presence. Godard does the inverse with
the shots of Edmund's silent wanderings and unexplained suicide: he creates
with them a rigorous connection that transforms the end of his itinerary
into the annunciation of the Resurrection. Edmund's conduct at the end of
Germany Year Zero, after he's snubbed by the schoolmaster whose notions he
thought he was putting into practice, amounts to a series of silent acts wholly
impervious to meaning: he walks, runs, stops, hopscotches, kicks a stone,
slides down a ramp, picks up a piece of metal that he makes believe is a gun
and that he points first at himself, and then at the emptiness surrounding
him. In the bombed out building, Edmund is separated from the world going
on below, from his father's burial, his freed brother returning home, and his
sister calling for him. Edmund's answer to this call will be to throw himself
into the void. Godard takes the radical disconnection of these scenes and
creates, using slow-motion, fast-forward, and superimpositions, a rigorous
connection that inverses the meaning of the episode. Edmund rubs his eyes
like someone just waking up, like the cinema learning to see afresh, and his
gaze meets the most innocent of gazes, Gelsomina's in *La Strada,* that other
icon of neorealist cinema. Between the gazes of these two "children," cinema
is reborn to its powers and duties to see, it recovers from the America and
Hollywood symbolized by the dancing couple in *An American in Paris.* The
extreme slow-motion Godard imposes on the end of the film transforms the
sister who bends over her dead brother into an angel of the Resurrection,
who rises towards us to show the perennial power of the Image to be restored
to life from every death.

Elsewhere, Godard condenses this resurrection into a single image, the
redemption of the sinner herself, the prostituted Babylon/Hollywood.
Godard rewrites an episode of *A Place in the Sun* and puts the love affair
between the beautiful heiress played by Elizabeth Taylor and the young
careerist played by Montgomery Clift in the light of the Image, reborn
from the death it had died in the camps that George Stevens filmed in 1945,
when a photographer with the American army. "If George Stevens had not
used the first sixteen-millimeter color film at Auschwitz and Ravensbrück,
undoubtedly Elizabeth Taylor's happiness would never have found a place
in the sun." Godard, once more, doesn't give us the chance to evaluate the

argument on its own terms, as the next shot literalizes this place in the sun.
The young woman stepping out of the lake appears encircled, iconized, by a
halo of light that seems to outline the imperious gesture of a painted figure
apparently descended from the heavens. Elizabeth Taylor stepping out of
the water is a figure for the cinema itself being reborn from among the dead.
The angel of the Resurrection and of painting descends from the heaven of
Images to restore to life both the cinema and its heroines. This is a strange
angel, though, who seems to have come down from heaven without wings.
And indeed, the halo of this character hovering in midair, the expression
in her gaze, and her red cape fringed with gold seem instead to belong to
a saint. But saints only very rarely descend from the heavens, and it is not
clear why this figure, where we recognize Giotto's hand, is here defying the
law of gravity for material and spiritual bodies. Nor is the profile that of
a saint famous for having practiced levitation, but simply the profile of the
preeminent sinner Mary Magdalene. She is now hovering in midair with her
arms reaching out to the ground because Godard rotated her image ninety
degrees. In Giotto's fresco, Mary Magdalene's feet are firmly planted on the
ground and her arms are reaching out to the Savior, whom she recognizes
near the empty tomb and who turns her away with his arms: *Noli me tangere*,
touch me not.

Godard, in the end, puts the final touches on his dialectic of the cinematographic image by resorting to a very specific use of painting. Giotto
holds a special place in the Western pictorial tradition, as the painter who
relieved the sacred figures inherited from Byzantine icons from their solitude
and brought them together as characters who form part of one and the
same drama and who all share a common space. Élie Faure, Godard's master
in matters iconographic, went so far as to compare *The Deposition of Christ*
to a photograph of a group of surgeons in the middle of an operation in
an attempt to get us to appreciate the painting's dramatic as well as plastic
composition. The full meaning of Godard's cutting and pasting is revealed
against this background. By cutting Mary Magdalene's profile, Godard
doesn't just free the pictorial image from the "original sin" of perspective
and history, as André Bazin and a handful of others wanted to do. Godard
releases the figure of the saint from a plastic dramaturgy whose proper sense
was absence, the incurability of separation, of this empty tomb that was for
Hegel the heart of Romantic art and the reason why this art was fated to
the play of metaphor and irony. He fills the place of *Noli me tangere* with the
absolute image, the promise descending from the heavens and raising the
rich heiress—and cinema along with her—from the tomb, like the speech

of the illuminato Johannes that brings the young mother in *Ordet* back to life.

Of course, this iconization is only made possible by the play of its opposite, the Romantic poetics of the "poem of the poem" that first undoes and then recomposes the works of the tradition and that introduces—between image and image, between images and their words, images and their referents—all the connections and all the short-circuits that permit the projection of novel flashes of meaning onto a segment of the story or of history. The short-circuits that Friedrich Schlegel's poetics had hoped to provoke when all it had at its disposal was the power of words can be infinitely multiplied today thanks to the possibilities available to video-editing. *Histoire(s) du cinéma* turns on its head the widespread contemporary *doxa* that accuses the fatal screen, the reign of the spectacle and the simulacrum. It brings into broad daylight what contemporary developments in the art of video have been intimating for some time: it is, on the contrary, from the heart of the videographic manipulation of images, where the reign of artifices and simulations of the machine are there for all the world to see, that arises a new spiritualism, a new sacralization of the image and presence. The prestige of videographic art transforms the melancholic discourse about the spectacle-king into a new sparkle of the idols of flesh and blood. It is true that the paradox could be read backwards. In order to bring the scenarios of cinema back to the pure icons of "non-manipulated" presence, Godard has to create the icons by force of montage. It cannot be done without the hand of the manipulator who cuts to pieces all the compositions of painting and all the links of film and then re-pastes them all as he sees fit. Godard has to enhance their pure presence with the same gesture that renders all images polyvalent: the image of the wind blowing on a woman's body must be seen as a metaphor of originary "murmuring," the "youngest of the ladies of the Bois de Boulogne" struggling with death as a symptom of the threat facing cinema, slaughtered rabbits as prefiguring genocide. Godard challenges the empire of language and meaning, but he cannot do without subjecting the links between images to all the prestiges of homonyms and word play. His cinema renews the perennial tension between the two antagonistic but complicit [*solidaire*] poetics of the aesthetic age: it affirms the radical immanence of thought in the materiality of forms, and it redoubles to infinity the games of the poem that takes itself as its object.

This is undoubtedly the most profound paradox of Godard's *Histoire(s) du cinéma*. He wants to show that cinema betrayed both its vocation to presence and its historical task. And yet the demonstration of this vocation and this betrayal suddenly turn into the opportunity to verify the inverse. The film denounces cinema's "lost opportunities," though all these "lost opportunities" are retrospective. If Griffith had not filmed the sufferings of martyred children and Minnelli two lovers dancing, if Lang and Hitchcock had not brought to the screen the manipulations of cynical and deranged calculators, if Stroheim and Renoir had not filmed the decadence of the aristocracy and Stevens the tribulations of a latter-day Rastignac, Godard would never have had the opportunity to tell a thousand new versions of the history of the cinema and the century with the fragments from their fictions. These "lost opportunities," in other words, are so many seized opportunities. Godard makes with the films of Murnau, Lang, Griffith, Chaplin, or Renoir the films they did not make, which are the films Godard would not have been able to make had those directors already made them, had they come ahead of themselves, so to speak. History, properly speaking, is this relationship of interiority that puts every image into relation with every other; it is what allows us to be where we were not, forge all the connections that had not been forged, and then replay all the "(hi)stories" differently. Here we come upon the source of the profound melancholy underlying this "denunciation." History holds the promise of omnipresence and omnipotence, and yet these are powerless to act on any present other than that of their performance. This "excess of power" denounces itself as guilty and calls upon the redemption of the naked image, though the price it must pay for it is one more excess, one more twist of the spiral. And this supplement is evidence of the contrary, of the infinite possibility and radical harmlessness of the great manipulation of images. It is understood that the figure of the "wrong man" haunts Godard's film. A "wrong man," for Hitchcock, is someone mistakenly thought to be guilty; for Dostoevsky, conversely, it is someone who struggles in vain to pass for guilty. Maybe the most intimate melancholy of Godard's project is that it demonstrates everywhere the innocence of this art that should be guilty in order to prove, a contrario, its sacred mission. The moral of the cinema is, much like its fables, thwarted.

NOTES

1. Jean-Luc Godard, *Histoire(s) du cinéma*, vol. 4 (Paris: Gallimard, 1998) 75–85.

2. A key to Godard's other allusions. In *I Confess*, Montgomery Clift plays a priest accused of a crime he didn't commit; he knows the identity of the real culprit, but cannot reveal it because he learned it in the secrecy of confession. The purse is the one in *Psycho*, full of the money stolen by Marion (Janet Leigh), who makes the fatal error of stopping at the Bates Motel for the night, where she's killed by Norman Bates (Anthony Perkins). In *Shadow of a Doubt*, Teresa Wright plays the young Charlie, crazy about her uncle and namesake, the widow murderer played by Joseph Cotten. The bus in the desert is the bus that Roger Thornhill (Cary Grant), sent to the middle of nowhere by his enemies, is waiting for in *North by Northwest*. In *Strangers on a Train*, the scene of Bruno (Robert Walker) strangling Miriam Haines is reflected in her glasses. Lastly, the musical score is integral to the suspense of *The Man who Knew Too Much*, where a diplomat is to be killed during a performance at the Royal Albert Hall.

3. Godard, *Histoire(s) du cinéma*, vol. 4, 99–120.

4. Élie Faure, *History of Art*, vol. 2, trans. Walter Pach (New York: Dover Publications, 1937) 64–72.

Index